THE BEST BUDDHIST WRITING 2010

A SHAMBHALA SUN BOOK

THE BEST BUDDHIST WRITING

2·0·1·0

Edited by Melvin McLeod
and the Editors of the *Shambhala Sun*

SHAMBHALA
Boston & London 2010

Shambhala Publications, Inc.
Horticultural Hall
300 Massachusetts Avenue
Boston, Massachusetts 02115
www.shambhala.com

9 8 7 6 5 4 3 2 1

First Edition
Printed in U.S.A.

⊗This edition is printed on acid-free paper that meets the
American National Standards Institute z39.48 Standard.
♻This book was printed on 30% postconsumer recycled paper.
For more information please visit www.shambhala.com.
Distributed in the United States by Random House, Inc.,
and in Canada by Random House of Canada Ltd

ISBN 978-1-59030-826-4
ISSN 1932-393X
2006213739

Contents

Introduction

It has never seemed more important to assess the role of religion in the world—in our own lives, in our society, in global affairs. It's certainly surprising that we find ourselves in this situation at the beginning of the twenty-first century. Who could have predicted that at the end of the Cold War the world would divide again on the ancient fault lines of religious identity? That American political and cultural life would fall into unprecedented animosity fueled by religious passions? That the struggle between "reason" and "superstition" would be seen as one of the most important philosophical debates of our time?

Religion is blamed, and justly I'm afraid, for much of the conflict and oppression in the world today. Yet religion is also an integral part of human existence. We need more—we *are* more—than the merely material. We need something that takes us beyond this life and the world immediately in front of us—or at least places them in a larger, spiritual context. We have a deep inner certainty that there is more than just the world of the physical senses, that there are questions, answers, and experiences beyond the powers of science, observation, and reason. We turn to religious practice for meaning, for morality, for deep peace and harmony. For all the problems of organized religion, we are spiritual beings. We know implicitly that there is more than just this body, just this world, just this lifetime, and we need to touch it.

So as the old joke goes, we can't live with religion and we can't live without it. Where does Buddhism stand in this dilemma? Sam Harris, the author of *The End of Faith* and one of the so-called new atheists, suggests that Buddhism can meet our innate spiritual needs while obviating some of the problems of the major theistic religions. Naturally, there is much that Buddhism shares with other religions, but there are important ways in which it is different. Let's look at some of Buddhism's unique characteristics and how they are reflected in this year's *Best Buddhist Writing* (while noting that much of what we're going to say about Buddhism also applies to the contemplative or mystical traditions found within all of the major faiths).

The great divide between Buddhism and the world's other major religions is the idea of God, a creator deity. Buddhism is a nontheistic religion: it is the religion with no God. The Buddha was a human being who practiced and achieved enlightenment, and if we follow his example and practice as he did, we can wake up too. If a religion has no God, everything changes.

In Buddhism, the starting place is a very human problem: suffering. Some people have accused Buddhism of being negative and obsessed with suffering. Buddhists call it realism. Life has its obvious sufferings, such as illness, loss, and death, and beyond that, all lives, even the most pleasant and privileged, are marked by an underlying sense of fear and unease.

Some of the most powerful and moving stories in this book are about coming to grips—bravely, openly, and realistically—with life's difficulties. I think Stan Goldberg's memoir of hospice work (and his own cancer diagnosis) that opens this book is a perfect example of the Buddhist approach to suffering, one of love and gentleness. In that context, a true meeting of human hearts can happen.

Elsewhere in this volume, Sylvia Boorstein tells us how we can connect with the universal truths of the human condition by sharing with each other our worries and concerns for those we love. Elizabeth Brownrigg struggles with a difficult caregiving situation, and the Zen teacher Norman Fischer suffers the death of his best friend. Daniel Asa Rose is having a tough time with his teenage son, but they are brought together by a century-old reminder of tragic loss.

If working with such suffering is the challenge, then the bad news, as we've already noted, is that Buddhism doesn't offer us an outside refuge or savior. It would be great if there were one—who wouldn't want that?—but the truth, at least according to Buddhism, is that we're on our own. The good news is that we can do it. We have the inherent resources—the intelligence, courage, wisdom, and love—to handle our problems.

Many schools of Buddhism call this our buddhanature. It is the opposite of original sin. You could call it original virtue. Our true nature is awake, open, and compassionate, and the ignorance and neuroses that obscure it are only temporary. This positive, hopeful view shines through many stories and teachings in this volume. The titles alone tell the story: "Joyful Wisdom"; "Natural Wakefulness"; and "You Are Here," in which the great teacher Thich Nhat Hanh explains that everything we need is right here, right now (and indeed where else could it be?).

None of this means it's going to be easy. We have only to look at the state of our world to know that our obscurations, if ultimately temporary, are still powerful and deep-seated. In Buddhism, it's all about mind. Our enlightenment and happiness, as well as our ignorance and suffering, are all a product of the mind.

Buddhism traces our problems back to ignorance. We fundamentally misunderstand what we experience—both our own nature and the nature of the world—and so we suffer. The path is working with the mind to remove the obscurations and reveal its original purity and goodness. In turn, the world's basic goodness is also revealed. This we do through the wealth of skillful means for which Buddhism is renowned, what we generally call meditation. Meditation taps into our inborn awareness and intelligence to wake up from our deep-seated belief in the solid reality of self and other and experience life as fundamentally open, interdependent, and joyful.

The best way to learn how to meditate is directly from a qualified teacher. Short of that, there is some very good meditation instruction in this year's edition of *The Best Buddhist Writing*. The Tibetan teacher Dzongsar Jamyang Khyentse Rinpoche offers a guided meditation instruction that focuses on the key point of Buddhist practice: doing nothing. Buddhist meditation is about stopping, not creating. It's not about changing who we are—the trying to do that is actually the root of our problem—it's about being who we are, simply and directly.

Who we are is naturally awake and joyful, and teachings by Yongey Mingyur Rinpoche and Gaylon Ferguson show us how to directly experience that enlightened mind, which is always present but usually unnoticed. Since the false belief in a permanent, ongoing self is said to be the root of our problems, Anam Thubten offers a meditation teaching that sums it up nicely: "no self, no problem."

Of course, we're missing the point if meditation is something we only do in formal practice. We have to take the insight we develop on the meditation cushion out into our lives. One of the most important American Buddhist teachers, Pema Chödrön, offers a powerful teaching on those key moments when we choose whether to take an open, courageous approach to our difficulties, or go down the dead-end road of denial. Sakyong Mipham Rinpoche offers a series of contemplations to start each day, and Carolyn Rose Gimian relates the advice of the late Chögyam Trungpa Rinpoche to "smile at fear."

Buddhism has all the philosophy, history, and structure of any organized religion, but meditation is its core, and in the West today there are many people who want to bring Buddhist-style meditation into their lives without necessarily adopting new religious beliefs. At the *Shambhala Sun,* where I am editor-in-chief, we feel that this is one of the most important developments in the growth of dharma in the modern world. We call it the "mindful living" movement, and it's changing the way millions of Americans approach their lives.

Two examples of this approach in this year's *Best Buddhist Writing* are "The Joy of Mindful Cooking," Laura Fraser's report on the Zen-inspired cooks who have had so much influence on the way we cook and eat, and "Mindful Eating," in which the Zen teacher and physician Jan Chozen Bays offers a mindfulness-based system for working with eating issues. Both show the way in which people can incorporate the clarity, enjoyment, and effectiveness of meditation practice into their lives without feeling they have to adopt a whole new philosophy. That's pretty much the way the Buddha himself first taught it, so it must be kosher.

These are some of the unique features of the Buddhist path, and they underlie all the writings in this book, in ways both lofty and down-to-earth. In Buddhism, the view is mind, not God. The ground is our inherent goodness, our buddhanature. The problem is suffering, which is caused by temporary obscurations. The path is meditation, working with the mind to reveal its original nature. The fruition is wisdom, awakening.

This is a different kind of spiritual path, one that is lonely but loving, profound but practical, sacred but deeply human. I hope you will get a good sense of it from this year's edition of *The Best Buddhist Writing*. Perhaps the teachings, essays, and stories that follow will help you decide where Buddhism might fit in your own life, and in the surprising, important debate about the role of religion in our world.

There is an old saying that Buddhist practice is like walking through a heavy mist. At some point on the journey, without even realizing it, you have become wet. Buddhism in the West is like that. It is ripening, deepening, and spreading in ways we're not even aware of.

This book reflects many people who are contributing to the maturing and spread of dharma in the West. First to thank, of course, are the teachers, writers, and practitioners who have contributed to this book. They are among the spiritual, intellectual, and community leaders of Buddhism today.

The publishers of Buddhist books are vital contributors to the development of genuine dharma in the West. Besides the mainstream publishers who continue to offer quality Buddhist-inspired books, there are the devoted people of the specialty Buddhist publishers, whose essential work all practitioners should support in these times of transition in the publishing world. These include Wisdom Publications, Snow Lion Publications, Parallax Press, and of course Shambhala Publications, the publishers of this series.

The Buddhist magazines—*Shambhala Sun, Tricycle: The Buddhist Review, Buddhadharma: The Practitioner's Quarterly, Turning Wheel, Inquiring Mind, The Mindfulness Bell, Mountain Record, Bodhi,* and others are the public square of Buddhism in the West. All offer quality writing and vital connection among those interested in dharma. Their future is important.

I would like to thank editor Beth Frankl of Shambhala Publications for her always excellent work on the Best Buddhist Writing series, and Peter Turner, the president of Shambhala Publications, for his friendship and support. All of my colleagues at the Shambhala Sun Foundation play an important role in the creation of *The Best Buddhist Writing,* and indeed in my life. Some are Buddhists, some are not, but all are friends and fellow travelers on a wide spiritual path. And finally, thank you to my partner Pam Rubin and our daughter Pearl. You are my teachers and companions as we learn together from this thing called life.

Melvin McLeod
Editor-in-Chief
The Shambhala Sun
Buddhadharma: The Practitioner's Quarterly

The Best Buddhist Writing 2010

Lessons for the Living

Stan Goldberg

Buddhism has been described in many ways—as religion, philosophy, ethics, psychology—but really it is a mode of being, marked by awareness, courage, love, and sensitivity to one's own and others' suffering. These qualities, no less heroic for being human and humble, are on full display in this story by Stan Goldberg about his first experiences as a hospice volunteer, shortly after his own diagnosis of prostate cancer. It also shows why Buddhism has had such a profound impact on end-of-life care in America.

The quality of mercy is not strain'd.
It droppeth as the gentle rain from heaven
Upon the place beneath: it is twice blest;
It blesseth him that gives and him that takes.
—WILLIAM SHAKESPEARE

There is a presumption when you're asking for forgiveness that you did something wrong. Until the cancer, I was reluctant to ask for forgiveness. I might half-heartedly admit that I "misinterpreted," said something "without thinking it through," or any of a dozen other rationalizations that allowed me not to use the words, "Please forgive me." I didn't realize what asking for forgiveness really meant until I met Jim.

My first shift was scheduled for Thanksgiving at the Zen Hospice Project's Guest House, a hospice in San Francisco. Although I had the option of starting the following week, something compelled me to start then, even though it meant missing Thanksgiving with my family and friends. I spent the weekend before my shift amassing as many facts as I could. That's how I tried making sense of things then: gathering information, numbers, and data. The book that had the greatest impact on me was *Final Gifts: Understanding the Special Awareness, Needs, and Communications of the Dying,* by the hospice-care nurses Maggie Callanan and Patricia Kelley. A recurring theme that Callanan and Kelley described about the experiences of people who were dying was their sense of embarking on a journey they said they were required to make, but for some reason couldn't start. One person talked about not having the key to open a locked door. A few people vividly described trips they were getting ready for but couldn't begin until something necessary, like a passport, was found. And others waited until they could say good-bye to someone. According to the authors, these were universal signals that something needed to be resolved before people allowed themselves to die. The idea that anyone could have control over the time of their death mystified me.

It was the Tuesday before Thanksgiving when I received an e-mail from the volunteer coordinator. Jim, one of the residents, was becoming confused, restless, and anxious. The coordinator asked if any volunteers could stay the night with him. Volunteer shifts normally end at 10:00 PM, and with only one attendant on the floor at night, someone needed to be at his side from 10:00 PM to nine in the morning, when volunteers returned. Since I would already be there, I thought a few more hours wouldn't be a big deal. When I discussed it with my wife, Wendy, she asked if I was sure I wanted to do that, since this was my first hospice experience since completing my training.

"Of course," I responded. "What difference would a few more hours make?" I was still minimizing the lingering effects of the surgery and the perpetual exhaustion I felt from the cancer treatments. I could tell Wendy was concerned, but given our history (she usually wanted to discuss my feelings about the cancer and I usually refused) she didn't persist. I called the hospice attendant to let her know I would take the Thursday overnight shift.

"What can you tell me about Jim?" I asked.

"He's sixty-seven and was a heroin addict on and off since age seventeen," she said. "The last time he was using was about five years ago." There was a pause and I could hear her turning pages.

"I'm looking at his chart and see he doesn't get along with most people. Scares them actually. He's quiet during the day," she continued, "but at night he becomes a different person. We think it's the toxic chemicals his liver is producing. You know, he has hepatitis C."

I didn't expect that my first patient would be contagious and I would need to use every universal precaution I had been taught. Unfortunately, I didn't remember all of them. *How do you take the gloves off? Do you turn them inside out with a free pinky, or was it a thumb? What do you do if there is contact?* Until then, dealing with a contagious person was theoretical. *Yes, put on gloves, don't allow their bodily fluids to come in contact with your open sores, and wash your hands after you take off the gloves.* Since we spoke in generalities, it never was threatening. Now, it was someone with a name, whose body was home to a virus even more deadly than my cancer. And the only thing separating us would be a thin layer of latex and as much physical distance as I could create without being embarrassed.

"After ten, he enters another world," the attendant said. "Two things happened last night. The first was he left his room, yelling 'Deuce' as he walked through the House."

"Who's Deuce?"

"When I asked him, he said Deuce was his drug dealer. Then it got really strange. After I got him back into bed and left the room, he called me back and pleaded that I ask them to let him go."

"Who?" I asked.

"He said the bakery workers wouldn't let him leave because he hadn't finished baking something. In a loud voice I said, 'Let Jim leave!' It didn't help. He kept repeating that they won't let him leave until his bread was baked."

She continued talking, but I heard little. Not only did the story resonate with those from *Final Gifts,* but I remembered a conversation I had had with the volunteer coordinator the previous week—I had offered to bake bread for the Thanksgiving dinner.

I drove to the House in the late afternoon on that warm Thanksgiving Day. I parked at the end of the block and walked on a sidewalk covered with leaves, their normally brilliant colors muted by the overcast sky. The Guest House was a Victorian home that maintained its 1850s splendor while surrounded by similar houses that had seen their prime decades before. There was nothing on its exterior that hinted about the remarkable things occurring inside. The only sign was a small bronze plaque next to the front door that stated this was a historical building. In every pastel-painted room except the kitchen, chandeliers descended from high ceilings through plaster rosettes. The people who were cared for weren't called "patients," they were "residents," a distinction that was more than semantic. At capacity, six adults could be housed.

I opened the unlocked door and smelled roasting turkey. I saw about ten people, each doing something related to dinner. The living room was transformed into a festive dining area with a large table in the center, covered with a purple tablecloth that shimmered as you passed by it. In the center was a beautiful flower arrangement, more glorious than anything in *House and Garden,* and on the mantel were at least forty cards with names written in calligraphy. *Forty?* I didn't realize there would be that many at the meal. As I wondered if I had baked enough bread, people greeted me. Some I knew, others were staff I'd seen but never met. An older woman, wearing a colorful vest that was probably vintage 1970s, offered to take the bread into the kitchen. It was still warm, and the smell stunned her. She called other people over to share the experience. One was a resident who had non-Hodgkin lymphoma. He was a huge man with letters tattooed on each of his fingers, from when he had been in San Quentin, sideburns down to his jawline, and a straggly mustache. I expected a deep rumbling to come out of his mouth, but his voice was amazingly soft as he told me his name, Paul, and then he introduced me to June, his wife. Although shorter than Paul, June blocked out his silhouette when she stepped in front of him. She immediately embraced me in a bear hug, kissing me as if I was a favorite nephew.

When June released me and moved to the side, I saw someone insisting on walking down from the second floor. His gaunt face was covered by a gray mustache and beard, his long thinning hair was tied in a ponytail, and his jeans were bunched in the front so they wouldn't fall off. After four steps, he couldn't move. Exhausted, he slowly sank onto a stair. It brought back memories of walking down the stairs in my house for the first time after surgery, each step sending a sharp pain through my body.

"Jim, would you like help coming down?" the woman in the vest asked from downstairs.

With his eyes closed and his upper body held upright by two volunteers, he nodded his head yes. They raised him and, using a fireman's carry, brought him down the remaining ten steps. After they gently lowered Jim into a wheelchair, he rested his chin on his chest. When his breathing slowed, he was wheeled into the dining room and a chair next to where I sat was removed. The table had twelve place settings precisely laid out as if on a grid. I wondered where the other twenty-eight people were and where they would sit. I waited for Jim to turn in my direction, but he didn't.

"Hi Jim," I finally said. The disease had so ravaged him, he was unable to move his head. He turned his upper body to see me, and our eyes met. He stared without blinking, without expressing anything. I thought his look was imploring me to say or do something. But what? The best I could say was, "I'm Stan. I'll be staying with you through the night. This is my first shift at the House, so if I screw up, please let me know."

He leaned toward me and in a barely audible voice said, "There's no way you can make as many mistakes as I have. Don't sweat it."

Shortly afterward, the remaining ten people sat down and someone suggested we remember those who died at the Guest House over the past few months. He gestured toward the place cards on the mantel. During the silent meditation period, I didn't think about the names. Instead, memories of my parents' deaths flashed back along with frightening images of what my own might look like. After we finished, Jim turned back to his food and tried to pick up a fork. Although he could hold it, his fingers didn't have the strength to grasp it firmly and it dropped to the floor. The person next to him, who was talking to someone across the table, took another fork without stopping his conversation and picked up a small amount of sweet potatoes. As he raised it, Jim opened his mouth and smiled at the volunteer. I looked around the table and saw nobody showed any interest in what was occurring; almost as if this was common.

After eating a few bites of sweet potatoes and some ice cream, Jim slowly hunched over. Was he dying right here in front of me? No one seemed concerned until someone casually asked him if he would like to go back to his room. He nodded yes, and was wheeled to the steps. Four people lifted the chair with Jim in it and gently carried him upstairs. My family and friends were joyfully feasting on turkey and listening to our annual playing of Arlo Guthrie's "Alice's Restaurant," a song in which the joy of a Thanksgiving meal turns into a bizarre adventure. I was in the middle of one, sharing food with people who were dying and had diseases that could kill me.

It was about eight when dinner was over. Paul and June went back upstairs to their room. Everyone else spontaneously started clearing the table. When I entered the kitchen, someone was doing dishes and another person was wrapping the food for tomorrow's meals. Everyone left except the attendant, Evan, and one other volunteer, Gary. Evan went upstairs to be with the residents while Gary and I finished cleaning. When we were done, we were expected to go upstairs and spend time with the residents. When I asked the volunteer coordinator before my shift began what I should be doing, she said, "Just be present." Although I nodded, signaling that I understood, I didn't.

I would be with Jim throughout the night, and Gary would stay with the other two residents until ten. Paul's wife would be taking care of him, and Evan would be there for everyone. Attendants were very special people. Some were certified nursing assistants (CNAs), and others had slightly less training; although I never could tell the difference in their duties. The residents referred to them as "angels." Whatever was needed by the residents they did, from changing soiled linens to monitoring medications to quietly sitting by the bedside holding someone's hand as he or she died.

I realized I was repeatedly vacuuming the same spot on the rug, dragging out the cleaning as long as I could. Downstairs, there was distance between Jim and me. It felt safe and, now, very clean. Upstairs, well, I didn't know how I was going to be "present."

As I climbed the stairs, the food odors faded, gradually overpowered by the smell of disinfectant. I asked Evan for the notes kept on each resident. I read that Jim only left his room when he had the strength. Since the prior week, he had been downstairs just once. Only a few people had come to visit since he arrived two months ago. And he was becoming combative and increasingly incontinent. Bowel movements were loose because of the colitis, and he often couldn't get to the commode in time, or, when he was delirious, he forgot to take off his pants and diaper.

I entered Jim's room and saw him sitting on a recliner with his eyes closed. According to Evan, Jim hadn't slept in his bed for two days. He preferred to sleep fully clothed on the recliner. I looked at the bed with its quilt and puffed-up pillows, trying to imagine how many people had died in it over the seventeen-year existence of the Guest House and wondering if the number would increase that night.

"Hi Jim," I said, sitting in a chair three feet away from him. He said something, but I couldn't hear what it was. I moved the chair closer and said, "Is there anything I can get you?"

He shook his head no.

"Anything I can do for you?"

Again, a no. I noticed he was wearing dress shoes covering socks whose elastic tops were indenting his skin. "Those shoes and socks look uncomfortable. Would you like me to take them off?" I asked.

He shook his head no, then slowly turned to me and waited until

I moved even closer. Reluctantly, I placed my ear a few inches from his mouth and wondered if he'd spray me with saliva. And if he did, how would I react? I prepared to pull away as he started speaking.

"They pinch my toes," he said, barely above a whisper.

"If they pinch your toes, why don't you want them off?"

"It keeps me awake."

I didn't know if he wanted to stay awake because he feared dying if he fell asleep, or because he wanted to talk. If it was the first, I didn't think I was ready for it. If it was the second, I would be less concerned, but unsure how to talk to him. Despite the role playing we did in training, I felt like a teenager about to meet a blind date. Our conversation began easily enough, with me asking him how long he had been at the House. He said three months. He asked me how long I had been doing this. I said, "Since dinner." He laughed. But as his laugh changed into a cough, I held my breath. When he finally stopped, I inhaled.

For a while, the easy talk continued. I asked how he liked the food. He said, "It depends upon who's cooking." He asked me how old I was. I said almost fifty-eight. Then after some more small talk came a shift in the conversation's tone when I asked him how old he was. "I'm sixty-seven and won't see sixty-eight." I tried changing the direction of the conversation. As a new hospice volunteer, I still wasn't comfortable talking about death. I asked how long he lived on the streets. "More than anyone should have to," he said. He was as persistent as a telemarketer trying to get you to buy penny stocks. I realized that no matter what I would say, he would pull me back to what he wanted to talk about, not just the facts of his life, which on their own were frightening enough, but most likely how he was feeling about his dying. Reluctantly, I gave in and asked about his pain. He told me with enough morphine even the worst eventually went away. I nodded my head, agreeing.

"How do you know about morphine?" he asked.

"I have prostate cancer. They gave it to me last year after surgery."

Jim wanted to know if I had family. Yes, I said. A wife and two adult children. I was no longer holding my breath as he spoke, and my chair was now touching the recliner. We were speaking with just inches separating our heads when he fell asleep. Earlier, I read in the notes he often did this—fell asleep, eyes wide open, then started speaking when he woke as if there never was an interlude. I sat and waited.

Ten minutes later he said, "How old?"

"My son's twenty-two and my daughter's twenty-six."

"How did you tell them about the cancer?"

Although it had been a year, I still wasn't comfortable talking about those conversations.

"It was hard," was all I said.

Jim kept looking at me as if he were waiting for more. I saw his eyes were glistening.

"Do you have any kids?" I asked. One girl, he told me, who hadn't visited. Jim didn't think his daughter knew he was dying.

"I haven't seen her in five years. She's in Illinois."

"Would you like to see her?"

As he nodded his head yes, the hints of moisture tipped out, forming thin streams that cascaded only an inch or so down his cheeks.

"Can anyone get in touch with her?"

"Her mother, but she won't do it. They don't speak. We don't speak." There was a long pause, and then he said, "I need to ask her to forgive me."

I asked him if he would like us to see if we could contact his daughter. With closed eyes he nodded his head yes, then slowly exhaled. When he fell asleep, I went outside the room and asked Evan if Jim ever talked about his daughter.

"No," he said. "This is significant. I'll see what I can find out after my shift is over. Then we'll try to call her."

I went back into the room and sat next to Jim as he slept. I thought about the times when I could have sabotaged my relationship with my children. I remembered when my son was nine and I had been under stress. I was directing a university program and enlarging my private practice. Between the two, I had little time for my family. As my son and I were walking together on a busy street near our house, he reached up and grabbed my hand. My thought was to withdraw it, and lecture him that nine-year-olds don't hold their father's hand in public. When I looked down at this face, I realized he was using a physical connection to compensate for the emotional one I was denying him. I held his hand tighter and turned away before he saw my tears. What if I had withdrawn my hand? Would Justin have become as distant as it appeared Jim's daughter was from him? And if I had rejected him, how would I ask Justin, as an adult, to forgive me? I wondered how Jim would do it. What could have happened to make a daughter not want to have contact with her father for five years? And would the knowledge her father was dying be enough to overcome it?

Jim woke again, and for the next three hours we talked as if we were lifelong friends sitting at a bar, delighted just to be with each other. Maybe this is what "being present" meant. He told me how he loved to sing classical music, but that he could barely breathe anymore. I told him about my love of fly-fishing in remote areas, but because of my hormone treatments I was too weak to go alone. Climbing steep canyons was no longer possible. Walking was even painful since I fractured my pelvis playing handball. I asked him if he'd like me to make French toast in the morning from the bread I baked. There was a long pause and then he slowly turned so he was looking directly at me.

"You bake bread?"

"Yes, I do."

"What kind?"

"Well, for tonight's dinner I baked challah, egg bread."

"Can you get me the recipe?"

"Sure, I'll bring it in next week."

He leaned back on the recliner, remaining silent for about a minute, then turned toward me, inhaling as much as he could to complete another sentence. "I want to make that bread, but I know I can't."

"We'll do it together," I said with a quivering voice.

He closed his eyes, smiled, and then fell asleep. As I watched him, death became more real and frightening. The real thing was in front of me in a body that was winding down and a brain that couldn't tell delusion from reality. I wondered if this is how I would die: watching my abilities fall away to the point where I couldn't even feed or wipe myself. My apprehension stopped when he woke.

"I'm hungry," Jim said.

Thank God! At least here's something simple. Something I could do without thinking. After all, how difficult will it be to feed someone?

"What would you like?" I asked.

"Ice cream."

"I'll go downstairs and see if there's any left."

The mantra at the Guest House was there are no emergencies in hospice. I was told people were there to die, not recover. In a hospital there is a sense of urgency when a life is in jeopardy. Here, everything moved slowly, deliberately, as if each moment was to be savored. But I forgot the mantra and painfully bounded down the stairs, each step reminding me my reduced bone density was putting me at risk for another fracture. In the freezer were quart containers of chocolate and vanilla. Plenty to satisfy the small amount I thought he would eat. I ran back up.

"There's chocolate and vanilla. Which do you want?"

"Both."

I went back down and put a large scoop of each in a bowl and again climbed the stairs.

"I have both in this bowl. Which one would you like to start with?"

"Both."

I took a small portion of each on a spoon. "I'm going to feed you, so let me know if the amount is too large."

He nodded his head, and I slowly placed the spoon into his open mouth. He closed it, allowing the ice cream to slide off as I pulled out the spoon. His eyes closed, and he slowly moved his tongue from side to side. With each movement of his tongue, his smile grew. Sometimes it took thirty seconds before the ice cream was gone and he was ready for the next spoonful. It was something so simple, so pleasurable, I couldn't understand it. Pleasure for me had always been complicated. I felt it when I made a perfect cast to a fish hidden behind a rock as I stood in my favorite stream in Wyoming. I experienced it completing a poem in which I merged thoughts into a unified line. But that night, it was just the taste of ice cream that seemed to bring more joy to someone than I could have ever experienced through complex manipulations of either my body or mind. We repeated the sequence for the next ten minutes until the bowl was empty.

"More please," he whispered.

I went downstairs, refilled the bowl, and we began again. After he finished, I sat next to him and tried to sleep when he did, propping my feet on a second chair. Shortly after one o'clock I felt a tapping on my shoulder and woke. Irma, the late-night attendant, introduced herself. She gave Jim a dose of Roxanol, a liquid derivative of morphine.

"Lie down on the couch," the tiny older woman then said to me. She was less than five feet tall, and she spoke quietly, with a South American accent. "You sleep. He'll go to sleep now." I later learned that Irma had come to San Francisco from Bolivia forty years earlier, when she was in her midthirties. Most of us at the hospice thought of Irma as the caring grandmother we all dreamed of having.

"But if I sleep over there," I said, pointing to the couch on the other side of the room, "I won't hear him if he wakes."

"Don't worry. I'll be here," she said.

She pulled a blanket and pillow from a second bed in the alcove and placed them on the floor between the recliner where Jim slept and the door. She had been doing this since the previous week when Jim began wandering. He would often wake and try to walk quietly down the stairs. Irma couldn't watch him and take care of the other residents by herself. That's why people had volunteered to stay with him throughout the night—every night until he died.

"Sleep, sleep," Irma said to me. I didn't need any encouragement. She lay on the floor and I crunched sideways on the couch with a blanket pulled up to my head. I almost immediately fell asleep.

"I need your help," Irma said in a whisper, as she gently tapped my shoulder. I looked at the clock. It had been less than an hour. "I'm sorry, but he's had an accident."

Although I was groggy, I knew what she meant. I reached into my back pocket and pulled out the gloves. Across the room I saw Jim.

"I'm sorry, I'm sorry," he said, standing next to the recliner. "Goddamn it. Look what I did," he said, staring at his soiled jeans.

Earlier in the evening I wondered how I would react to cleaning another person, especially someone contagious. Worse, would it be a preview of my future? Looking at Jim apologizing over and again, my fears and the odor that filled the room both disappeared. In their place, I saw someone devastated by probably one of the most embarrassing things an adult can do in the presence of other people.

"I'm sorry, I'm sorry. Look what I did," he repeated.

"It's all right Jim," I said.

Irma and I helped him to the bed, where it would be easier to clean him. He stopped apologizing as she told him where to move his legs and what we would be doing. Irma directed each of my movements like a choreographer preparing a child for his first dance recital. When I hesitated, she would gently take my hands and place them where she wanted them.

It took almost thirty minutes to clean him, change his clothes, and replace the bed linens. When we began, my hands moved hesitantly, almost as if my fears pulled them back. But when I stopped trying to analyze everything and just let my concern for him lead me, a flowing rhythm developed. I didn't have to wonder if I was rubbing him too roughly or too lightly. It was as if I were transported back to when I changed my children's diapers, and my hands instinctively knew what to do.

Finally done, I slept on the couch until six, when Jim woke. He asked to go back to the recliner, and I gently led him there. He turned his body so he could look out the window on the other side of the room. It was a typical gray San Francisco morning.

"It's going to be a good day," he said, then fell back to sleep.

Evan came to the House at 8:00 AM even though his shift didn't start until late afternoon. He stood outside Jim's room and motioned to me. We walked down the hall so Jim wouldn't hear us.

"I asked the house manager about Jim's daughter," he whispered.

"Can we contact her?" I asked.

"No."

"Why not? He wants to see her."

"She said she died five years ago."

"But we talked about a daughter in Illinois. Are you sure there isn't another one?"

"No. That was Jim's only child. She's buried there. The family blames him for his daughter's death. Nobody here knows how it happened, and the family didn't want to talk about it."

At 9:00 AM, after spending eighteen hours at the Guest House, I left to go home. The street seemed cleaner, the sky bluer, and I was becoming less afraid of my emotions. I confronted my fears of contagion and death that night, not by talking but by doing. I was experiencing Jim's dying, and I was imagining what might happen to me. I wondered if he agreed with his family and blamed himself? I was so overwhelmed by my experiences that I had to concentrate on remembering to stop at traffic lights and stay on the right side of the road as I drove. I felt as if I were dropped from a sensory deprivation chamber into the middle of a Rolling Stones concert. Only ten minutes more, then I'd be home.

"How was it?" Wendy asked as I walked through the door. I couldn't speak. I started to cry and hugged her as my grown children looked on. After my night with Jim, I felt more alive than I ever had. During my shift, there wasn't time to think about the past or future. My mind remained in the present, unlike the previous six months, which I had spent wallowing in the past—trying to relive experiences that I would never have again—or leaping into the future, creating goals that would affirm a long life—one that I might not have. For the next three weeks, I stayed overnight every Thursday after the end of my shift. One week, I stayed overnight on two consecutive days. Although there were peaceful times, Jim was acutely agitated at least half of the time. One night, he even tried to punch Irma when she was giving him morphine.

"Is that the best you can do?" he shouted as I caught a left hook before it could hit her face. I don't remember ever reacting so fast.

"Jim, it's me, Irma," she said to him sweetly, not flinching. Their faces were inches from each other as I struggled to hold back his arm. Instead of moving away, Irma kept talking. "Remember? You said I was like a grandmother to you. Remember?"

He looked at her intently. Finally, there was a look of recognition, then he said, "Hey, Irma. How are you, darling?" A smile came over his face, and I felt his muscles relax. Then I watched his eyes close.

This pattern repeated itself for the next few weeks. Jim became agitated, believing he was on the streets again, ready to fight all comers whether they were imaginary street people trying to steal his stash or the little Bolivian grandmother who was trying to comfort him. When the delusions stopped, and if he was conscious, he apologized profusely, repeatedly asking everyone in the room to forgive him. As he ate less, his body began consuming its own fat, revealing a wiry, muscular physique. If you didn't know his condition, you might assume he was an aging boxer. Then, with little fat left, his muscle started breaking down.

Volunteers agreed to stay at his bedside twenty-four hours a day. The nurse told me the toxic chemicals his dying liver was producing caused the agitation. I thought it was more than chemistry. He struggled constantly with things that needed finishing before he died. His comment at Thanksgiving dinner that I could never make as many mistakes as he did was the first sign. Then came the conversation about wanting to reestablish a connection with his daughter. As our friendship developed, he talked about wanting to ask for forgiveness from scores of people he hurt. Some had already died; others he didn't know about. Family, other than his brother, wouldn't speak to him.

Whatever mistakes Jim made in the past didn't appear correctable, or, if they were, I couldn't seem to help him find a way to do it. Perhaps I didn't have the experience, or the wisdom, or the willingness to open myself even more than I had already. The only thing I could do was listen. Other volunteers were more successful at calming Jim than I was. One woman got in bed with him when nothing helped the pain and restlessness. She caressed him until he fell asleep, the way a mother caresses a frightened child. I was humbled watching her, wondering if I could ever become as compassionate. But even with her, Jim's agitation stopped only for short periods. Few friends visited. After repeated phone calls from Jim to his brother, his brother agreed to come and stay with him for two days. When he heard his brother would be visiting, we talked about forgiveness. He wanted to ask for it, but was afraid to.

I never saw Jim's brother smile, and I never saw him talk to any of the volunteers or staff. During the first day of his stay, I heard their conversation through the open door of his room. It started pleasantly, with both of them recollecting their childhoods, then adolescence, and finally adulthood. As they progressed through the years, joviality was gradually replaced by accusations. He reminded Jim of every thoughtless thing he ever did, using words that sounded to me as if they were burning the inside of his mouth. Jim sank lower into the recliner as his brother vividly described painful events for twenty minutes.

Tearfully he said, "I'm sorry, Rick, please forgive me. I'm sorry for the pain I caused you."

"Really? You should have thought about it before you went back to using."

"I know."

"Even if I forgive you, your daughter is still dead because of you."

I didn't hear any words indicating that he was shocked. I had wondered since our first night if he really believed his daughter was still alive. When he started crying, Rick left the room. I entered quietly and sat next to him.

"It didn't work," he said. "I've done some terrible things in my life," he continued.

"We all have."

"No, you don't understand. You can't. Not bad things. Terrible things. There are things I can't be forgiven for. I know that when I die, people will celebrate. And they should. I wanted my brother to forgive me, but I didn't think he would. Actually, I knew he wouldn't, but I had to try."

As he cried, I put my arm around him. I had never done that with Jim. Hugging and cradling were things he always wanted from female volunteers. Firm handshakes were for men. As I held him, he leaned toward me. This was the closest we had ever been physically. I started thinking about things I did throughout my life that I was sorry for. The list seemed endless. Eventually he became quiet.

Looking at me he said, "You're a sweetheart."

"That's not something I'd expect to hear from a street-smart guy like you. I don't even hear that from my wife," I lied. He laughed. We were both becoming more comfortable expressing our feelings.

"Is there anything I can do for you, Jim?"

In a clear voice, he said, "Shoot me."

"Sorry. Anything, but that," I said. He smiled and leaned back in the recliner waiting for the morphine to take effect.

I knew he would be in physical and psychological pain until he died. I didn't admit it to anyone, but I hoped it would happen soon. I saw aspects of Jim's life in my own. I looked back on times when I wanted to ask for forgiveness but didn't. I wondered if my father's death twenty-five years ago would have been any different if I had been able to ask him to forgive some spiteful things I said years before he died. Would his last few hours have been more peaceful if I were able to express gratitude for all he gave me? I was slightly better with my mother's death. I always wondered if she knew how important she was to me. I knew I should have told her, but I wasn't able to then.

I was spending Tuesday and Thursday overnights with Jim. But one Thursday in December, all the volunteers were required to attend a training session at another location. The first presentation was by a nurse who had been working in hospice for fifteen years. As she described her interactions with patients, I realized I still wasn't able to deal with an idea that had been presented during my training: being able to fall in love with those I served and then let them go without regrets. I wouldn't say I'd fallen in love with Jim. Maybe I felt the type of friendship that occurs when you share experiences so wrenchingly authentic that they create a bond that defines the relationship forever. I knew I would miss him like a crotchety old uncle who, years after his death, is only remembered for his good qualities.

"How do you accept the loss when someone you love dies?" I asked.

She immediately replied, "Love can take many forms. The love I experience for my patients involves feeling I've done everything I could have to make their death as peaceful as possible. I knew every one of the thousands I cared for would die within six months. If I focused on that, I'd go crazy or quit. But when you know you're helping them on a journey, your love is different. So is your sense of loss. Yes, I miss most of the patients I've worked with, but that's minor compared with what I think I gave them."

There was another speaker, but at the end of the nurse's presentation, I began feeling intense pains in my abdomen. Even though my surgeon had told me that when the cancer returns it wouldn't give me dramatic pain, I excused myself and left anyway, feeling a little panicked.

The next morning I received an e-mail announcing that Jim had died at nine o'clock the previous night. I realized my pains began shortly afterward. I had never believed in prophetic feelings. Those that I had experienced, I always credited to coincidence. When other people would tell me about theirs, I would listen politely and think, "Give me a break! Who could believe that?" Now I don't question them.

The e-mail said his body would be removed from the House at eleven in the morning. Anyone who would like to say good-bye could sit with him until then. I arrived at nine and sat alone at the side of the bed. It was the first time I saw him looking peaceful. I felt I was looking at the face of a sixty-seven-year-old baby, content to just be. When I went home, I reread one of my favorite passages from the Buddha's teachings:

> This existence of ours is as transient as autumn colds.
> To watch the birth and death of beings
>   is like looking at the movements of a dance.
> A lifetime is like a flash of lightning in the sky,
>   rushing by, like a torrent down a steep mountain.*

After Jim died, I asked my wife and children to forgive me for a number of thoughtless things I had done. Fortunately, they weren't in the same league with the death of Jim's daughter, but I often ask myself, *What if they were?* How could I ask for forgiveness for something that was "terrible"? I'm not sure I could, although after Jim I was inspired to help other people do the same thing. I helped one woman write a letter asking for forgiveness from her adult daughter, whom she felt she had neglected as a child. For another patient, a phone call to an answering machine was all he could do. It seems to me that asking for forgiveness is redemptive, not necessarily in any religious sense, but it seems to remove something that makes the journey more difficult.

There's an old Buddhist story about a monk who would walk around with two bags of pebbles tied to his waist. One bag contained white pebbles and the second, black ones. Whenever he did something virtuous he took out a white pebble and put it in his pocket. Whenever he did something that was hurtful to someone, he took out a black one. At the end of the day he looked at the number of white and black pebbles in his pocket. If the whites outnumbered the blacks, it was a good day. Since seeing the pain of someone who

---

* From the Diamond Sutra, in Sogyal Rinpoche, *The Tibetan Book of Living and Dying* (New York: HarperSanFrancisco, 1994), 25.

desperately wants forgiveness before they die, I understand how important it is to ask now—and to forgive others now, too. I've found that when I ask for forgiveness for something I did that was thoughtless, some of my black stones magically become white.

The Whole Way

Joan Sutherland

Traditionally in Asia, meditation and enlightenment were the province of monastics and yogis, while laypeople generally followed a path of faith and gathering merit. In the West a different model is evolving, in which lay practitioners meditate and seek enlightenment while still pursuing a life of family, career, and social engagement. The Zen teacher Joan Sutherland, one of Western Buddhism's most insightful and elegant writers, argues that the new model is truer to the spirit of Buddhism, making the depth of the dharma available to many more people and relevant to all aspects of life.

Being human is a complicated affair, and Buddhism began and continues to evolve as a response to this challenge. It describes in great detail what is unsatisfactory and why, and then it offers practices, philosophy, and art to help transform this unsatisfactoriness into awakening—or, more accurately, to help us see the awakening that was always right there, inextricably a part of the very life we considered unsatisfactory.

There are many forms of Buddhism and a variety of Buddhist practices, including meditation, ceremony, study, service, art, and devotion. Practice is key, because it bridges idea and embodiment; it helps make the Way real. In the Asian cultures in which Buddhism first arose, there has been, broadly speaking, a distinction between monastic and lay practice. There's obviously much that they share, but monastics and laypeople have often had different aspirations, which has led them to different forms of practice.

To a larger extent than we sometimes realize, Westerners have inherited this split. It's easier to recognize if you think of monastic practice as including the retreats that laypeople attend, with the perennial end-of-retreat question about how to bring the experience into daily life. So I'll speak of cloistered practice, which is meant to include both monasticism and lay retreat experience, and daily life, which is pretty much everything else.

Many of us take for granted that we're moving from one world into another as we leave the retreat center and head for home. Some of us believe that the truer practice, the one that will lead to enlightenment, is held in the monastery or the retreat, and that anything else is second best. Some would argue that only lay practice and immersion in the world can open the Way. Do we have to choose one over the other, or reconcile ourselves to the idea that the disjunctions between them are inevitable? Is awakening really the province of one mode of practice more than the other? Or is there a perspective that unites them into something whole, an uncompartmentalized and onflowing Way?

❖   ❖   ❖

When buddhas don't appear
And their followers are gone
The wisdom of awakening
Bursts forth by itself.
       —Nagarjuna

Last year I moved to the high desert of northern New Mexico, where the presence and absence of water are never far from our thoughts: monsoon rains in the summer, winter snows, water held for a season by rivers or a few hours in *arroyos* that flood and go dry again, water held for centuries in aquifers, bubbling up as natural springs. And from time immemorial we humans have joined the great cycle of wet and dry with our wells and irrigation ditches. Even with modern reservoirs and sewer lines, there's the strong sense here that life has been sustained by deep wells and a net of *acequias,* the ditches that run through fields and along the sides of roads, even in some neighborhoods of the state capital.

This is how I've come to think of awakening. It's everywhere—as sudden and complete as the crash of thunder on a summer afternoon, as promising as a distant smudge of cottonwoods, revealing the presence of water. There are times of drought, too, when the very idea of awakening seems to have dried up under an unrelenting sky. We might think of awakening as something that happens inside us, but, as with a landscape, we also happen inside of it.

In moments of awakening, it's clear that what our heart-minds experience—what we sense and see and feel—is entirely continuous with the world we ordinarily think of as outside ourselves. There is no longer observer and observed but a single field, and this field is what I'm calling awakening. From this perspective, awakening seems like a force as fundamental and all-pervasive as gravity or electromagnetism, and we see that it is inside us and we are inside it.

And so we try to establish a relationship with it, tap into the resource, coax awakening into causing our particular corner of the world to flourish. We practice, and it's just as though we're digging wells and ditches. At times we concentrate our energy and go deep into the underground sources of water. At others we stand on the earth and open the acequia gates, letting our awareness pour across the land like water, which makes life possible wherever it spreads. Each is essential; neither has power without the other. A well without acequias is a hole with water at the bottom; an acequia without a source of water is a dry ditch. Our practice is a collaboration with awakening to discover its expression in our particular human life. To do this we have to touch the deep pools of awakening that are hidden from our ordinary gaze, and we have to do something out in the open with what we discover.

In this spirit, some people have adapted practices developed in a Buddhist context so they can be shared with others for specific ends like pain or stress reduction. Others have taken what they've learned from practice into prisons, hospitals, hospices, environmental work, corporations, social work, political action—the list is long and growing. Family life, friendship, art, and culture have all been affected, sometimes explicitly and sometimes without saying a Buddhist word. Making accessible the ideas and methods that might be useful to people whether they're Buddhist practitioners or not is the very Way itself—generous, creative, skillful.

If the flow of ideas and methods was initially from cloistered practice into daily life, it moves in both directions now. The field of awakening grows stronger and more tangible as silence and speech converse; stillness and action learn from each other in the new exchanges made possible by crossing the boundary from meditation hall to marketplace and back again. If the question arises whether it would be better if we were all doing the same kind of practice—choosing the cloister or a householder's life—just pull the camera back. The hermit in her meditation cave, the Buddhist midwife, and everyone else whose heart has turned toward the Way—there is a field large enough to hold us all. It is our shared awakening, to which we all contribute. Its evolution might be achingly slow and full of setbacks, but it continues—because of, and in spite of, all our best efforts.

◆ ◆ ◆

Someone is standing on a solitary mountain with no way to get down. Someone is in the middle of a crossroads, not facing any direction. Who is ahead and who is behind? It has nothing to do with householder and bodhisattva.
    —LINJI

In what follows there's an artificial purity in the distinction between cloistered practice and daily life. Each, of course, contains elements of the other, and neither always lives up to either its ideal or its shadow. Neither, in other words, is wholly the pure land nor wholly problematic; both are much more complex and interesting than that. Perhaps I'm speaking to that part of ourselves that tends to see things with unrealistic purity; perhaps I'm inviting a little boundary crossing and border-town mixing it up.

Both the well of cloistered practice and the acequias of daily life have their mysteries, their beauties, and their difficulties. To be sure, some things happen more readily in one mode or the other, but if our aspiration is for an awakening that leaves nothing outside itself, this seems like an argument for the complementary nature of cloistered practice and daily life, for the ways they need each other. Many Westerners seem to be making this assumption, as we apprentice to awakening in the world and the cloister simultaneously.

Even as we do, retreat practice and daily life can still appear to be in conflict with each other. This is probably rooted in a split between a cloistered and a worldly turn of mind that many of us bring to practice. In the midst of one, we long for the other.

When we're awake in the early hours doing our taxes, the starlit, pine-scented walk to the meditation hall can sound like heaven. It goes the other way, too: A woman's old sailing buddy calls to say that while she's in retreat he'll be out on the open sea in the yacht she used to crew on, and she wonders for a few moments about the turn her life has taken. Someone wakes up in the city every morning, pierced by a deep longing for silence and solitude; someone else is surprised by the urgency with which she wants to see her young son on the last day of retreat.

The institutions of Buddhism can, wittingly or unwittingly, reinforce this split. Most of the Buddhism that first came to the West in the twentieth century had a strong monastic cast, even when it was being practiced by laypeople. Over time many established centers have actively encouraged the development of householder practice, while new ways of practice have emerged that don't make the monastic assumption at all. But there's still a pretty strong, often unconscious bias toward cloistered practice, with householder practice seen as an adaptation of it. When inner conflict meets institutional authority, it can create an inertia that's difficult even to see clearly, let alone question.

Let's do it anyway.

Why do many of us assume that this split is inevitable? Why, in point of fact, do many of us experience it that way? What is the nature of longing? Is it just that humans are wired to yearn for the thing that isn't there? Is it instead a deep desire for wholeness? Is it the symptom of something not yet resolved or out of balance in the ways we practice—a symptom that, if we paid attention to it, might lead to greater health? Are we unwilling to accept that true apprenticeship offers a great deal and also asks for sacrifice? How does longing relate to aspiration and to *bodhichitta,* the desire for enlightenment so that one can be helpful to others? What about when the longing, the feeling that something is missing, eventually drops away, because, whatever the circumstances, nothing seems to be missing anymore?

The more we don't take the split between the cloistered and the daily for granted, the more a rich field of inquiry opens up, as many have discovered. Individuals and practice communities can respond to these questions in lots of different ways and come to very different conclusions. The important thing is that we keep holding the questions, keep examining our assumptions and conclusions, because all of this is still very much a work in progress. It's alive, it's exciting, and this exploration might end up being one of the West's great contributions to the onflowing Way.

◆　　◆　　◆

. . . the love that is enlightenment because it is the unity of experience.
—Vimalakirti

Over time, someone in apprenticeship to awakening is not so buffeted by the movement from cloistered practice to daily life. She becomes aware that there's really only one practice going on, and its location at any given time becomes less and less critical. The pure lands on either side of the boundary are receding, while the border town grows. This unified practice gets at once simpler and more pervading; it's like breathing. Inhale and exhale. Turning away and turning toward. Down and deep, out and wide. Wells and acequias.

What once seemed like two activities or focuses of attention are now aspects of one. You can't hold your breath forever, and you can't breathe out forever, either. We don't call this inhale-and-exhale; we call it breathing. In the same way, the apprentice begins to experience a one whole practice, a one whole path, under her feet wherever she is.

Awakening is the unity, the breathing that is made of inhale and exhale. It's the through line and the base note of our lives. If at the start the apprentice has a sense that the continuity in her life is provided by the self, a profound shift of allegiance eventually occurs. She sees that the self rises and falls; she climbs into the self when she needs it, and sometimes when she's deeply absorbed in meditation or art or physical exertion it disappears altogether. Underneath it all, awakening unfolds with each new experience, and it won't be complete in this lifetime until she draws her last breath.

This awakening isn't thicker or more accessible in some places than others. Awakening happens in the meditation hall, and it also happens on the freeway and in the sickbed. In any moment of any day, awakening is already there, and in any moment of any day we might come to experience it. We can leave that to chance or we can practice, which puts us in collaboration with awakening rather than making us exclusively reliant on grace. Most of us have figured out that practice isn't something we do only at specific times and in specific ways, but something we're doing in all the moments of our lives. What the apprentice to awakening comes to see is that she's not bringing something she gets from formal practice into the rest of her life; she's allowing that practice to change her, to soak in and stain her completely, so that she is now that stained person in every moment of her life. Awakening is also her willingness to be soaked and stained by other things—to feel the caress, to take the hit, to be devastated by a bit of news from the other side of the world, to let an encounter with beauty change her mind about everything. Allowing all these things to break open her heart is an essential part of the apprenticeship, because without it awakening can't be whole.

Sometimes the long arc of awakening is punctuated by great breakthroughs. In an instant, the true nature of things becomes vivid. The apprentice sees the emptiness of everything, meaning that she experiences how big and radiant everything is, and how everything is connected to everything else. People have these experiences in the meditation hall after years of practice, and they have them spontaneously as children, or in the most unlikely of circumstances. Awakening isn't snobbish about where and when it reveals itself, so we probably shouldn't be, either. A breakthrough will leak away, though, unless we ground the experience. Without a way to deepen and broaden it, to maintain a living relationship with it, it tends to fade into a fond or frustrating memory of what might have been.

Here's where the practice of daily life can be helpful. Awakening doesn't happen only like a bolt of lightning; sometimes it's a dawning awareness that the sky has been gradually getting lighter for some time. In the midst of our daily lives, we become aware of domestic, local moments of seeing the emptiness of things. A man starts to tell a familiar story whose meaning was set sometime in the last century about some relationship, and he finds that he can't get past the first sentence; suddenly the habitual narrative seems unreal, completely made up, even ridiculously funny. That's also seeing emptiness, just a particular emptiness rather than the emptiness of everything all at once. If we let the floor be pulled out from under us and for a moment fall freely, that moment of falling freely is a moment of breakthrough. With practice, we won't try to catch ourselves too soon, to reconstitute the self that has for a moment vanished. Crucially, if these moments of falling freely are recognized and appreciated, they tend to leak away less readily than the big breakthroughs; they accumulate and cause lasting change, and this can be tremendously encouraging. If the breakthroughs give us the biggest perspective of all, this falling freely shows us what that looks like in any moment of any day.

The fundamental promise of Buddhism is that any of us can awaken. As Buddhism has evolved, it has become clear that awakening is not just an individual matter. We are all in this world together, and we are all awakening together. So a matter of great importance is how we encourage practice that compromises on neither the awakening of the individual nor awakening in the field that holds us all—that sees both as essential to the uncompartmentalized Way. What an extraordinary, what a beautiful, challenge to be given.

That Bird Has My Wings

Jarvis Jay Masters

Jarvis Jay Masters has been a prisoner in San Quentin since he was nineteen years old. He is now on death row, convicted as an accessory in the murder of a corrections officer in what his many supporters call a miscarriage of justice. What is certain is that he has undergone a profound personal and spiritual transformation in his years behind bars, and has become an eloquent voice of the dharma. In this chapter from his new book, he describes with humor and amazement an unexpected few hours of freedom. All of us would benefit from seeing the world with such fresh eyes.

One morning I'd awakened to another day, when a guard called down the tier, "Masters, you have a medical escort. We'll be down in five minutes to pull you out!"

What medical escort? I thought to myself. *Can't be me! I'm not sick!* I couldn't help but feel suspicious. It was June again, always the hardest month.

"Wait! Hold up!" I yelled as the guards opened the front gate of the tier. "I never asked to see a doctor!"

"Are you going or not?" was the cold response. "It's up to you, Masters! Are you refusing?"

A few seconds passed. "Yeah, yeah, I'm going," I answered. "Whenever you guys are ready, I'm ready." And to myself, *Let's just get whatever this might be over with.*

Two guards came onto the tier and ordered me to undress. I pushed my clothes through the slot and turned around, naked, in front of them. After searching through the clothes, they pushed them back in. Then they reached through the slot and placed me in hand restraints. They called out my cell number to another guard off the tier who controlled the switch for the door to come open.

As I was being escorted off the tier, all my senses panned for even the slightest of unusual vibes that would tell me something, anything. But there were no clues. They placed me in a "waiting cell" without saying a single word to me, and I began reciting the Buddhist Red Tara mantra, *Om Tare Tam Soha.*

My Vajrayana Buddhist teacher Chagdud Tulku Rinpoche had given me many meditation prayers to say in moments just like this. I thought this prayer to Tara, the female Buddha, the embodiment of wisdom, might help the most. *Om Tare Tam Soha*—"Please be aware of me; remove whatever obstacles I'm here to face." As I said it, my eyes welled up as the image of Chagdud came over me.

On death row your closest fear is of your own death. This can be so consuming that it seems as if everyone you love on the outside is guaranteed to outlive you. They seem immortal. But Chagdud Rinpoche had recently died.

I adored him as both my teacher and my father. I felt so blessed that he had walked inside San Quentin to sit with me. In later years, through all his illnesses, Chagdud had rolled his wheelchair into the visiting room. He was the one who gave me my spiritual path. His students and other Buddhist practitioners had become my friends, forming the core of a support group that has worked tirelessly to appeal my death sentence.

A guard I'd never seen before took off my hand restraints and handed me an orange jumpsuit. It looked like a carrot costume. "What the hell is this?" I asked. "Where am I going?"

"Put it on," he commanded.

The words *Om Tare Tam Soha* struggled against *What the fuck is going on?!* The last time I had worn a jumpsuit was over a decade earlier, during my death penalty trial. So where was I going now? I had heard rumors that some death row prisoners were transferred to Pelican Bay, another prison many hours' drive north.

I was placed in a waist-chain—a chain fitted around the waist with hand restraints welded to it. It kept my hands close to my sides, but allowed more movement than handcuffs.

Three guards escorted me out the front door of the adjustment center. A small car was waiting for me, its four doors already open. As I sat down in the back seat, a guard reached over me and pulled a strap across my chest. I felt like an astronaut being prepared for lift-off. I'd never worn a seat belt before.

One guard took the driver's seat, one took the passenger's seat, and the third got into the back seat with me. The driver spoke into his handheld radio, and off we drove toward the back of the prison. Unfamiliar sights—the general population lower-yard, the prison industry buildings—passed by my window like a movie. I hadn't been in a regular car in over twenty-two years. The ride was so smooth, without the slightest sound—only by looking out my window could I *tell* we were moving. It felt dreamlike.

We drove on a narrow street along the shore of the bay, uphill toward the visitors' entrance. We were going a lot faster than I would have preferred. Being shackled in waist-chains with a weird seat belt across my chest while speeding around narrow lanes made me nervous.

We passed through several security gates—I could see Mount Tamalpais right across San Francisco Bay—to get to the front gate. We passed the prison parking lot, and there was my unit counselor, briefcase in hand, closing the trunk of the car. I made a mental note to tell him that I'd seen him. I was trying to distract myself from the feeling that I was in a car with three *assassins*—a car that made no sounds and told no tales.

When the east security gates swung open, we proceeded down the street to a stop sign, turned left onto a ramp, and then drove onto the freeway. I vaguely remember this from when I'd gone to court. *So maybe,* I thought, *I'm going back to court.* But noticing more and more sights I hadn't seen before, I felt a sick sway inside: this was not the direction of the Marin County courthouse.

A sign on the freeway made my heart drop. It read EUREKA. I knew that was next to the Oregon border.

So that's it, I told myself. *I'm being transferred to Pelican Bay, all the way up north, far from my friends in the Bay Area.*

At that moment the guard in the back seat spoke for the first time. "So, Mr. Masters, what's going on with you? What's the problem with your ears?"

Seconds passed. I could hardly piece together the words. "What?" I said. "My ears?"

"Yeah, your ears," he said. "Why are we taking you to see a hearing specialist?"

"Woah! Wait a minute!" I said. "Is that where I'm going? To see a hearing specialist?"

"Yeah. We have you scheduled to be at Marin General Hospital for a 9:30 appointment."

"You're shitting me!" I said. I tried to bring my hand up to my head to scratch my brains clean, but the chain from my waist didn't reach half that high.

"Nah! I wouldn't do that," he answered flatly. "You have an outside appointment to be examined by a hearing specialist."

More seconds passed. Then it all came to me.

Nine months before, I'd gone to see a doctor in order to get authorization to use the visiting phone for people with impaired hearing. I'd been having serious difficulty hearing my visitors in the noncontact visiting booths. The only visiting booth with a telephone was designated for the hearing impaired. But the doctor said that he couldn't provide me the permission slip I requested; I would need to be examined by a "hearing specialist." It never occurred to me that he'd place me on a list to be seen by one, let alone that I'd be taken out of prison to go to Marin General Hospital.

I felt light as a feather. I wanted to fly, to open my eyes, to look around and remember everything. I couldn't shift gears fast enough! Now I was on an outing, a sightseeing tour of the world that I hadn't seen since I was a teenager. The summer sun reflected off the car window, and as I peered out I wished everything could slow down. My eyes became a camera lens, snapping pictures of cars, trees, and houses. I could breathe the air of freedom—sweeter than anything I could remember.

As I stayed glued to the window, I also began to remember how I'd lost my freedom, and all the pain I'd caused for so many people—those awful times. I felt the violence crushing me. As we passed a supermarket, I remembered how I'd once jumped up on a store counter shooting a gun. The thought froze me. How could I have done something like that? I became scared of myself, scared by those years. How could I have compromised my freedom, my sanity?

My spirit was now struggling to be free—free from the chain tight around my waist, free from the handcuffs, free from the conversations I was having with myself, free from the conversation with the guard about my ears and the hearing specialist.

Minutes passed. We got off the freeway and came into a lot of traffic. People of all ages were walking down the street, riding their bikes, sitting and waiting for the bus.

"So, Masters," said the guard, "Do you know how long this examination is going to take?" My nose was almost pressed against the window as I focused on a shopping center. "Well," I said, "Let's hope you guys won't get back in time to be reassigned to more work, and let's hope I won't get back to my cell too soon, you know? Hell, guys," I asked, "Isn't there some *long* way we could take?"

Along Sir Francis Drake Boulevard I saw all different types of cars. I once knew the make of every single car I saw, but now I couldn't tell a Chevy from a Toyota. I saw joggers, some wheeling strollers as they jogged, while others ran with their dogs on a leash.

As we drove through the midst of everything and I looked at all the people, I felt that each one was sharing that day in their life with me. *What if it had been them, these real faces, that I had stolen from? That I had shot at?* I thought to myself. I didn't know how I could have done what I did. I felt so much regret. *How was I not able to feel all this before?* I wondered.

Whenever we came to a red light, I was in the best moment—being there, not going any place, just waiting, thinking. Narrowing my focus, I could see small things like the names of businesses on building walls. Widen my lens, I could take in the bus benches and the pair of gray pigeons walking along as if they owned the sidewalk. I saw the beauty of life inside the canvas I wanted much to be a part of. I wondered: *would I, could I, ever fit back into society after so damn long?* I really felt that I could. But would I ever be allowed to?

Every time we drove through a green signal, I felt a bit disappointed. I even wished we'd find ourselves in a traffic jam for hours. I know such waiting usually frustrates people, but it is heavenly compared to San Quentin's death row.

It didn't take as long as I wished to get to Marin General Hospital. The car parked in front of the lobby door, and I got out, looking like an overgrown carrot with legs. In the hospital lobby sat a large number of people, including children. Walking in wearing that orange jumpsuit, under the escort of three uniformed guards, I felt like a character from *The Silence of the Lambs*. People stared at my waist-chains. I wasn't sure if a smile would make things better or worse.

A man reading the *Marin Independent Journal* slightly lowered the newspaper as I walked by. For an instant, we looked at each other. Then he hid behind his sunglasses. Something was wrong, but what? I could swear I'd seen the ghost of my adjustment center counselor; I'd just seen him in the prison parking lot. No way could my counselor be sitting there.

We went down a hallway to the hearing specialist's waiting room, where a middle-aged white woman finally came out and called my name. She explained the tests she would do and asked me if I had any questions. She acted as if she hadn't noticed that I was a prisoner. The guards escorting me stood down from their "this is a hardened criminal."

The testing area was a space no larger than my prison cell, all decorated like a children's nursery. The specialist put earphones on my head, instructing me to raise my hand whenever I heard a sound. Then she and the guards left the room.

While I was listening for beeps to come into my ears, the word "sunglasses!" inadvertently came out of my mouth. The man reading the newspaper had been wearing sunglasses—that's what was bothering me. Why would somebody wear sunglasses while reading a newspaper inside a hospital lobby?

When my hearing test ended, the specialist said there were still many charts she needed to read, but already she could see I had some deficiencies. She assured me that her final assessment would be forwarded to the prison.

"In a month or so?" I asked her.

"No, not even that long," she replied as I walked out of her office into the hallway.

Speaking so comfortably to the hearing specialist gave me the courage to speak again, despite my carrot jumpsuit. I noticed an elderly lady walking by, completely bent over her cane. She was struggling so painfully with every tiny step, I wanted to reach out. I stopped, caught her eye, and asked, "And how are you today? You look so beautiful this morning, ma'am." And she did look beautiful to me, walking like I could imagine my own grandmother walking.

She beamed up at me. Then, nearly in tears, she responded, "Oh, thank you, young man," in a voice so loud that everyone in the lobby spun around, including the hospital employees behind their desks. Then I noticed her hearing aids; she wasn't aware of how loud her voice carried. Some of the people were smiling at our exchange.

I knew I'd been impulsive, but I just had to say something to somebody! Outside the prison, people didn't seem to talk to each other. Was it the orange jumpsuit? The several pounds of chains around my waist, and the restraints around my hands, that were to blame for the hush-hush in the lobby? Everyone in the lobby kept their own space, even when they were seated next to each other. Nobody seemed to acknowledge that someone else was sitting right there—not even the kids! I would have been so hyper at their age, but they weren't saying anything, not even bouncing around in their chairs. They were too well behaved, just frozen stiff.

As I was escorted out, I again noticed the guy with the newspaper held up over his face. I couldn't help but ask, "Dickerson, is that you? Is that you, Dickerson?" He didn't look up at first. I could feel a guard giving my waist-chain a tiny push to say, *Keep moving*, when the newspaper came down. Behind the glasses was my counselor, cracking a smile. He let the glasses slide down his nose so I could see his eyes.

"Man, Dickerson," I said. "I thought that was you! What in the world you doin' here?"

My counselor still didn't say a word, but gestured to the guards that I could stop walking. He looked down, folded the newspaper, then looked up at me again, leaning back in his seat, grinning. His eyes were signaling me to take a look around to see for myself why he was there. In the thin second it took me to scan the lobby, I saw familiar faces here and there—even behind the front desk—of both men and women. They were all prison guards dressed in plain clothes, scattered all over the lobby.

Holy shit! I said to myself. I couldn't believe my eyes. *Where did they all come from?* My counselor got up from his seat. Through subtle hand movements, quietly and effortlessly, he directed all the guards to begin their exits, with some in front of me and others behind. There were more guards stationed outside in the parking lot.

When my escorts put me back in the car, I saw the plainclothesmen searching the bushes around the parking lot. Then state cars pulled up alongside them, picking them up one by one. I turned to the guard beside me. "Man, what is all this secret service stuff? Some sort of presidential escort you guys got goin' on?"

"Well, Mr. Masters," he answered, "you're a very important person to the state of California. We don't want to lose you."

"Aw, come on! Give me a break!"

"No, seriously," the guard responded. "We know your supporters want you out of San Quentin. We just tryin' to make sure it doesn't happen today!"

"You thought my supporters would be here at the hospital waiting to break me out? Is that why you were all hush-hush about where I was going?" I asked.

"All I can tell you," he said, "is that we'd rather be safe than sorry! Whenever we transport a prisoner outside the prison, especially a condemned prisoner, every precaution is taken to ensure that we get you where you're going and return you safely."

As we drove out of the parking lot, I saw a state car in front of us and two others directly behind, all carrying plainclothes guards. "Tell me something," I asked the guard. "Have all these other cars been with us since we left San Quentin? Because I know I saw Dickerson walking out of the prison parking lot, and I've been wondering how he could have been sittin' in the lobby when we arrived."

"You're going to have to ask Dickerson that," he answered.

I hoped the ride would be slowed by lots of red lights.

I watched the walkers, joggers, and bicycle riders with such a smile across my face, as if this was my own walk on the boulevard. I also noticed the lack of social interaction among people, which was painful. *Where has all of that gone—turning to talk to each other?* I seriously wondered.

I saw whole groups of people waiting together to cross the street without looking at each other or speaking. People sitting right next to each other on a bench waiting for the bus just looked ahead as straight as an arrow, as if nobody spoke the same language. They seemed robotic. It reminded me of a science fiction series on television, *The Outer Limits.*

I watched two sets of parents almost side by side, pushing their babies in strollers. Only the babies tried to communicate, their tiny hands reaching toward each other, gesturing in thin air while the parents ignored each other. Drivers in the cars alongside us wouldn't turn their heads to look at me, though some of them seemed to be talking to themselves. I could relate to that.

"Well, I guess folks would just rather talk to themselves nowadays—they've just become more accustomed to talkin' to themselves!" I mumbled. The guard beside me started laughing. I laughed too. It was sort of crazy, like San Quentin.

"Nah, that's not true," he said.

"Oh, yes, it is!" I insisted.

A minute later a car drove up beside us, as if to prove my point. There it was again—another person talking to herself. I made double sure she didn't have a cell phone in one hand before I pointed her out to the guard. "So, hey—you tryin' to say she's not, that she's singin' or somethin'?"

The guard started laughing again. "Mr. Masters, how long you been in prison?"

"Doesn't matter," I said. "I know what I see! And she, that woman, is holdin' a serious discussion with herself! Can't you see? She has both hands on the steering wheel. And look, just look, she's in some serious discussion, just a-laughing and giggling to herself."

"Look closely," the guard told me. "Look very closely, Masters. There's a pair of thin headphones on top of her head. You see 'em? And right in front of her mouth, look real closely. You see that little piece of equipment?"

"Yeah, I think I can see something. You're talkin' about that curled piece of wire in front of her mouth, right?"

"Yeah, that's it," said the guard. "That's a telephone. That's an actual cell phone."

"Nah, you kidding me," I said, embarrassed. "You mean to tell me all the people I saw that I thought were talking to themselves had on somethin' like that?"

"Mr. Masters, this is Marin County," explained the guard driving the car. "If it's out there, you'll see it first in this county!"

"Well, I guess you learn somethin' new every day, huh?" I mused, wanting to scratch my head again for some reason. At that moment I realized just how distant San Quentin was from this whole society, like an island unto itself, even though it sat right in the center of the Bay Area. And I'd been confined behind its walls for over two decades. On this day I'd seen a world I hadn't known before.

Over the years I've tried hard to remember things as they were, to hold on to something that I could reach back to and reflect upon, so that I might not feel altogether severed from the world I wished to reenter. Now my memories started to shred. The impermanent nature of everything left me nothing to hold on to. Everything had changed. I asked myself: *Hey! Would you want things to stay the same? Especially if that means you never grow in any way?* When the castlelike shape of San Quentin suddenly came into view, I had so much to think about, so much to reflect upon.

How fortunate I had been compared to all the other condemned inmates on the dreadful first tier of the adjustment center, perhaps the most crazed in all of San Quentin. I'd actually gone outside the prison, if only for a couple of hours—and in order to have my ears tested! My spirit soared, wanting to rejoin life, wanting to redeem myself, wanting to do it a different way, regretting that I had not gotten it right the first time, and that I'd terrorized others in the process.

When the cell door slammed shut behind me, I thought I could hear more clearly the noise of the tier. Then I realized that I was hearing the voice of my own heartbeat telling me that I did not belong here in San Quentin or in any other prison—the voice of my longing to be free.

You Are Here

Thich Nhat Hanh

Nirvana is usually described as a state of peace, but it can also be understood as the cessation of struggle. While some religions recommend a spiritual path of internal struggle, Buddhism suggests we take an attitude of gentleness and loving-kindness toward ourselves, even our flaws and faults. As Thich Nhat Hanh says in this beautiful teaching, Buddhism is a practice of love, nonviolence, and nondualism, and so we do not turn ourselves into a battlefield between good and evil.

Every twenty-four-hour day is a tremendous gift to us. So we all should learn to live in a way that makes joy and happiness possible. We can do this. I begin my day by making an offering of incense while following my breath. I think to myself that this day is a day to live fully, and I make the vow to live each moment of it in a way that is beautiful, solid, and free. This only takes me three or four minutes, but it gives me a great deal of pleasure. You can do the same thing when you wake up. Breathe in and tell yourself that a new day has been offered to you, and you have to be here to live it.

The way to maintain your presence in the here and now is through mindfulness of the breath. There is no need to manipulate the breath. Breath is a natural thing, like air, like light; we should leave it as it is and not interfere with it. What we are doing is simply lighting up the lamp of awareness to illuminate our breathing. We generate the energy of mindfulness to illuminate everything that is happening in the present moment.

As you breathe in, you can say to yourself, "Breathing in, I know that I am breathing in." When you do this, the energy of mindfulness embraces your in-breath, just like sunlight touching the leaves and branches of a tree. The light of mindfulness is content just to be there and embrace the breath, without doing it any violence, without intervening directly. As you breathe out, you can gently say, "Breathing out, I know that I am breathing out."

Buddhist practice is based on nonviolence and nondualism. You don't have to struggle with your breath. You don't have to struggle with your body, or with your hate, or with your anger. Treat your in-breath and out-breath tenderly, nonviolently, as you would treat a flower. Later you will be able to do the same thing with your physical body, treating it with gentleness, respect, nonviolence, and tenderness.

When you are dealing with pain, with a moment of irritation, or with a bout of anger, you can learn to treat them in the same way. Do not fight against pain; do not fight against irritation or jealousy. Embrace them with great tenderness, as though you were embracing a little baby. Your anger is yourself, and you should not be violent toward it. The same thing goes for all of your emotions.

So we begin with the breath. Be nonviolent with your breathing. Be tender with it. Respect it, and let it be as it is. You breathe in—there's an in-breath, that's all. If the in-breath is short, let it be short. If the in-breath is long, let it be long. Do not intervene, or force either your in-breath or your out-breath. It's like looking at a flower: letting it be as it is, mindful of the fact that it is there, a kind of miracle. See the flower as it is. See the breath as it is. We let the flower be as it is, and we should not do violence to our breath either.

Then we move to the physical body. In practicing sitting and walking meditation, in practicing total relaxation, you embrace your physical body with the energy of mindfulness, with great tenderness and nonviolence. This is the practice of true love in relation to your body. In Buddhist meditation, you do not turn yourself into a battlefield, with good fighting against evil. Both sides belong to you, the good and the evil. Evil can be transformed into good, and vice versa. They are completely organic things.

If you look deeply at a flower, at its freshness and its beauty, you will see that there is also compost in it, made of garbage. The gardener had the skill to transform this garbage into compost, and with this compost, he made a flower grow.

Flowers and garbage are both organic in nature. So looking deeply into the nature of a flower, you can see the presence of the compost and the garbage. The flower is also going to turn into garbage; but don't be afraid! You are a gardener, and you have in your hands the power to transform garbage into flowers, into fruit, into vegetables. You don't throw anything away, because you are not afraid of garbage. Your hands are capable of transforming it into flowers, or lettuce, or cucumbers.

The same thing is true of your happiness and your sorrow. Sorrow, fear, and depression are all a kind of garbage. These bits of garbage are part of real life, and we must look deeply into their nature. You can practice in order to turn these bits of garbage into flowers. It is not only your love that is organic; your hate is, too. So you should not throw anything out. All you have to do is learn how to transform your garbage into flowers.

In the practice of Buddhism, we see that all mental formations—such as compassion, love, fear, sorrow, and despair—are organic in nature. We don't need to be afraid of them, because transformation is possible. Just by having this deep insight into the organic nature of mental formations, you become a lot more solid, a lot calmer and more peaceful. With just a smile, and mindful breathing, you can start to transform them.

If you feel irritation or depression or despair, recognize their presence and practice this mantra: "Dear one, I am here for you." You should talk to your depression or your anger just as you would to a child. You embrace it tenderly with the energy of mindfulness and say, "Dear one, I know you are there, and I am going to take care of you," just as you would with your crying baby. There is no discrimination or dualism here, because compassion and love are you, but anger is too. All three are organic in nature, so you don't need to be afraid. You can transform them.

Let me repeat: In the practice of Buddhist meditation, we do not turn ourselves into a battlefield of good versus evil. The good must take care of the evil as a big brother takes care of his little brother, or as a big sister takes care of her little sister—with a great deal of tenderness, in a spirit of nonduality. Knowing that, there is a lot of peace in you already. The insight of nonduality will put a stop to the war in you. You have struggled in the past, and perhaps you are still struggling; but is it necessary? No. Struggle is useless. Stop struggling.

So I take care of my breath as if it were my tender little baby. I breathe in, and I let my in-breath proceed naturally. I rejoice in the fact that my breathing is there. Breathing in, I know that I am breathing in. Breathing out, I know that I am breathing out. I smile at my out-breath. This is how you can practice. You will get a great deal of joy out of it right away, and if you continue for a minute, you will see that your breathing is already different. After a minute of practicing breathing mindfully, without discrimination, the quality of your breathing improves. It becomes calmer, longer; and the gentleness and harmony generated by your breathing penetrates into your body and into your mental formations.

Try to breathe in this way when you experience joy. For example, when you are looking at a sunset and are in contact with the beauty of nature, practice mindful breathing. Touch deeply the beauty that is before you. I am breathing in—what happiness! I am breathing out—the sunset is lovely! Continue that way for a few minutes. Getting in touch with the beauty of nature makes life much more beautiful, much more real, and the more mindful and concentrated you are, the more deeply the sunset will reveal itself to you. Your happiness is multiplied by ten, by twenty. Look at a leaf or a flower with mindfulness, listen to the song of a bird, and you will get much more deeply in touch with them. After a minute of this practice, your joy will increase; your breathing will become deeper and more gentle; and this gentleness and depth will influence your body.

Mindful breathing is a kind of bridge that brings the body and the mind together. If through mindfulness of the breath you generate harmony, depth, and calm, these will penetrate into your body and mind. In fact, whatever happens in the mind affects the body, and vice versa. If you generate peacefulness in your breathing, that peacefulness permeates your body and your state of mind. If you have practiced meditation, you have already discovered this. If you have been able to embrace your in-breath and your out-breath with tenderness, you know that they in turn embrace your body and your mind. Peace is contagious. Happiness is also contagious, because in the practice of meditation, the three elements of body, mind, and breath become one.

So as you breathe in, respect the in-breath. Light up the lamp of mindfulness so that it illuminates your in-breath. "Breathing in, I know that I am breathing in." It's simple. When the in-breath is short, you take note of the fact that it is short. That's all. You don't need to judge. Just note very simply: my in-breath is short and I know that it is short. Do not try to make it longer. Let it be short. And when your in-breath is long, you simply say to yourself, "My in-breath is long."

You respect your in-breath, your out-breath, your physical body, and your mental formations. The in-breath moves inward, the out-breath moves outward. In and out. It's child's play; but it provides a great deal of happiness. During the time you are doing it, there is no tension at all. You are here for life; and if you are here for life, life will be here for you. It's simple.

Answers to Children's Questions

Thich Nhat Hanh

The author of a number of children's books, Thich Nhat Hanh often begins his talks with teachings especially for the children in the audience. In every program he sets aside time to answer questions from children and young people, and as you'll see, he doesn't dumb it down for them. They ask good and important questions and his answers deliver clear, strong dharma that all of us can benefit from.

*W*ho was the Buddha?

The Buddha was a person, just like you and me. He was a prince named Siddhartha, who lived in Nepal about 2,600 years ago. He had everything he could want: a beautiful palace, wealth, the best foods, luxurious vacations, and plenty of power. He was a very good student. He learned very well. He grew up, got married, and had a little boy. But he wasn't happy. He knew something important was missing in his life. Although his father tried to hide all human suffering from him, Siddhartha saw how much people were suffering, and he saw how little his father, the king, was able to do to help them.

His father wanted him to become king, but Siddhartha didn't want to be king. Instead, he determined to become a monk, in order to liberate himself from suffering so that he could help others. Siddhartha left the royal palace during the night, leaving behind his wife and his son, and he went to the woods and practiced as a monk for many years. Finally he became a buddha, a fully enlightened person. Then he began to teach. He taught for forty-five years and helped many people—rich people, poor people, all kinds of people—and he had many students. He died at the age of eighty. His teaching has been handed down through the generations, and now we are his students.

The Buddha said that every one of us can become a buddha like him. If we have love, understanding, and peace, if we can transform our anger, our jealousy, then we can become a buddha like him. And in the cosmos there are many other buddhas. Wherever there are human beings, there is the possibility of a buddha, or many buddhas, manifesting.

What does "dharma" mean?

The dharma is the practice of love and understanding. The dharma may be in the form of a dharma talk, or perhaps in the form of a book. The best dharma is the living dharma embodied by a practitioner. When you look at that practitioner you see the presence of peace, loving-kindness, understanding, and compassion. That is the living dharma. When you practice mindful breathing, calming your mind, calming your feelings, that is the living dharma.

The Buddha passed on the dharma to many generations. Now you and I are the continuation of the Buddha, and thanks to our practice, we keep the dharma alive so that we can pass it on. The dharma is the essence of a buddha. With the dharma, people suffer less and they can be happy and loving. Without the dharma inside, the Buddha is not a buddha. Without the dharma inside, a sangha [Buddhist community] is not a true sangha. Your practice is to keep the dharma alive and growing every day, for your own happiness and for the happiness of other people. When you embody the dharma in that way, we call it the "dharma body."

What is the most important thing we can do to become enlightened?
Enlightenment isn't something that's far away. You don't need to practice for a long time to get enlightened. You can be enlightened right here and right now to some degree. It's like health and well-being. When you drink your tea and you know that you're drinking your tea, you're concentrated, you see that drinking tea is something you like to do. So drinking tea mindfully is a kind of enlightenment. There are many people who drink their tea but who don't know that they're drinking their tea. They're so absorbed in their anger, their fear, their worries, and their projects that they don't even notice the tea.

Being mindful of what's happening in the present moment is enlightenment. When you walk like a sleepwalker, there's no enlightenment. When you walk mindfully and enjoy every step you make, enlightenment is already there. When you eat mindfully, there is enlightenment. We call it mindfulness, but mindfulness is the beginning of enlightenment. If we continue to live mindfully every moment of our daily life, our mindfulness will grow strong and powerful. That's why we have the saying, "There's no way to enlightenment, enlightenment is the way." Enlightenment must be in the here and the now. You drink your tea, you walk, you breathe, you sit, you wash your clothes in such a way that happiness is possible right now and right here. That is our practice.

What is the best way to meditate?
We can meditate in the sitting position, but we can also meditate while we're walking or standing. Meditation can be very informal. Suppose you're standing in line, waiting your turn to serve yourself some food. You might practice mindful breathing in and out, enjoying yourself and the presence of the people around you. When you ride your bicycle, if you ride mindfully, enjoying your

in-breath and out-breath, you're practicing meditation. When you wash the dishes, if you enjoy breathing in and breathing out and if you smile, the dishwashing becomes very pleasant. So meditation is possible in all kinds of positions, whether lying down, standing, walking, sitting, or doing things. Everything you do, if you do it mindfully, is meditation.

How do we overcome fear?

First you must find out whether your fear has been born from your wrong perception. The practice of mindful breathing in and out, deep and slow, can help you to look deeply into the nature and roots of your fear. People are afraid of dying, people are afraid of getting old, of being abandoned. People are afraid of being sick. People are afraid of losing what they cherish today, of losing the people they love today, of losing their jobs and so on. The Buddha advises us not to try to run away from our fear, but to bring up our fear and have a deep look into it. Most of us try to cover up our fear. Most of us are afraid of looking directly at our fear. Instead of trying to distract yourself from this fear, or ignore it, the Buddha proposed that you bring the seed of fear up and recognize that it's there and embrace it with your mindfulness. Sitting with your fear, instead of trying to push it away or bury it, can transform it. This is true of all of your fears, both small ones and big ones. You don't have to try and convince yourself not to be afraid. You don't have to try and fight or overcome your fear. Over time you'll find that when your fear comes up again, it will be a little bit weaker.

How can we deal with anger?

Sometimes we're angry, but we don't accept that we're angry. In that case we need a friend who's honest enough to say, "Dear friend, you're angry." But if you're a good practitioner you don't need a friend to tell you, because you practice mindfulness and you're aware of what's happening inside you. When anger comes up, you know it's there. So you practice mindful breathing and say,

> Breathing in, I know anger is in me.
> Breathing out, I take good care of my anger.

Don't say or do anything else, because saying or doing something in anger can be very destructive. Just go home to yourself and continue to practice mindful breathing and mindful walking to embrace, recognize, and bring relief to your anger. After that, look deeply into your anger and ask yourself what has caused it.

We may be the main cause of our own suffering and anger because often the seed of anger in us is already too big. As soon as we hear or see something unpleasant, that seed in us is watered and we become angry. So, our suffering comes mostly from us, and not from another person. The other person is just a secondary cause. Look deeply into your anger, and you might see that your anger has been created by your wrong perceptions, wrong views, and misunderstanding; and when you realize that, your anger is transformed.

I worry so much that it's hard for me to do whatever I need to do. How can I stop worrying?

The practice is to learn to take care of the present moment. Don't allow yourself to be lost in the past or the future. Taking good care of the present moment, we may be able to change the negative things in the past and prepare for a good future. We tend to worry about what will happen in the future. The practice helps us to come home to the present moment, to our body, our feelings, to the environment around us. When we breathe in and breathe out mindfully, our mind is brought back to our body and we are truly there in order to take care of the present moment. If there's some stress, some tension in our body, we practice mindful breathing in order to release the tension, and that brings us relief. If there's a painful feeling in us, we use mindfulness to embrace our feeling so that we can get relief.

The key point is that you are fully there in the present moment, in the here and the now, to take care of yourself and what's happening around you. You don't think too much about the future or project too much about how it might be; and you're not trapped too much in the past. You have to train yourself, to learn how to go home to the present moment, to the here and the now, and to take care of that moment, to take care of your body and your feelings in this moment. That is the most effective way to deal with anxiety or worries.

As you learn how to handle the present moment, you'll gain faith and trust in your ability to handle the situation. You learn how to take care of your feelings and what's happening around you. That makes you confident, and as your confidence grows, you're no longer the victim of your worries.

Seth and Willie

Daniel Asa Rose

The first truth of Buddhism is impermanence, which is really just another word for death. Buddhism doesn't focus on the reality of death to make us morbid or depressed. As this story by Daniel Asa Rose so poignantly illustrates, when we contemplate the reality of death it opens our hearts and connects us to all sentient beings, past, present, and future, who must share this universal experience.

Why are you in such a sucky mood?" I asked.

My fourteen-year-old came up to my face, the machinery of his teeth glinting. "Because my whole mouth is on fire, OK?" he replied.

I remembered to breathe. "Just because you got your bottom braces put on, that's no reason to take it out on your little brother," I said. "Demonstrate a little courage."

The sullenness worsened.

That's when I proposed the bike ride.

"I don't want to take a bike ride! I'm hungry but I can't even eat. I can't put anything in my mouth!" he replied. "Everything's too germy anyway. Why would I even *want* to take a bike ride?"

"Maybe it'll make you feel better. We can ride to the ball field and watch your brother play."

So that's what we did. After his little brother was picked up by a classmate's father to go to the game, we rode. The sun was still high at 7 PM. I pointed out the long shadows, the purple crowns of clover so plump in the evening air, the stalks of grass straight and firm. I was trying to coax some sunshine into his being, or at least help console him through the distemper of being fourteen with a mouth full of biting metal. He grunted and moaned. Nothing soothed him. He slumped over the handlebars like something wilting.

We passed a sign that said "Free Rabits." It was leaning against a telephone pole all by itself, the "rabits" long gone. It might have looked forlorn except for the stately rods of green swaying against the base, their tops gleaming in the slanting light. So strong and stalwart. The perfume of cut grass was everywhere, liquory enough to make you drunk. I could hear mowers working throughout the countryside.

"Don't be discouraged if I go faster than you," I said. "I do this year-round so I'm in pretty good shape."

He pedaled even slower. Was he hanging back on purpose or were the teenaged years really so full of fatigue? I tried a new tack.

"Sometimes when I'm feeling out of sorts, I just pedal a while and, like magic, pretty soon I feel better."

Neither did this solve the world's problems. "Do you mind if I wait for you at the next turn?" I said, losing a measure of patience. "If you lose your way just keep going straight."

"I'll mess up!" he cried.

I went ahead anyway, not to be a prisoner to his mood. In a meadow a lamb bleated. Lucky lamb, I thought, with all this grass everywhere, swallowing the town. After a while I stopped to relieve myself. "This is the end" blasted out from inside a nearby garage. Not half bad for a garage band, I thought, then realized it was actually the real recording by The Doors. I saw my son pedaling, in a kind of lethargic nervousness, down the road by himself. God knows what he was thinking. When he got to me, I said, "We're about to pass the saddest gravestone in the world."

"I don't want to stop," he said.

"It's right on our way."

He huffed some more, distressed.

When we got to the graveyard, we parked our bikes outside the little stone wall. I found the double gravestone right away, though I hadn't been there in fifteen years, since my first set of boys was the age this pair was. My wife had left me in despair, hers or mine was not clear, and I had the boys every weekend. The rest of the time I kind of wandered around, alert for things like this.

I kneeled in the dirt and put my hand on the yellow lichen growing so adroitly on the small, low stone. When he joined me, I read aloud:

SETH A.   WILLIE W.

Died Jan. 4, 1878

In the 11th year of his age   In the 9th year of his age

Children of Gilbert A. and Rachel B. Horton

In the morning these two brothers,
Left their home on ice to play,
But were drowned beneath the waters,
Early on that painful day.

When I looked up, I saw with a shock that Spencer had tears in his eyes.

"Me, too," I said.

"Yup," he said.

I rubbed the stone a while. Though the stone dated from 1878, it felt like rubbing the hair of my sons just this morning. I was glad I had two sets of them, for safety.

I stood and patted the taller monument, my height.

"These are the parents, Gilbert and Rachel," I read. "They lived till 1905 and 1916, all those years after their sons died."

Spencer sniffed. I didn't point out how the stone did not use the words "dreadful" or "unspeakably horrible"; "painful" was sufficient. Nor did I tell him the saddest part—that there were other children buried nearby, all around us, siblings of Seth and Willie. The parents had outlived them all.

We remounted our bikes. "Life is complicated," I told him. "Everyone you see, even the mean ones, they all have their struggles and their troubles."

"Yup," he said.

When we got to the ball field, I borrowed a piece of paper from the scorekeeper and sat on the rough wooden bleachers with the other parents to write this down. The pen skipped over the splinters.

"You signing autographs?" one of the fathers asked.

"Just writing something that just happened," I said.

"Right here?" he pursued. "You rock."

No I don't. I just wanted to write this down. Out of the corner of my eye I saw that Spencer had put a blade of grass in his mouth and was chewing on it.

Saltwater Buddha

Jaimal Yogis

The goal of Buddhist practice is to weaken the hold of ego, the illusion of a permanent self to which we so desperately cling. But the ego is a clever beast who can turn even Buddhism into a source of pride and self-satisfaction, particularly when it is joined with a worldly pursuit, say, becoming a really good surfer. Jaimal Yogis put his Zen in the service of ambition, and he wasn't happy with what he became. An unlikely friendship was the cure.

All my favorite Zen masters said everyday life is the path. And since surfing was my everyday life, I sat at the ocean's feet. She always had lessons. And she didn't tithe. She didn't have a hierarchy (even if some of the other surfers did), and she didn't ask me to obey secret codes. She just ebbed and flowed, demonstrated impermanence, and slapped me around when I needed it.

So as summer turned to fall and the monarch butterflies migrated through Natural Bridges State Beach, I left my studio to be a full-time ocean devotee. I parked my van along West Cliff and slept on the cold beach and didn't care that I went to class with sand in my hair. I surfed and surfed and surfed and sat in cafes and drank lots of tea and meditated in the verdant hills.

It was kind of fun. For a while.

Eventually, of course, living in a van in Santa Cruz and puppy-dogging after a girl who never had enough time for me stopped working for me. I really missed hot showers. So I moved away, to Berkeley, and took classes at Cal and eventually fell in love with a responsible girl.

But I hated *driving* to the surf. I really hated it. I began to go completely insane, and no amount of meditating could cure it. My girlfriend was wondering if I had some strange illness. I *needed* to get back to the sea, I told her. But I didn't want to go back to Santa Cruz, to the Surf Nazis and cold water and the gurus. I'd had enough of that Pure Land.

So I used the old fallback. I executed my familiar escape routine once again: one-way ticket to Hawaii, upheaval with loved ones, deciding which island to go to, blah blah blah. You've heard it. And I know you think I was just running away (again). Hell, even I thought I was just running away. But I figured it was OK. I mean, I was making progress, right? This time my trip had a responsible edge. I applied to the University of Hawaii at Hilo—yes, possibly the worst-ranked university in the country, but *still* a university—as a religious studies major.

After my time living in the monastery I could write Eastern philosophy essays with my eyes closed—which meant ample time for surfing, and that's what mattered.

Surfing really, really mattered.

Having been away from warm water for two years, on this trip I got fanatical. I woke at five AM to check the waves. I surfed twice a day. My back muscles turned to rocks and my nose peeled in perpetuity. When there wasn't surf, I ran and lifted weights and swam long distances to stay fit. I daydreamed about waves. I nightdreamed about waves. When I meditated, I visualized myself tucking into waves, endless barrels—my new version of Zen emptiness.

I didn't realize how much I was obsessing until Aran, with whom I usually had deep conversations about love and philosophy and politics, called me one night from California. He told me about everything going on in his life and wanted to know about mine.

"Uh, I don't know," I found myself saying. I honestly couldn't think of anything I was doing but surfing. No deep thoughts. No life outside of the weather patterns.

"Well, tell me about surfing," he said.

"Well, I do it a lot."

My mind was saltwater.

I drifted farther from formal Buddhist practice and everything else that didn't peel or tube or pitch. My grades suffered. I still sat my daily *zazen* session. But it became shorter and shorter until it almost wasn't there. Which was OK with me. I saw "merging with the waves" as my new practice. Surfing was becoming my official religion.

It's not that I was giving up on Zen. But I saw surfing as the best Zen practice. By this point, I'd done weeks and weeks of formal Zen retreats in lots of different monasteries. I didn't think I was any hotshot meditator, but I'd experienced some interesting meditative states—but so what?

And after all that, it still seemed to me that the mind brought forth while surfing a wave was as close as I'd come to Zen. The great ancestor Sengcan described the Zen mind by saying that the subject disappears without objects, objects vanish without a subject. And centuries later in Japan, Master Dogen talked of the dropping off of one's body and mind, and the body and mind of others. Riding a wave, this happened naturally. The wave demanded such hyperfocus, there wasn't room for judging. On a steep, hollow wave, there wasn't even time to differentiate between one's body and the wave. There was only *this* and *this* and *this*. Just power and presence.

And, I thought, if I could only hold that focus when the wave ended, I would be a Buddha. But I couldn't. The wave always ended. The special meditative state always ended.

Impermanence was inescapable, omnipresent.

When there weren't waves in Hilo, or when it was raining too hard to see them, my friends and I would go to impossible lengths to find surf. We drove and hiked down every dirt road and path on the island. We skipped class and camped in deserted valleys and flew to other islands and paddled to distant reefs. In the beginning, it was fun even when there weren't waves. We were seeing sights— living the dream. Surfing videos had assured us that the endless hunt for perfect waves was the best life anyone could live. And we were *doing it.*

But I was also slowly beginning to question whether it was the best life. The more I obsessed with "getting good" at surfing, the more I noticed myself getting frustrated with mediocre waves and genuinely pissed off when the ocean was flat. Surfing was my religion, my one true love. But at the same time, it was slowly becoming an unwholesome relationship with all kinds of unhealthy expectations and needs.

The Buddha talked a lot about not attaching to the good stuff and not running from the bad stuff. Suffering, he said, arises from the mind's incessant attraction and aversion. He wasn't recommending people abandon their commonsense attraction and aversion. Putting your hand in fire hurts for a reason. Eating healthful food feels right for a reason. But the Buddha encouraged cultivating a more even-keeled mind.

I thought about the Buddha's teaching in reference to surfing. On good days, I could observe my obsessive chasing of the pleasurable waves and how it often led to dissatisfaction—but somehow, even then, the idea of "getting better" trumped that awareness.

I just *had* to be a good surfer. I couldn't slow down the search. And I definitely couldn't stop it.

I immersed myself deeper in surfing, deeper in the waves. For a few months there, I was surfing better than I ever have. My best friend at the time was an insanely good athlete named Tim. He grew up in Hawaii and was a sponsored bodyboarder, one of the best on the island. He pushed me to ride waves I never would have and took me to all the famous breaks on Oahu: Pipeline, Backdoor, Off the Wall.

Around campus, I even developed a minor reputation as a good surfer. "Dude, I saw you pull that snap the other day," a stranger at a party told me one night. "You really rip. I just wanted to give you props."

"Um, thanks," I said. But then other people told me. And it was hard to believe. Having started surfing later than most, I never thought I'd impress even my own mom. But apparently my hard work was paying off.

And then came my downfall, running up to me in a yellow bikini, eyelashes batting. The cute surfer girl I had a crush on, Emily, was saying, "Jaimal, I saw you out there. Maybe you should start competing."

That's when my mind warped.

In my mind, I started seeing myself on the cover of *Surfer* magazine, women fawning, cameras flashing. Result: I gradually started becoming the thing I most despised.

It started with me seeing myself as having some divine right to waves. I was still a small fish in a big pond of incredibly skilled surfers. I still knew my place (almost). But I began to see the beginners as somehow *undeserving* of waves. Sometimes, much as I hate to admit it, I didn't even like going out with my friends from school who were still learning. They embarrassed me. My *reputation* was at stake.

My attitude was trickling into my life outside the water, too. I found myself doing things I never would've done before. I caught myself in little lies. I got in a screaming match with one of my best friends over money. And the weirdest part was, I could even observe the process happening. Worse still: I didn't care.

Then one day I snapped. It was a sunny day at Honoli'i and there were tons of waves, more than enough for every surfer to get dozens. I had surfed plenty, but I still wanted more. And that was when some oblivious tourist—looking much like I once looked in those first days on Maui—dropped in right in front of me and fell, ruining a very nice wave, my wave.

This had happened a hundred times before and I'd never cared much. "No worries," I usually said, and paddled on. But this time, I lost it. The words just spilled out of me. "Watch where the fuck you're going," I growled. I startled even myself. The kid looked terrified. "Sorry, man," he said. "I'm so sorry. I didn't see you."

I looked back at him—teenager, not even with any tan yet. He had the same exact look I'd had at sixteen: innocence, excitement, fear. And that's when it hit me. I'd really gone too far. I was becoming a Surf Nazi, an extremist. I paddled over to the kid. "Look, don't worry about that fall," I told him. "Sorry I flipped. I was just worried I'd hit you."

He looked relieved. "No, that's alright. It was my bad."

I felt like such a jerk, like I wasn't any better than the Surf Nazis who I found so difficult to bear. The whole reason I'd started surfing was to find a life that was free.

Surfing was my religion—but in my confusion I was twisting it into something unrecognizable, mistaking the method for the goal, the means for the end.

I guess it happens all the time, to religious fanatics of all stripes.

The Buddha understood this problem of attaching to methodology, even though he also took great care to hone the methodology he did teach. He warned his students about engaging in unproductive practices that were all the rage in India at the time: rubbing your body in ash, worshipping fire, having sex with skulls. (I'm not sure how popular that last bit was, but it was popular enough to make it into the Buddhist rulebook.) But then he went further: He said even his own teachings were not to be taken as Ultimate Truth. He asked his students not to worship him like a god or make statues of him. He said that his teachings, to borrow a Zen phrase from centuries later, were merely a finger pointing at the moon, not the thing itself.

He also compared his teachings to a raft. The raft could be employed to cross the river of delusion and suffering. But once that shore was reached, the teachings had to be let go of. It would be foolish, he said, for someone to reach the opposite shore—of enlightenment, of freedom from suffering—and still carry the raft around on his head.

I knew very well I wasn't enlightened. And the day I screamed at the kid, I finally understood that I was carrying my surfboard around on my head and it wasn't getting me any closer to freedom. In fact, it seemed to be making me into an asshole.

So I let go a little. I surfed once a day instead of twice. I got my grades back up. I even did my own weeklong silent retreat up in a little cabin on the volcano. And I got a job.

And amid all my studies of world religions, each with its own strengths and pitfalls, I saw that Buddhism, though it too had its flaws, was still a pretty good raft, at least for me. If I could get a little better at steering it.

But I still didn't want a guru.

Naturally, a guru showed up.

He didn't come as I imagined he might. I wasn't climbing up a misty mountain. And he wasn't a fat old Zen master, or a Shaolin monk who could balance on a pin, or a 110-year-old yogi who could see the future.

His name was Lambert.

And he was a Hawaiian insurance agent who spent most of his day watching television. He had a passion for three things: poke (a kind of Hawaiian salad made out of raw fish, pronounced "po-kay," by the way), detective stories, and—surprisingly enough—church.

I admit that Lambert was a strange sort of guru. He didn't know anything about Buddhism. Or want to. Lambert actually thought Buddhism was kind of weird.

"I just really love Jesus," he told me one day when we were talking religion.

"Me too," I said.

"Then why are you a Buddhist?"

"I can't be a Buddhist who loves Jesus?"

"Uh, I guess. Well, I don't know. I don't see why not. But I think that makes you a Christian who likes Buddhism."

"Fine with me. But you're just trying to convert me. I mean, maybe you're a Christian who loves the Buddha and you don't even know it."

"Yeah, but I don't need to find out. I'm fine with just Jesus."

"Suit yourself. But how do you know Jesus wasn't a buddha?"

"Because he was God. I thought you said Buddha wasn't a god."

"You might have a point there. But I think it's primarily a vocabulary problem."

"You're weird."

"*You're* weird."

At first I couldn't see Lambert's teaching. I thought I was teaching Lambert. I told him about all the very profound things I learned in my religious studies classes. And since Lambert was a Christian, and I had to read the Bible a lot for class, I read Lambert the Bible almost every day. Usually, he'd just fall asleep.

"Man, this is *your* religion and *you're* sleeping," I'd say. "Have a little respect."

"I'm just taking it in on a very deep level," Lambert muttered dreamily.

But most striking was this: we laughed a lot. And I soon learned that that was Lambert's main teaching. He always had bad jokes. And when he wasn't dropping those on me, he was making fun of me for being a vegetarian, which seemed to be an endless source of entertainment for him. He couldn't believe anyone could live without poke and beef.

"You're not going to live very long if you don't eat meat," Lambert told me all the time.

"Well, I'm doing a little better than you are, Mr. Carnivore."

"Ha ha. Very funny."

This wasn't a very good joke, actually. And I never would've said it if Lambert didn't have an incredibly good sense of humor. Lambert was the biggest optimist ever; that was his other teaching.

Because considering his condition, it was amazing Lambert could even smile.

Lambert couldn't even get out of bed.

He could barely move.

Lambert had a rare sickness called neurofibromatosis—Elephant Man's disease. He had gotten bouts of it through his teens and twenties and he'd beaten them, somehow. But the most recent one had nearly paralyzed him.

I'd like to say I volunteered to take care of Lambert. But I met him because I needed some money and responded to a job posting for a caregiver position that also included free rent. Lambert and I hit it off right away. Suddenly I was Lambert's roommate and caregiver.

At first, I thought it would be nice just to help the guy out and save some money. I felt rather proud of myself for being a do-gooder again: Saving Lambert. I could almost picture the movie. What a hero I was. But after a couple weeks, it became clear that movie really would have to be called *Saving Jaimal.*

Lambert had been a handsome competitive athlete in his youth, a swimmer who was great at science and math. He had strong Hawaiian bones and huge, shiny black eyes and a big, sincere smile. But the disease ruined his body. It made his bones swell up. His skull got lopsided. His elbows bulged. His fingers were stuck in a half fist. He couldn't be left alone even briefly or it was likely that his lungs would fill up with fluid and he'd drown in his own mucus.

I admit that taking care of him was sort of painful at first. For one, I missed out on some of the best surf sessions of the winter. Plus, I was always tired because Lambert needed fluid sucked out of his lungs with a special machine every few hours, so I never slept more than a few hours at a time. When I did sleep, I was on the floor next to his bed so I could wake up to do the lung clearing.

But the more time I spent with Lambert, the more I liked being with him and didn't mind missing the surf, didn't mind the intimately mundane parts of the job: stretching Lambert's legs, bathing him, emptying the bed pan, cooking for him. Lambert was always upbeat and I could never maintain an emotional slump around him. Not even I could keep sulking when a paralyzed man with a fatal disease was telling jokes. It was free therapy. Lambert's family almost never came to visit him. But he didn't complain—ever. His main social interaction was with his caregivers. But his caregivers all seemed to linger when they came to visit. They didn't want to leave. I guess they knew they were going to have to go care for a bunch of bitter patients who were angry about everything, and understandably so: most of them were dying.

Lambert was dying, too. But he didn't take it out on those around him. He never got mad at me when I messed something up—which as you might imagine happened all the time.

And that is why he's still my guru. His life is a perfect teaching. It doesn't need any clever words. The way he just abided in his life exactly as it was. This was a perfect demonstration of the core truth of the Buddha's teaching: true contentment does not come from external circumstances.

From a whole year of frantic searching for perfect waves, fanatically living my surf-religion dream, Lambert's teaching was the one lesson that really stayed with me.

So: Thank you Lambert.

PS Lambert, I'm sorry I haven't written. Also I know you don't need it, but I can't help reciting Amitabha Buddha's name for you once in a while. So if you see a big golden buddha, don't freak out. I'm betting he and Jesus know each other.

It's All Happening to All of Us, All of the Time

Sylvia Boorstein

The mind of the Buddha is called bodhichitta, *literally "awakened heart–mind." Bodhichitta has two aspects: wisdom—profound understanding of the nature of reality, and compassion—love for all beings and the desire to free them from suffering. Bodhichitta is actually our true nature, and through various practices we can develop this innate wisdom and compassion. The beloved Insight Meditation teacher Sylvia Boorstein found one way for people to share and expand their natural love and care for others.*

I've been leading a two-hour, Wednesday-morning class at Spirit Rock Meditation Center for more than fifteen years. Of the seventy or so people there on any given week, there are the folks who have been coming regularly since the beginning, new people coming to see what it's like, and visitors to San Francisco who come because they are in town. I've begun to think of it as our local church. We always begin by greeting newcomers. I then give some meditation instructions and we sit quietly for thirty or forty minutes. In the last minutes of the sitting I remind people that they're welcome to mention the names of people they are particularly thinking of, people facing a special challenge, so that we could, as a group, think of them with shared concern and support. I often start by naming someone I know—"I am thinking of my friend Allison, who is recuperating from surgery for ovarian cancer"—and wait for others to speak. People say a name, a relationship, and a challenge.

"I am thinking of my cousin Joan, who has macular degeneration."

"I am thinking of my daughter-in-law Louise, who just had a miscarriage."

"I am thinking of my brother Tom, whose son just lost his job and his house."

"I am thinking of my friend Michael, who has lung cancer."

". . . my Uncle John, who has emphysema."

". . . my son Tim, just diagnosed bipolar."

". . . my friend Bernie, who lost most of the retirement savings for him and his wife."

". . . my neighbor Virginia, whose daughter died in a car accident last Sunday on her way back to college."

I don't call on people to speak. In random order, from different parts of the room, voices speak out names, and relationships, and special circumstances. Sometimes I recognize a voice, or a name. More often not. Sometimes the naming goes on for what seems a long time. There is always a space between the voices, as if people are reflecting on what they've just heard. I think we share the sense that there is no hurry to get finished, no activity more important to arrive at.

Not all of the special circumstances that people mention are dire, although it seems that sad situations are usually the ones that come up first. Then, in between difficulties, someone will say, "I'm thinking of my daughter Jessica, who has just been accepted into three colleges and needs to choose." Or, "I'm thinking of my son and daughter-in-law, who are on their way to Peru to meet their newly adopted baby daughter." Or, "I'm thinking about my college roommate from Michigan, who has remained my friend for fifty years and who is arriving tonight for a visit."

I don't think I am imagining the communal sigh of relief or appreciation that follows happy news. Those moments seem like opportunities in which my mind, perhaps everyone's mind, can "catch its breath" and remember the pleasures that punctuate life and make it seem desirable to go on in the face of difficulty.

Sometimes the listing of names and circumstances goes on for some minutes:

" . . . my grandson Jason in his second tour of duty in Iraq."

" . . . my sister Ruth with breast cancer."

" . . . my friend Claire, whose life savings were invested with Bernie Madoff."

" . . . my niece Renee, who is nine months pregnant and whose husband just lost his job and their insurance."

" . . . my husband's mother, Ruby, who is dying of Alzheimer's disease."

At some point the room becomes quiet again, and we sit a while longer. I say a blessing for all the people we've mentioned, and for all people suffering everywhere, and I ring the bell. Usually, we all just sit there and look at each other for a while. Often, I find myself feeling speechless, stunned both by the array of pains that body and mind are heir to and humbled by our communal courage not only in carrying on in spite of challenges in our lives but in being willing to share them with each other.

What more compelling evidence could there be, apart from personal testimony, of the inevitable difficulties of life? Every week, as we listen to each other and hear about sicknesses of young people and old people, about disappointments and losses at all ages, we directly confirm that it is impossible to be a human being connected by affection to others and not be vulnerable to pains beyond our own. My sense is that hearing the implicit message that most of us carry on in spite of our difficulties builds strength and courage. I'm sure that's true for me, and I think it is for others as well. At the end of each Wednesday I feel remarkably freed of any grievances or ill will I might have had before class. I feel kinder, more connected, through both sorrow and joy shared with the people in the room and, past them, with people everywhere.

Life is difficult, the Buddha taught, for everyone. Suffering, he said, is the demand that experience be different from what it is. Of course we do what we can to address pain. Sometimes illnesses are cured. Sometimes relationships are mended. Sometimes losses are recouped. Sometimes, though, nothing can be done. The Buddha's teaching of liberation was that peace of mind is possible, no matter what the circumstances.

I recall hearing, for the first time, the legend of the young mother rushing with her dead son in her arms to plead with the Buddha, who was known to have miraculous powers to restore her child to life. I knew at once, as you will too if you are new to this story, that when the Buddha responded, "I will do it if you bring me a mustard seed from a household in which no one has ever died," the boy would not live. The mother, disconsolate, returns from her quest knowing that everyone dies and that the heart can survive grief. To me, the instruction "bring me a mustard seed" means: "Look around you. You are supported by everyone else in the world." I understand the end of the legend, the mother bowing to the Buddha and becoming his disciple, as her miraculous healing.

I feel myself supported by the awareness that everyone struggles. At Spirit Rock on Wednesday mornings, when I hear someone whose voice I don't recognize say, "My Aunt Claire, who has Parkinson's disease . . . " I remember my friend Claire, who doesn't have Parkinson's disease but has something else, and Phyllis, who does have Parkinson's disease, and my aunt Miriam who, until her recent death, was the only person left in my family older than I am. A woman's voice saying, "I'm thinking of my son Jacob in his second tour of duty in Iraq," reminds me of my cousins, whose son Jonathan is back in Iraq for his third tour, and I think about everyone with sons and daughters in wars all over the world. When I say, in the final dedication of merit at the end of the class, "May all beings be peaceful and happy and come to the end of suffering," I mean it with all my heart.

On one particular Wednesday morning when the list of special circumstances had been especially diverse and the kinship connections unusually wide-ranging, someone said, "Everything happens to everybody." I thought, at the time, that the remark was a response to the vast numbers of complex situations, sorrows, and joys that happen to people. What feels more true to me now is that when I *am* paying enough attention I realize that everything is happening to everyone collectively, and I feel appreciation and compassion for us all.

Dawn Light

Diane Ackerman

There's a lot of debate these days about religion versus science. Diane Ackerman, the best-selling author of The Natural History of the Senses, *shows one way that they are reconciled. As she contemplates the dawn light one early morning, her deep knowledge of the natural world becomes not a materialist straitjacket but a gateway to the mysterious, beautiful, and ineffable.*

Waiting for dawn, much is sensible, if not visible. To us, anyway. Some other creatures—bats, moths, fireflies, owls, raccoons, cicadas, spiders, mountain lions—get by just fine. For me, dawn begins before the sun and below the soil, and extends up through sky and weather to the canopy of stars. The visible stars that is. So much surrounds us that we can't see. Life on other planets, but also the missing matter in the universe. Computations show that stars, planets, galaxies, and all the rest of the visible matter make up only four percent of what actually exists. Where is the rest, the so-called dark matter and, even stranger, dark energy? A yard or street is partly full of the invisible weight of the universe.

At the doorway of the senses, the self chances upon the world. Yet, for the most part, we live a life of surfaces; otherwise we'd buckle under an avalanche of sensations. When we turn on the radio in the morning and hear static or interference as we switch between channels, do we need to know we're divining lightning strikes on other continents and the hissing death throes of galaxies? Probably not. But, when we do, the aperture of the mind widens as it travels to distant continents and galaxies and back again.

After the black dawn, the white dawn arrives laced with pink fire. Dawn light brings a clarity that's missing from noon glare or smoggy sunset, however pretty their filters. Sitting on a rusty wrought-iron chair, I turn my thoughts to the beauty of rust, which dissects metal so meticulously, creating freeform bronzes, brown bubbling sandwiches, gritty red icons, supine statuettes, ragged perforations, flaking black-orange memorials to time. We underestimate rust, which may well have sponsored all of life on Earth. In the explicit light, rust declares its past.

Some think it's easy for life to emerge, for primitive cells like bacteria to form anywhere in the universe. For instance, in the deep ocean trenches, several miles below the sunlit waves, hyperthermophiles bloom—hardy bacteria that breathe iron and thrive in water hot enough to sterilize surgery tools. Hugging the scalding vents, they reproduce in boiling water and can abide at 266 degrees Fahrenheit where minerals abound. Of the many heat-loving microbes haunting the deep ocean, *Geobacter metallireducens* can even generate its own electricity.

All you really need is rocks and water, and everything else happens by itself. When iron sulfide (rust) from Earth's hot core meets cold water, the shock creates honeycombed chimneys where the first living cells could have grown. Subject oxygen and carbon dioxide—so plentiful on the young Earth—to heat and high pressure, with rust as a catalyst, and a metabolism naturally ensues. The earliest microbes would have left those cradles to colonize the land. We still carry some of that primordial iron in our cells today. Rust is a very slow fire, and like fire it releases energy as it devours. It also gains in size, prying apart steel in a process known as "iron smacking." Iron corrodes especially fast when exposed to an electrolyte like water, and, for better and worse, the human body is awash with an electro-lyte broth.

"Rust, I bow to you," I say silently, not wanting to disturb the birds that have begun to pipe, trill, and bark, chasing each other at speed across the sky. My rusty, weathered chair is rich with the fetch-ing poverty the Japanese call *wabi sabi.*

Wabi originally meant living miserably alone in nature, far from human society, and feeling gloomy, bleak, comfortless. And *sabi,* whose beauty comes from the patina of age, originally meant "chill," "lean," "withered." But the phrase *wabi sabi* changed in the sixteenth century, when the hermit's life of chosen isolation in the woods seemed to offer a spiritual richness society lacked, and the words came to mean an intimacy with nature and delight in the rustic de-tails of daily life. The hermit's eye turned toward the minute, the crude, the cracked, the incomplete, those objects with interesting crevices—especially if something were rusted, weathered, or worn, revealing the passage of time. It's a nice felicity that the Japanese word for rust is also pronounced *sabi,* returning us once more to the rusty origins of life and the rust at the heart of the word "rustic." Partly as a rebellion against the glory of the decorative arts, wabi sabi favored the purity of humble forms, but unlike European modern-ism's ideal of smooth, streamlined, futuristic creations, wabi sabi valued the organic, imperfect, faded nature of earthy things that were handmade one at a time, not mass produced, and all the more appealing when worn through loving use. Wabi sabi relies on intui-tive, right-here right-now observation, without any glance toward the future or even the idea of progress.

A pastoral aesthetic, wabi sabi not only accepts nature as unruly and uncontrollable, it welcomes nature's rule, beyond the scope of any technology we can create, however sleek and obedient. So, wabi sabi embraces the idea of corrosion, decay to the point of disintegra-tion, and ambiguity, in warm fluid shapes and quietly resonating earth tones. Poetry, too, can be wabi sabi, if it arouses serene melan-choly, an acceptance of reality at its most exquisitely mundane, a reality in which things and people break down, but are no less beautiful for that.

Japanese also has many names for beauty. One feels *awaré* while appreciating the ephemeral: say, the transient beauty of decay in the luminous green moss spreading over rotting trees, the mushrooms and toadstools rising from the rich soil, the patches of brilliant gold and red lichen. After a bird has flown, one may feel *yoin,* silent reverberations that remain. It's this sensation that poet Wallace Stevens writes of in "Thirteen Ways of Looking at a Blackbird," when he celebrates both "The blackbird whistling / Or just after." One may also experience the poignant beauty known as *yugen,* described in this way by thirteenth-century author Kamo no Chômei (in *An Account of My Hut,* 1212): "It is like an autumn evening under a colorless expanse of silent sky. Somehow, as if for some reason that we should be able to recall, tears well uncontrollably." Or: "When looking at autumn mountains through mist, the view may be indistinct yet have great depth. Although few autumn leaves may be visible through the mist, the view is alluring. The limitless vista created in imagination far surpasses anything one can see more clearly." Solar energy lights our days and fuels the plants that prey animals eat before they're eaten by predators. We eat the sunshine stored in those plants and animals, burning it for energy, which we spend to work, cook, make love, play music, pursue games. And so we're connected to every other life-form on Earth in a skein of interrelated victories of fire, including rust. The universe is most likely littered with planets as rusty as our own. Are they florid with life? If so, how well, and how long, have their life-forms survived?

That question almost qualifies as a koan. Koans are capsules of thought, psychic knots that resist unraveling. In some Buddhist sects, students are assigned phrases or situations to meditate upon, to focus the mind and free it from the bear-trap of reason. For example:

1. "A man is sitting atop a hundred-foot pole. How does he get off it?"

2. "A wheel maker makes two wheels, each with fifty spokes. Suppose you cut out the hubs. Would there still be wheels?"
3. "On a windy day, two monks are arguing about a fluttering banner. The first says, "The banner is moving, not the wind." The second says, "The wind is moving, not the banner." Who is right?
4. "Two hands clap and there is a sound; what is the sound of one hand?"
5. "What is the straight within the bent?"
6. "Pull a five-story pagoda out of a teapot."

Inexhaustible, koans are intended for live practice between master and student, with illumination as a goal, not interpretation, because, as an old saying goes: "It's easy to confuse the pointing finger with the moon." As Zen teacher Norman Fischer explains: "This practice consists of living with and sitting with phrases, until they become very large and very strange, and reveal themselves to us. That is to say, through them we are revealed to ourselves."

There's no right answer to these puzzles designed to focus the mind, and I sometimes dwell on koans while waiting in the dark for first light. This morning, I've been thinking a little about *mu*, though I appreciate it's not something understood by occasional thought. *Mu*, which translates inadequately as *nothingness*, often appears in Buddhist practice, and sometimes in this venerable koan: "What is mu?"

As I sit under a coliseum of stars, awaiting the dawn, mu is the everythingness of everything fed by and in time with the everythingness of everything else, except that its particles are too small to be captured in the net of words like "every" or "thing" or "net," which, like life-forms and galaxies, are only temporary clumps of the stridently irrational mu, a mutable, ultimately manic, mute, munificent force that strings us together as it does the farthest stars. And I am only using the unwieldy symbol of "force" because we are the sort of beings who do, to communicate the shred of universe we homestead and can perceive, when of course there is no force, no we, no universe, not even mu-mesons: only these molecules, this energy pooling here for a short while as Diane, and never again in the same way.

I once read of a Zen master who became enlightened like this: "When I heard the temple bell ring, suddenly there was no bell and no I, just sound." Imagine no distinction between yourself and the bell, the sound and the universe. Sometimes when I'm swimming, the waves don't feel separate, the water's history and my history melt together, and I sense my particles breaking apart and scattering, returning now and then like a school of fish to form what appears solid, pattern, thing, but happens only to be a temporary sack of cells turning together. As sunlight hits the prismatic water, the walls and floor of the pool become a luminous cage holding nothing but thought. Ever since I was a child, for whole minutes at a time, I have effervesced out of my self in an ecstasy of communion with the cosmos at the level of atom and leaf. And yet, I also spend most of each day not in that state, with my zaftig "I" sprawling all over the mind furniture, a slovenly and selfish guest. So, is enlightenment sustainable? Jack Kornfield, of Spirit Rock Meditation Center in northern California, explains that enlightenment isn't continuous; one still has to do the laundry. But surely *how* one does the laundry is what matters? Fine, but one still has to go to work, not always with equanimity. Unless one lives in a monastery, it's not easy to prolong a calm, serene, cheerful equilibrium, which one nerve-jangling phone call can quickly convert to anxiety. In the stir of the world, I'm glad to find slender moments of dawning, when the ephemeral cape of being simply fits.

In the end, life is the best koan—not the word, but the process of living. An endlessly mutating koan created by water, minerals, and heat in the cold furnace of the atom, without meaning or purpose. From that evolved creatures stricken by meaning, afflicted with purpose. But it has always been about rust, the ancient, unknowable, nearly unthinkable rust that created all life, and the rust that obliterates us, intimately, one by one.

Natural Wakefulness

Gaylon Ferguson

Enlightenment is such a big word. It feels like a far off goal, probably unreachable for people like us. But in fact we are naturally awake, and flashes of enlightened mind happen to us all the time. The path then is one of recognizing, understanding, and deepening what is always present but usually unnoticed. Here is a clear and helpful presentation of this view from one of the most eloquent Buddhist teachers in the West today.

In meditation retreats over the years, I've been asked many times: "Why is it natural to 'wake up'?" After some conversation among the group, circling around the deeper meaning of "awake" as our natural state of being, someone will occasionally grow bolder still and raise a hand to wonder out loud: "If it's so natural, why do I need to meditate?"

Meditation is the natural path of spiritual awakening. The Buddha discovered a "middle way" of developing our innate human potential, an approach to meditating that avoids the twin traps of trying to force the mind to be still or letting it run wild. Right meditation skillfully joins our basic awakened nature with the practice of gently training the mind and heart.

The word "buddha" means "awakened one." Imagine that one day, walking among the fresh vegetables of your local farmer's market, you suddenly see someone with unusual presence—calm, compassionate, clear. What are the signs of this? It might be the graceful way the person moves: body and mind in easy harmony with each other. It might be the person's gentle tone of voice, the friendly way of speaking to the checkout person. It might just be the bright clarity and steady kindness of the gaze; the eyes can be the windows of wakefulness.

Seeing such a person, we might wonder: Who is this? Where did this wise person come from? How is it that someone could be radiating such peace and sanity in the midst of so much anxiety, aggression, and speed? The most important question we might ask ourselves is: how did this person get to be this way? As soon as we begin to contemplate awakening, wondering about it—where it comes from, how to get there—we are already on the path to enlightenment. Our curiosity is a sign of inner wakefulness uncoiling itself.

The Buddha's powerful yet gentle presence inspired many similar questions among those he met: "What are you? Are you a supernatural being? Is there a way for us to become more at peace with life, more grounded and open—the way you are? What should we call you?" Smiling, he answered: "I am awake, so you should call me, 'Awakened One'—and here is a noble path to your own awakening."

This name, "Awakened One," is an answer—but also a question: Awakened from what? Awake to what? Clearly the famous "awakened state of being" involves more than just rising with a yawn and a few stretches from an ordinary night of restful sleep to face the challenges of another day. We are concerned here with deeper senses of "asleep" and "awake." We are beginning the journey to complete realization by contemplating the meaning of enlightened wakefulness and spiritual sleep.

The first step of true awakening involves realizing our habitual, everyday, walk-around state of being "asleep." Our distracted, daydream-filled life has been compared to sleepwalking. As we know, sleepwalkers often dream on in relative comfort—until they suddenly bump into a wall or step off a staircase. The resulting "ouch!"

experience corresponds to the discovery of what the Awakened One called "the noble truth of suffering."

Certainly the Buddha's own spiritual path involved first waking up to his sleepwalking state. Suddenly—with a penetrating glimpse of the painful realities of human life outside the cozy comfort of his parents' palace—he saw that he had been living in a pleasant dream. The bubble of indulgent life at court was a seductive trap, lulling him into a false sense of security, keeping him from seeing the bright truth of real life. For Prince Siddhartha, recognizing confusion was the crucial first step on the way to enlightenment, a milestone in his journey to complete freedom from confused suffering.

This is the victory cry of the unbroken lineage of awakened ones: there is a path that leads to liberation. We can free ourselves from the automatic, habitual thoughts and emotions that so often bind us into familiar psychological prisons. The good news is that liberation is possible. Our first major challenge is facing the trap of self-imprisonment, for the path to true freedom begins with insight into our routines of self-deception. Our initial awakening is to the sleep state, our lack of self-awareness.

Checking In with Our Experience

If we are at all unsure about the truth of distraction in our ordinary state of being, our everyday life, then let's pause for a moment to check, to see for ourselves how it actually is right now. It's crucially important that we test these teachings on wakefulness against the truth of our own experience. So, please put the book down for a moment, sit comfortably, and then just take notice of what is happening physically and mentally for you at this very moment. Take two or three minutes to notice and inquire in a curious and friendly way: What is happening with the body—notice the play of physical sensations, perceptions, feelings. What is happening in the mind? Any thoughts? Are these mostly thoughts about the future? Thoughts about the past? Any hopes or anxieties? A mixture of the two?

Feelings of happiness? Sadness? Boredom? Excitement? Just notice your own state of being—body, mind, and heart, as you are right now. Are there just a few thoughts—like a tiny trickle from a faucet? Or is it more like a gushing waterfall, thoughts upon thoughts upon thoughts, one after another, rushing forward in a continuous stream? Look. Take note of what is happening, inquiring with loving-kindness. If you find your mind repeatedly drifting to last night's dinner conversation or next week's planning meeting, notice that—and instead of jumping into the details of the past (why did she say that?) or future (what will I do when I get there?), gently return to this focused inquiry into the present: what is happening in body and mind, right now? Look with gentle curiosity, and see what is actually happening.

As we are inquiring into our present state, doubtful, skeptical thoughts about the whole process may emerge: "I don't feel like I'm distracted by thoughts of the future or the past. Many of my thoughts are about the present. Sure, I'd rather be doing something (anything) else right now. What's the point of this exercise, anyway? I don't think I'm sleepwalking through life, at least not most of the time. Has it been three minutes yet?" Again, the truth is not a matter of belief or accepting some traditional dogma. Truth is uncovered by closely examining our own experience. Answers are discovered through seeing what is actually happening in our body and mind. Here, the proof of the recipe is definitely found in the taste of the pudding. Cook—and then taste-test for yourself. Just look and see what is happening at present. Don't take anyone's word for it. Look—honestly and directly.

Just notice—and then notice again, noticing what's happening in the next moment and then the one after that.

Don't Reject Anything

Even this simple exercise of precise awareness and honesty involves bravery—we're letting go of our preconceived ideas about what our experience is (or should be) and taking a fresh look for a change.

We're letting go of old judgments. We're not trying to make anything in particular happen or achieve a specific state of mind. We're not meditating. We're just noticing what is already going on in the present—without any manipulation. Don't try to hold on to what occurs: If it feels relatively pleasant to sit simply for a moment like this, let it be that way. If it feels like nothing special is happening, then let that be as well. Similarly, if it feels slightly uncomfortable and unfamiliar, let that feeling of awkwardness arise. Does it linger and then dissipate? Above all, don't condemn or reject anything that's arising in your experience: "Is this really the way my mind jumps around all day long—like a grasshopper that's had too many espressos? That wasn't a very loving thought, now, was it? Why am I still thinking about that? What comes next, what comes next, what comes next? Is this what's supposed to be happening? What's wrong with me today? I think I was more present last week—what happened?"

In Robert Heinlein's science-fiction novel *Stranger in a Strange Land,* he describes several truthful, evenhanded beings called Fair Witnesses. Adopt the attitude of "fair witnessing" toward all your experiences for a moment, gradually relaxing the pervasive compulsion to grasp and hug the best and happiest moments while avoiding the ugly, unpleasant ones. As much as possible, return again and again to noticing, noticing, just noticing, with a simple, nonjudgmental attitude of curiosity and gentle inquiry. What is happening here and now for you, within your own experience? Notice with the open attitude of a good friend you haven't seen for a while. This is the friend who genuinely wants to know your state of being, who asks and then listens carefully to hear the answer to the question: how are you? Listening in your own experience for the answer to this contemplative question is the essence of genuine self-reflection.

More Than a Fair-Weather Friend to Ourselves

In this simple way, we begin to make true friends with ourselves in a thorough and profound way instead of being a fair-weather friend.

We say, "Jack and Jane are mostly fair-weather friends," meaning these are friends we can spend time with when all is going well and sailing along smoothly, but during high-stress times of grief and loss, illness, or divorce, Jack and Jane don't come around. The invitation of a daily meditation practice is to move beyond such a superficial, fair-weather friendship with ourselves.

After all, it's fairly easy to love those aspects of ourselves that others approve of, the facets of our personality we are rewarded or admired for. What about the less praiseworthy aspects of our being, our less savory emotional habits? Losing our temper over a minor hassle. Endlessly procrastinating. Pushing ahead in traffic without regard for the feelings and needs of others. Waffling back and forth with fearful, worried indecision. Covering over our moments of insecurity by faking it, blustering our way through any conflict or challenge, afraid to show our true feelings to anyone. Part of the power of genuine spiritual practice is that we sit in meditation with ourselves during all the seasons of our life, during the falls and winters of trouble and defeat no less than the springtimes and summers of victory and celebration.

This is the royal road to enlightenment, approaching meditation as a process of making friends with oneself. This is the path of meditation as loving-kindness practice—we begin by first extending gentleness and kindness to ourselves.

This noticing, this wakeful, caring interest in our present state of mind and body, is itself natural. Appreciative inquiry expresses our true nature. We all have an inborn, native sense of care for ourselves. Attention expresses respect. Awareness of our own state of being is the basis of self-respect. Awakening starts with appreciating this natural interest and then gradually expanding the appetite for self-knowledge. Self-knowledge is the vanguard of wisdom. We begin with this innate appetite for knowing, and we return to it again and again, going with the grain of our own deepest inclination. We want to go beyond the illusions of sleepwalking to wake up to ourselves as we truly are, so we inquire: what am I sensing, feeling, thinking now? This basic level of self-awareness and self-reflection is readily available to all of us. Self-knowledge is the essential ground for the entire spiritual path.

WHAT IS NATURAL WAKEFULNESS?

The term "natural wakefulness" echoes similar phrases from the Buddhist tradition: original nature, fundamental wisdom, basic goodness. Are these different words for the same thing? Perhaps. What's more important than the menu is actually tasting the meal. We live in a time in which we doubt the fundamental trustworthiness of our experience. This has become so pervasive that we wonder if it isn't just as natural to be selfish and distracted as it is to be open and kind. To clarify this essential point, let's return to the relationship between natural wakefulness and meditating.

Our original nature is the single most important element on the path of waking up. Why? Because it is the essential ingredient—without the natural impulse to wake up, there cannot be a path of meditation or a spiritual journey at all. Practicing meditation without this original wisdom-nature would be like gardening all summer without any seeds—we could prepare the ground and water the soil, even pick away the weeds and insects, but without seeds, we know that nothing will grow.

Similarly, no movement along the path is possible without this primary motive force. It would be like setting out to travel across town but not walking, running, biking, driving, or using any other means of transportation. How could we possibly move without motivation? True nature is our motive force.

Chögyam Trungpa Rinpoche urged us to study the sayings of an ancient Indian Buddhist wisdom teacher named Tilopa. Tilopa—whose name means "sesame-seed person"—used the analogy of sesame seeds to point to the importance of our fundamental nature. Without the seeds we cannot obtain the inner essence, the sesame oil, the fruit of the meditative path. Even if we dutifully press sand or gravel for hours upon hours all day, every day, for a month, we won't find any sesame oil. This simple analogy illuminates a profound truth: the spiritual path is not just a matter of effort and forceful will. Success on the path—what's sometimes called "realization"— is never the product of sheer exertion, of trying and trying to get there. "Realization" means realizing what is always already here in potential form. From the beginning, the oil is present in the seed; it simply needs pressing to draw it out.

The awakened state lies dormant, an ignored potential within us, but we need consistent training in meditation to awaken this sleeping giant. There is a saying in the traditional Buddhist teachings of Tibet: "The ultimate materialism is believing one has to manufacture the buddha-wisdom." All our grasping after unusual experiences or higher spiritual states comes from lack of confidence in the power of this original nature.

How Do I Gain Confidence in Natural Wakefulness?

The analogy of the sesame seeds also illuminates the second most important aspect of the spiritual path—training. Here we are primarily exploring the topic of training in the discipline of the sitting practice of meditation. Training, cultivating—actually doing something to draw the inner essence out, to develop it—is absolutely necessary. Merely thinking about practice, intending to get to it someday soon, is not enough. As Tilopa explains: "If by the combination of mortar and pestle and hands, the beating and extraction are not done, one cannot obtain the oil." If we simply sit staring at the bowl of sesame seeds in front of us, wondering when the sesame oil will magically appear, nothing happens. It's not enough just to think, "Open sesame!" As it says in the genealogies of the biblical scriptures, nothing begets nothing. No pressing of the seeds, no sesame oil.

The seed of our awakened nature is an essential ingredient; it's absolutely necessary, but it's not sufficient by itself for awakening. If we don't apply our attention and fully engage body and mind, stagnation soon sets in. Sleepwalking continues to reign. The net result? We find ourselves repeating the same scenarios, living out the familiar routines of habit, again and again and again. The accumulated power of our ingrained distraction is so strong that it easily overrides our momentary good intentions, like floodwaters snuffing out a matchstick's flickering flame. We make a New Year's resolution not to lose our temper, but then two weeks into January we hear ourselves snapping at someone at home or at work. Facing a tough deadline, we catch ourselves cursing at a slow driver on the freeway.

So, just as the teaching of an originally wakeful nature tells us that the path is not a matter of just working at it, the complementary teaching of training—particularly training through the discipline of meditation practice—tells us that just trusting in the fundamental goodness of our original nature is also not enough. As we know, it's not enough merely to believe that exercise improves our well-being—actually getting to the gym or going out for a walk or a run is another, crucial matter. Similarly, it's not enough simply to have naive faith or belief in the goodness of our original nature.

Why Not?

Why isn't original goodness enough? If we're naturally awake, why do we need to train?

Particularly at first, our trust and confidence in basic goodness are based largely on ideas and concepts. We have heard or read about inherent enlightened nature, and we say, "Yes—this makes some sense to me; it sounds good. Yes . . . yes, I think I believe in basic goodness." This is fine, to begin with—where else could we start except with a somewhat vague sense of belief, a slightly naive faith in this possibility? Again, we have to start where we are. Wisdom is already there in our initial inspiration.

However, remaining with just this vague outline—the "finger-painting level"—would be like skipping the meal and instead continuing to chew on the menu in a good restaurant. ("Hmm, this cardboard could use more salt.") Menus are helpful and often whet the appetite, but the point is to actually taste the tomato soup. Training in meditation corresponds to actual experience—smelling the aroma of a simmering stew, biting into a carrot, chewing and swallowing, feeling the sense of satisfaction as outer elements nourish and strengthen our inner being. Even the best menu is a pale and superficial imitation of enjoying a delicious bowl of soup. Just having a conceptual belief in basic goodness doesn't provide real spiritual nourishment.

The two most important aspects of the path of awakening, then, are nature and training. Both are essential. Without a natural interest in meditation, we cannot begin, continue, or reach the goal; without actually setting out on the journey to awakening, we will never arrive. Wakefulness is natural—this is the essential point, and we need to actually walk the path of meditation. Confidence in our original nature comes from skillfully combining these two.

Do Nothing

Dzongsar Jamyang Khyentse Rinpoche

Because Buddhism traces both our problems and potential back to the mind, the key to the religion is working directly with the mind through the powerful tools of meditation. Here is an opportunity to learn mindfulness meditation directly from a modern Buddhist master. This teaching is in the form of a guided meditation—you listen as the teacher speaks and take a minute or two where indicated to practice his instructions. Even if you don't want to take it quite that literally, you will benefit from these teachings on the essential points of Buddhist practice.

I'm going to talk a little about *shamatha* meditation, and I thought it would be good to try and actually do the meditation as we go along. The actual technique is very simple. All the great meditators of the past advised us to sit up straight when we meditate. When we sit up straight, there is a sense of alertness, a sense of importance—it produces the right atmosphere. In this particular instruction, I'm going to suggest we don't use an external object, such as a flower, but instead follow the standard Theravada tradition of using our breath as the object. So we concentrate on our breathing: we simply follow our breath in and out. That's it. Our mind is focused on the breathing, our posture is straight, our eyes are open. That's the essential technique: basically doing nothing.

Let's do that for a while.

Short meditation session
We simply sit straight and we watch our breathing. We are not concerned with distractions, with all the thoughts that occupy our mind. We just sit—alone, by ourselves, no reference at all. Us, the breathing, and the concentration. That's all we have.

Short meditation session
So we sit, we concentrate on the breathing, nothing else. Then some thoughts may come, and any number of distractions: things you talked about yesterday, movies you watched last week, a conversation you just had, things you need to do tomorrow, a sudden panic—*did I switch off the gas in the kitchen this morning?* All of this will come, and when it does, go back to the breathing. This is the slogan of shamatha instruction: just come back. Every time we notice that we've gotten distracted, we remember the instruction and we come back to the breath. Let's do this for a while.

Short meditation session
If we have ambitions—even if our aim is enlightenment—then there is no meditation, because we are thinking about it, craving it, fantasizing, imagining things. That is not meditation. This is why an important characteristic of shamatha meditation is to let go of any goal and simply sit for the sake of sitting. We breathe in and out, and we just watch that. Nothing else. It doesn't matter if we get enlightenment or not. It doesn't matter if our friends get enlightened faster. Who cares? We are just breathing. We just sit straight and watch the breath in and out. Nothing else. We let go of our ambitions. This includes trying to do a perfect shamatha meditation. We should get rid of even that. Just sit.

The beautiful thing about having less obsessions and ambitions—and just sitting straight and watching the breathing—is that nothing will disturb us. Things only disturb us when we have an aim. When we have an aim, we become obsessed. Say our aim is to go somewhere, but somebody parks right in front of our car, blocking us. If something gets in the way of our aim, it becomes a terrible thing. If we don't have an aim, though, it doesn't matter. Meditators often have a strong ambition to achieve something with their meditation. But when meditators get distracted, they go through all kinds of hell: they lose their confidence, they get frustrated, they condemn themselves, they condemn the technique. This is why, at least during the first few moments of meditation, it doesn't matter whether we are getting enlightened or not, it doesn't matter whether the hot water is boiling in the kettle, it doesn't matter whether the telephone is ringing, and it doesn't matter whether it's one of our friends. For a few moments, things don't matter.

Short meditation session

You don't have to meditate for the sake of attaining enlightenment. If you are not interested in enlightenment, you can practice shamatha to be natural—to not be so swayed by circumstances. Most of the time we are not in control of ourselves; our mind is always attracted to, or distracted by, something—our enemies, our lovers, our friends, hope, fear, jealousy, pride, attachment, aggression. In other words, all these objects and these phenomena control our mind. Maybe we can control it for a split second, but when we are in an extreme emotional state, we lose it.

Letting go of ambition is a bit like the renunciation that Buddhists talk about. The Buddha renounced his palace, his queen, his son, and his parents, and went out in search of enlightenment. You can say that the Buddha was trying to diminish his ambition. At least, he was trying to see the futility of it, and he was letting go. Letting go is quite important if you want to become a shamatha practitioner. We do shamatha meditation so we can achieve this power to let go.

Meditation is one of the rare occasions when we're not doing anything. Otherwise, we're always doing something, we're always thinking something, we're always occupied. We get lost in millions of obsessions or fixations. But by meditating—by not doing anything—all these fixations are revealed. Beginners might find this a little frightening, but slowly they will gain inner confidence, and these fixations will automatically lessen. The classical meditation instruction texts say our obsessions will undo themselves like a snake uncoiling itself.

Short meditation session

Thoughts are coming and I'm telling you to go back to the breathing. You automatically interpret this as, "We should stop the thoughts." This is not what I mean. I'm not saying you should stop thinking. All I'm saying is, concentrate on the breathing. When thoughts come, don't stop them, don't increase them, don't encourage them, don't discourage them. Your job is to concentrate on the breathing. That's it. Stopping the thoughts is not your job. It's important to understand the difference: thoughts are going to come; all you do is just concentrate on the breathing. That's it.

Short meditation session

When we are doing shamatha and the mind gets distracted, it is important that we remember the antidote. The antidote here is very simply to go back to the breath. We call this "applying the antidote."

But sometimes we apply the antidote too much, which can cause both dullness and agitation. You got that? If you keep applying the antidote—antidote, antidote, antidote—it's like applying the antidote when there's no poison. That becomes a problem.

Short meditation session

Always do short but frequent shamatha sessions. I'm talking especially to beginners. If you're going to meditate for fifteen minutes, start fresh at least thirty times. Over time we can start doing longer sessions—in a fifteen minute session, we can do it fifteen times with a break in between. And when you take a break, take a *real* break—walk, stand up, do something else. Don't just linger there half meditating, half not meditating. After a while, you can practice seven times within fifteen minutes.

Keeping it short is important because if you do too much at the beginning, you'll get fed up with the technique. We are human beings—we don't like to get bored. We like to change what we eat, we like changing our clothes. We like change.

Likewise, the spiritual path is a long process, and we need a lot of patience. We need to like the path, so keep the meditation short and precise and frequent. That way we develop strong habits. Later on, it becomes part of us. It's like drinking alcohol: when we first start drinking, we drink a little; we don't drink two or three bottles at one time. If we did, we'd get so sick we'd never touch it again. So practice shamatha for a short time but many times. That way you'll get habituated. This is necessary. Shamatha should become part of your life.

And during the off-sessions, also, if it's possible, remember you are breathing. We always forget that we are breathing.

Also, you should not limit your meditation to only in the morning or only in the evening: you should do it any time, all the time. Practice time is always now—it's never in the future. Don't ever leave your shamatha thinking, "I'm going to do it next weekend, next month, or next year." Do it now. Anyway, you're only doing it for about forty-five seconds, if you're a beginner. It's easy. You can do it anywhere. It only requires this: to sit straight.

Short meditation session

As we meditate, we simply sit straight and watch the breath. So what does that do? It creates space. In fact, the technique itself is just a trick. The main point is to recognize all these thoughts and distractions that are constantly bombarding us. We still get angry, but we know that we are angry—this kind of anger has so much humor. We can actually drive it in certain directions—we have more control.

The frustrating thing about our life is that there is no control over these emotions. That's why there's no fun. The whole purpose of Buddhism is to have fun, isn't it? And in order to have fun you have to have control. If someone else has control over you, that's it: there's no fun.

Short meditation session

Shamatha involves a lot of discipline. Lamas often advise us to do meditation in a group, because when we are doing meditation in a group, we want to be the best, the fastest; we have so much pride and ego, and we're so competitive—why not use this competitiveness as a tool on the path? It's like working out—if you buy the machines and bring them home, you do three or four days and the machines end up in the garage. But if you go to a gym, you see the other people who are diligently doing it, and all the other beautiful bodies, and it gives you inspiration. What a wrong motivation! But at least it will lead you somewhere.

Keep it simple, don't make it complicated. Concentrate on the breathing, sit straight—that's all. Every day, do a few minutes, and, on top of that, do it spontaneously in different places—not just in front of the shrine, but everywhere. There's so much merit in just sitting there.

How Will I Use This Day?

Sakyong Mipham Rinpoche

There are many types of Buddhist meditation. Some, such as the technique taught in the previous selection, involve simple awareness of whatever arises in the mind, body, and environment. Others are more active, consciously directing our thoughts and intentions in a positive direction. Sakyong Mipham Rinpoche suggests a series of such contemplations that will help us carry the awakened state of mind into our busy day.

We are always meditating—constantly placing our minds on an object and becoming familiar with it. But are we getting used to things that will take us forward on the path?

Our modern culture does not encourage awakening, and without a sense of inner strength, we are easily invaded by the difficulties around us. If we don't orient our day toward spiritual growth, the speed of our life takes over, fueled by habitual patterns. While some habitual patterns are a source of inspiration, others just drain our energy. Meditation trains us to notice these patterns, which create the fabric of the entity known as "me."

When we wake up in the morning, our first meditation is often "What about me?" We can loosen this pattern by setting a different kind of view. Instead of "What do I have to do today?" or "Will I ever get enough sleep?" we can ask ourselves, "How can I use this day to let the dharma change my thoughts, words, and actions? What positive qualities shall I cultivate?"

Carrying this view to the cushion will enrich our morning meditation. Yet no matter how well our meditation goes, entering into everyday life presents a schism: "I finished my practice and now I have to go to work." It's an insidious dilemma that lowers our energy and hampers our growth. Thinking practice is over when we leave the house weakens our ability to engage wholeheartedly with the world outside.

So how do we carry a dharmic view into the day? By seeing the day as our life, and our life as the path, we learn to regard everything we meet as an opportunity to practice. There are seven facets of awakened mind that we can consciously cultivate to enhance the pathlike texture of our life.

The first is *egolessness.* In order to grow, we must be willing to give up territory. We may look fervently for the teacher, teachings, or situation that fits into our comfort zone, but the path is not going to happen on our own terms. Are we prepared to abandon our habitual patterns—to give up the support of concepts, opinions, and comforts? To make progress, we need to be willing to change.

The great Tibetan saint Milarepa said that to give up territory we have to understand impermanence. If we don't understand impermanence, we don't have a sense of immediacy. Without a sense of immediacy, we remain under the influence of the protracted illusion that we are eternal. In other words, we become very comfortable in our habits. Our practice is lazy and our mind tends to be thick. So every day we need to cultivate the willingness to give up the habitual patterns that warp our experience.

The second element to awaken is *faith.* The word "faith" often has the sense that even though we're not really sure about something, we believe in it anyway. The faith we're talking about here is based on knowing what we're doing, not in hoping for the best. It's as if we've checked our boat for holes and found none, so we set sail with a yearning to be completely engaged in practice because we're certain that the teachings will work. The active ingredient of our yearning manifests as strength and compassion.

There are three kinds of faith. First is the faith of inspiration. Seeing a teacher, hearing the dharma, or visiting a meditation center, we feel an immediate inspiration. Faith suddenly arises as a very powerful hit. It hooks our mind and we become excited about it. We just *know*.

But that kind of faith is not sustainable. We must supplement our inspiration with curiosity, from which the second kind of faith arises, understanding. We ask ourselves, "What made that person that way? Why is this place so powerful?" Unless we investigate our inspiration, we will lose our motivation to practice. So we get curious—reading, studying, and hearing dharma. That's how we increase our understanding, which leads to a deeper kind of faith because we know why we were inspired in the first place.

The third kind of faith is following through. Having been impressed, then curious, we now think, "I want to be like that, so I will follow this through." The three kinds of faith naturally sequence into a potent driving force, combining inner strength and compassion.

Being willing to give up, having trust, and yearning to go forward, we now need to be *daring*. But to do what? We dare to jump out of our samsaric habitual tendencies into more dharmic ones. When we see ourselves falling into the "me" meditation, we emerge from our hallucination and courageously take a leap into a more open place. This can be as simple as giving up our place in line to someone in a hurry.

If we dare to jump out of laziness, we might become slightly aggressive, so we also cultivate *gentleness*. That means slowing down so that we synchronize our intention with our speech and action. Our intention is to use the day as a spiritual path. What is the path? It is a place to grow. With gentleness, we provide the space and warmth for growth, but we don't force progress—our own or others'. If we're not in a rush with our own mind, we have the patience to let things unfold naturally.

If we become too gentle, however, we might become feeble. So *fearlessness* comes next. In terms of how we engage in our life, we're no longer second-guessing ourselves, because we're not afraid of our mind. We can look at it head-on. Although we encounter obstacles, we steadfastly move forward; we're not afraid of giving up territory or taking a leap. Fearlessness has a decisive element, too: at some point we can respond to a situation with a simple "yes" or "no"—the "maybes" go out the door.

With fearlessness comes *awareness*. No longer cloaked in habitual pattern, no longer using hope and fear to manipulate the environment, we are aware of what's happening in our life. We have more energy because we're not burdened by trying to maintain the concept and polarity of "me." Our practice becomes more three-dimensional.

The last entry on this list is a *sense of humor*. I haven't met any great practitioner who didn't have a good sense of humor. It's a sign of pliability and intelligence. Who wants to be a brow-heavy practitioner, squinting hard as we try to push out realization? With a dharmic eye, we're able to see things with some levity because we're connected to our wholesomeness.

Each morning we can choose one of these elements as a daily contemplation and practice. Throughout the day, we can train ourselves to bring the mind to "egolessness," "faith," or "gentleness"— as words, then actions. In the evening, we can take a moment before going to sleep and reflect on what happened: "How did I use this day to nurture my mind and heart?"

Training to increase our dharmic habitual tendencies is a perpetual source of inspiration and strength that provides a standard for decision making at every level. It's how we become perpetually forward-thinking, visionary people who can use every situation as an opportunity to cross over from the transcendent to the practical—and back.

In the Wild Places

John Tarrant

A dying father, a grown son. Past pains put aside in an atmosphere of love. Sometimes such times are the best a parent and child ever have. How much more so with dharma quietly present in the background.

> People go to wild places to search for their true nature. Where is your true nature?
> —Zen koan

My father, Max, lived alone for some years in Launceston, Tasmania, on a steep hillside with a view of the mountains and the town. He liked the light and the smell of the bush, the wallabies thumping their tails against the side of the house as they went down to drink at dusk. Then his health led him to move in with my sister, in Adelaide.

He said on the phone that he was dying and it would be nice to see me. I flew into Adelaide via Auckland and contracted a flu along the way. My body felt hot and gritty inside, and when I closed my eyes there was a dark swirling followed by lights that flashed and disappeared, like luminous plankton on a long night journey in tropical waters.

When I opened my eyes, Adelaide was there, turning from summer to autumn, and showing signs of global warming. The trees were gasping in public parks and had shed their leaves in the heat. Everyone spoke about rain, wanting rain, whether it would rain, the last time they had seen rain.

The hospice was in an old building of pleasant brick with new bits added on and trees around. He greeted me with delight: "Who are you? Never saw you before in my life!" He seemed to be playing with the idea that his relationship to consensus reality couldn't be taken for granted anymore. We shook hands.

Wild places exist in people as well as in landscapes. When my mother was in hospice, she was resolutely herself. With the integrity of an animal, or of an archetype, she was prickly and hostile and sweet in a rhythm belonging to her alone. She didn't adapt, and made few concessions to the requests of the living. In practice, this made her journey quite private.

I had unconsciously expected Max to follow the same path. He did something unexpected, though. He took off the jackets he had worn; he became interested in his dying, and in the complexity of his life. This brought him into a world in which wild places could be shared. The margins between us dissolved, and we were in no-man's-land together: it was frightening, breathtaking, and satisfying. There was a feeling of a large awareness, both real and happy, in the room, holding us both. I came to see that my father and I had, without intending to, over many years, worked out ways of being together in the wild places.

He had found an ease with metaphor and art. My brother-in-law brought a TV into the windowless room and looped the cable around the overhead rail of the bed. Max waved at the spiral loops and said, "I appreciate the corroboree"—a corroboree is an aboriginal ceremonial dance. And in the room there were perhaps twenty origami cranes, made by my daughter during a recent visit. They had the bright patterns of wedding kimonos.

There were negotiations. He mentioned walking to the bathroom a few times until I said, "Well, I'll help you up." Then he ignored me. This happened a few times. Finally, I pushed things a bit and said, "I'll help you up now, if you wish."

With a large, childlike grin he said, "You are asking for a punch on the nose."

I took this to mean that he wanted to get up but was in too much pain to carry out the plan. This sort of assessment was going on all the time. He was doing it and I was doing it, and the staff was, too. The method was to listen and guess, followed by more listening and guessing. I got him up a couple of times and he tried a few times more, but then he surrendered and didn't get up again. He had no particular shame about having to be helped, but he was very aware of being caught in the ancient coils of having a body, eating, getting rid of the waste.

Then there was the matter of drugs, ordered by his oncologist. The monastic discipline of the medical profession is a worldwide phenomenon; the doctor was intelligent, well trained, practical, decisive, and willing to answer all my questions. "The source of the cancer could be prostate or lungs, but we didn't want to put him through an extra biopsy, and it doesn't matter, does it?" He was also inclined to the stoic and bleak, or perhaps I could say that his consolations were those of the scientist who adheres to the data at hand and makes few speculations about whether life has meaning.

"What's the likely course?"

"Well, the metastases in the bone will eventually collapse the spine onto the nerves and stop his breathing, probably in his sleep. Three weeks."

I took his clarity as a kindness. I had a week to spend with Max before I was to teach a retreat in California.

Hospice patients have acute conditions; they either die or move out, and their doctors tend to whack the pain with a blunt instrument. The drugs made Max miss his own experience, though, and he understood this in some animal way and backed off from them. When he fell behind the pain, the nurses gave him a large dose and he was loopy again. This unsatisfactory cycle went on until a palliative-care doc took over and gave him a pain patch. Meanwhile, we brought him single malt whiskey, which was a good placebo.

When I stepped out into the sunshine after my first visit to the hospice, I was disoriented. I zipped off in my dad's VW diesel, wondering for a puzzled moment why all the traffic was coming toward me on the wrong side of the road.

I wasn't aware of any need to say deep things or to improve my relationship with my father, so when the pain negotiations were finished—something my sister accomplished with persistence and verve—the question became a matter of what Max and I would do together.

When I've been sick, for example with fever, I can be happy as long as I listen to what the universe, represented by the state of my body, allows me to do. It's as if there is an awareness inside that knows what that is. This awareness treats my thoughts as hypotheses. I have the thought "I'll watch a movie," and, no, it won't let me do that. "I'd like to eat." No, not that. "How about reading?" Yes, but barely—not physics, try fiction. Nothing appeals. "Well, then, I'll lie here and be here." Yes, that. The awareness is not always minimalist; it might let me walk in the garden but not discuss business.

I don't know if that was what was happening with Max, but that was how it was for me to be with him. I sat with him, and nothing much else was needed or possible. I had no impulse to read or chat. He was clearly glad of the company. And now and then we would talk.

A hint of openings to come had appeared on a previous visit, more than a year earlier, when he had said, "I'd like you to give me something."

He just bought a car, I'd thought, I wonder what he wants? "I'd be happy to," I said. "What would you like?"

"Just something you use every day, like that traveler's clock you have. Something that's yours, so I can put it on my chest of drawers and think of you when I look at it in the morning."

Now, in the hospice, he was wandering in the dark at first, but his mind cleared when the pain meds changed. When he was clear, Max's stories gave shape to his life. In his generation there were men who talked about the war incessantly and paraded in uniform, and others who rarely mentioned war or medals and never paraded. He was of the second type. The war stories he did tell were in two categories. They were stories either about life and sensibility in the Jane Austen mode, slightly poignant, or of the clash between ability and circumstances. Either: "I was kicked out of the Army because they found out I had lied about my age—too young—and that's how I ended up in the Air Force." Or: "I sat in the back of the math classes for the officers, though not being an officer I couldn't get credit. 'It's a pity you are not an officer,' the instructor said, 'you would be top of the class.'"

He also told antiheroic stories about how he kept getting sent to the wrong place an hour before the Japanese Army took Amban (or, another time, Lae). The CO swore at him to make him feel better about leaving and told him to get his bloody useless men back on that bloody DC3 and go the hell back where they damn well came from, and that's how he escaped from being finally and completely dead at that time. In another antiheroic story, he told about shooting down a plane that was firing at him; it turned out to be an American Wildcat—the pilot was trying to draw attention to himself because he was disabled and being chased. "I had to buy the pilot a case of beer. He was decent about it." These stories, like other comedies, were about how lucky it is to be alive.

In hospice, he began an experiment in discovery and improvisation. Each morning, I asked, "How are you?" Apart from dying, I meant. One morning he gave me the force of his predicament:

"I have a problem. I want to get home, but I can't work out any way to do that. I can't work out how to solve the problem. I really, really want to go home, but I just can't work it out."

"Yes."

I was struck by the thought that this is the way you take on koans. The situation is insoluble and you hang around with it and something shifts to another level. At its simplest, the problem was that he needed more care than he could get at my sister's home. At other levels, in which having a body is a metaphor as well as a shape to breathe in, I wasn't sure: he seemed to be free sometimes as we talked through the long afternoon. And he was at ease with the contradictions of being human, the way characters in Shakespeare are. A predicament automatically thrusts you into wild places. Sometimes he was moved to make a small speech.

"You know what little presence there has been of you in my life—what little presence, no one's fault, of course—I've enjoyed."

"Indeed. And I have enjoyed our meetings too."

My father and I had separated when I was seventeen and hadn't reconnected until I was living on the far side of the world.

Max had an easy, catlike quality and had taught unarmed combat during the war. His litheness was enjoyable to be around and translated to other dimensions of life. I learned classic moves for meditation and poetry from that quality. He also showed me a few fighting tricks with the air of someone who thinks that the tricks might be useful but that they don't really touch what life is about.

It was a working-class world and fights occurred, not often, but memorably. I had an aversion to them, stemming from laziness, cowardice, or intelligence, it wasn't really clear. I could usually, not always, think my way past fights that were casually offered. The difficulty with my father belonged with me, though, and couldn't be dodged. Our generations were set against each other by the times; to him, Vietnam looked like World War II. Ideas were separating people everywhere you looked.

One time we faced each other in the living room as if we were in a western. The living room was a small space in which Danish modern furniture with skinny wooden arms and green cushions had recently and proudly replaced the walnut nineteenth-century chaise lounge and sideboards.

A street fighter hits you just before you have convinced yourself to fight, but something more complicated was going on with us. We were listening and guessing. He was more skilled, but I was an athlete, fitter and quicker, and it wasn't clear to me who would win or if it would be good to win. In the middle of that waiting, time began to spread out and we relaxed. This might have been a bad sign, meaning that the posturing was over. But then the space around things got larger still. No time was taken up by this expansion, but during the interval it came to me that fighting was not a good idea. An explanation of this would be that if I lost, I lost, and if I won, I lost—we would walk through a one-way door—but it wasn't a reasoned decision. The clarity was an absence of reasons. We didn't like each other any better, and there was no satisfactory resolution, but the seriousness and tension drained away, and this became a moment of seeing through things, the emptiness of plans—the emptiness of what we each thought was crucial. Zen happened to us.

In the story of the Buddha's early life, there is a moment when, as a child, Siddhartha sees things just as they are, without wanting anything to be different. Later, his awakening builds on this simple discovery. This moment with Max seemed like such an opening in time. Not a mystic revelation, but not delusion either—simply a piece of clear-mindedness, a gift. If consciousness is always making up its best story, these are moments when it doesn't—when it is not really committed to the way it thinks things are.

Now, this is not such a big deal, really, but the important moves in consciousness are the small moves that bring about larger shifts. It's not that my dad and I were wise; we just stopped holding our prejudices, and it became obvious what to do, which was mainly what not to do. The opposite of hell was not heaven but an unselfconscious simplicity.

Back in the hospice we moved him to a room with a slant of precious sunlight and a potted palm outside the French door. It seemed a blessed tree.

"So how are you, Dad?"

"I've been thinking. I've changed a lot since I was young."

"You have?"

"Yes, I have."

"How so?"

"Well, I'm a lot more easygoing than I used to be."

I took this dialogue as an acknowledgment of past difficulties.

"I've changed a lot, too."

"Really?"

"Yes, I have."

"How is that?"

"I'm a lot more easygoing than I was."

He smiled a quiet, private smile, and that was it for working through our past.

I had made my first visit home to Tasmania in 1984, after over a decade, returning on the plane across Bass Strait as something incomprehensible—a Zen teacher, exploring the deep passages of the mind.

I wrote a poem about the cottage in which I grew up, where he and my mother still lived. They were kind enough to take the poem as an offering. It begins like this:

The Source

> No memory warned me
> how particular and true
> the doll's house where I grew would be,
> the kitchen smell of rosemary, my father's
> cough, the green spots
> on the bells of the snow drops.
> Sap rises in the almonds to
> the first of bloom,
> the blossoms open one and two and three
> like stars at evening.

In the hospice he was still sorting his life.

"You know I really loved Alison, I really loved her, but you know how you sit down with someone and you get some paper and draw the lines and make squares. And then you move the squares around together till they connect. No matter how I tried to line them up, it didn't work. No matter how hard I tried."

There wasn't any blame in this—he was trying to make out the pattern in his relationship with my dead mother. And it was true that you could work things through with him, but she didn't do that. Sitting with him in the hospice, it was clear that the deep passages of the mind were not alien to him after all. Sorting took other forms, too.

"The flight lieutenant said to me, 'You are a strange, intelligent bird, Tarrant, what should we do with you?'

'I don't know, sir.'

'Well, we'll find things for you to do.'

They got me to run an anti-aircraft battery. They were fifty-caliber machine guns. We weren't meant to shoot anything down, just to keep the Japanese bombers honest and force them up to a height at which the ack-ack could come into play."

He told me about another moment of seeing through the forms of things.

"Some of those Japanese pilots could speak English, you know. We shot one down and had him in the cells. I had a bad feeling that night, so I dropped in for a visit. The guard was knocking the pilot around. Oh, he was a nasty piece of work. Withers was his name. I told him, 'You can stop that right now and clear out.' He wasn't happy about it at all, didn't want to go. The pilot spoke English because he had grown up in Hawaii, you see. Quite good English—a polite feller."

"What did you do, though?"

"Oh, Withers. I put my rifle on him, and told him I'd shoot him on the spot. I had him transferred the next day."

A couple of things stand out for me in this story. One is that he remembered the process by which he made the decision—he had a bad feeling and listened to it. The other is that, at the most intense moments, objectivity and clarity appear in the form of empathy. Max was a teenager then; that clarity must be a natural possibility in consciousness, something available to us at any time.

"What are you thinking about today?"

"I'm wondering about my attitude . . . well, not my attitude to the butcher, but my attitude to my attitude."

He thought that dying was difficult sometimes and matter-of-fact at other times, but then what did he think about what he thought about? Here was afternoon sunlight and conversation and the great palaces of memory that seem to fling their doors open at the end of life. Even though everyone says that you review your life, you actually do review your life. And the bare act of noticing is harder than it looks. This attempt to look at your attitude—what you are feeling and thinking and the frame that holds it, and then your attitude to your attitude, is one of the routes to freedom.

I had always assessed my father in various ways, and I had hoped to change my assessment in a positive direction. Lots of psychology hopes for such results, but it takes effort, and I have no talent for it. What was valuable was to stop assessing each other—that was the intimate thing. We could meet there and be happy.

In a dream nine months after his death, I bought licorice with my dad at a shop down the hill from our house in Launceston. I bought other sweets as well, and felt a bit ashamed at how many. We walked back slowly, his feet splayed out for balance like Charlie Chaplin's, patiently lifting and extending and placing themselves down as we walked up the hill toward my childhood home. He seemed older. Death had not stopped that process.

If we had decided that Max's dying would hurt unbearably, that would have been all right. But we didn't decide anything; we decided to step into an open paddock together. Something more interesting than hurting happened.

I mentioned that I was leaving the next day a couple of times. There was no reaction.

"This is my last day here." My third repetition.

"I'm very well aware of that."

Oh, silly me. Then, when it was actually time to leave, to leave the *bardo* of the hospice and go back to the other bardos that I think of as my life, I said, "I'm leaving in the morning. Is there anything you would like to say?"

"Yes, there is."

"What is that?"

"I would like you to do something about the weather."

Happily Ever After

Steve Silberman

Here's a love story so classic, so storybook, it could only lead to marriage. And who would stand in the way of something so wholesome? Who, indeed! Here's how Steven Silberman and his now-husband Keith, with the help of Buddhist practice, persevered in the face of prejudice until they could finally live as they wanted—as a happily married couple.

On a hazy August afternoon in 2001, I knelt on one knee and asked my beloved, "Will you marry me?" We were standing on a breakwater in front of a weathered house on Cape Cod that my family had been renting for nearly forty years. Keith looked tenderly at me with his big blue eyes. "Of course I will," he said, and we both burst into tears.

Though we didn't know it, my mother, father, and sister were watching this drama unfold with their faces pressed against the window. After being my best friend for seven years, Keith—a blond, soft-spoken young science teacher from the Midwest—was already treasured as a welcome addition to my hyperverbal East Coast Jewish family. The next morning, my mother filled a flowery hatbox lid with sand from "our" beach and spelled out *Happiness is Steve and Keith!* on top in plastic letters, like a pre-wedding cake.

We figured we would host a ceremony for our friends and families in San Francisco, where we live, the following summer. We knew we wouldn't have any of the rights and benefits of other wedded couples, because marriage between same-sex partners wasn't yet legal. But we wanted to celebrate the truth of what we had found together in the presence of everyone we knew.

Keith and I weren't planning on starting a gay marriage revolution, outraging the religious right, or even committing a noble act of civil disobedience. We just loved each other a lot. We grew up in the same culture as everyone else, in which the fairy tales of childhood end with the phrase "and they lived happily ever after." Trying to live happily ever after just seemed like the next step of our deepening commitment to one another.

Even my future father-in-law, Kent, who was a church-going Republican mayor of a small town in Illinois, seemed to understand. The first time I met him, he took me aside and said, "I know you are very special to Keith, so that means you are very special to us." There was such simple, human, Midwestern forthrightness in that statement. No banner waving, no Biblical injunctions, no soap-boxing. Just a clear and compassionate message: *We love our son, and we trust his ability to make the most personal decision of all.*

A month after our engagement, our plans changed unexpectedly when my mother looked across the Hudson River one morning and saw an airplane explode into the World Trade Center. Suddenly asking all our friends to fly out to the West Coast didn't seem like a good idea. We decided to wait another year.

Keith and I had our ceremony in 2003 at Greens Restaurant, where I had waited tables as a Zen student in the '80s. Our officiant was a gnostic Jewish Buddhist cancer survivor named Judith, and our recessional music was Frank Zappa's "Peaches en Regalia." We vowed to love, honor, and cherish one another, and exchanged rings inscribed with a line by Walt Whitman: "Every atom that belongs to me as good belongs to you." Then we threw a big party.

The only person to talk politics that day was my father, Donald, a college professor and lifelong advocate for social justice. My coming out in high school had been tough for him to accept, but he went on to become a champion for equality in the American Federation of Teachers. He gave the fight to legalize gay marriage a rousing toast, and even my new contingent of blue-eyed relatives cheered.

A few months later, our mayor, Gavin Newsom, began granting marriage licenses to same-sex couples. The first to wed were Del Martin and Phyllis Lyon, pioneering gay activists and advocates for women's health, who had been waiting fifty years for that day.

Newsom's bold decision launched a firestorm of angry words about defending the sanctity of marriage from "activist judges" and brazen interlopers like Del and Phyllis. Gay people were accused of mocking the sacred institution of marriage with their flamboyant tuxedos and gowns. After a Texas court overturned a law against sodomy, U.S. Supreme Court Justice Antonin Scalia unleashed a torrent of disdain from the bench. He equated homosexuality with "fornication, bigamy, adultery, adult incest, bestiality, and obscenity."

Suddenly Keith and I found ourselves at the flash point of a raging culture war. Did we have to call it marriage? Wasn't that an unnecessary provocation for those who take that word to mean getting to the church on time? What about framing our commitment with a less confrontational term like "civil union"?

Certain words, however, have alchemical power. A humble noun or verb can become a transformative mantra. Embracing the word "marriage" had a subtle but profound effect on our relationship, like unlocking a door to a secret garden that only other married people know about. Now our job was to care for that garden together—to nourish it, weed it when necessary, and give it the compassion and space it needs to grow and flourish.

Knowing the way to that garden proved to be a great comfort shortly after that, when my seemingly healthy, vibrant father suffered a heart attack at a union meeting and died a few days later. My heartbroken mother moved to San Francisco to live near us. And that same winter, our beloved house in Provincetown was torn down by the guys we had rented it from for years.

We had planned to make our marriage legal, but we didn't get the chance. In the months after dozens of couples like Del and

Phyllis were wed, further court decisions put a stop to the celebration at City Hall, and retroactively stripped these couples of their marriage licenses. State after state began passing bans on same-sex marriage, and President Bush announced his support for inscribing such a ban in the U.S. Constitution.

My mother, my beloved, and I returned to our beach one more time. My mother leaned on Keith's arm as the ashes and bones of her best friend for fifty-four years tumbled into the water.

Keith and I were finally able to get legally married a year ago, following yet another court decision. My mother was one of our witnesses, with a box of Kleenex in her lap. We already felt married, but it felt good to take those humble vows again in front of a county clerk. The corridors of City Hall were full of beaming gay couples who had been together for decades. My father would have been happy that day too.

The election season was upon us, and I was doing full-time volunteer work to help put Barack Obama in the White House. One day, we received a glossy brochure in the mail featuring smiling portraits of Barack and his wife, Michelle, urging us to vote for Proposition 8, an amendment to the California constitution to ban marriages like ours. I knew that Obama was on record as being against the amendment. But his statement, "I believe that marriage is between a man and a woman," was emblazoned at the top of the brochure.

At the same time, the ads opposing Proposition 8 seemed to convey an extreme wariness of offending anyone. "No matter how you feel about marriage . . . " they began. And there were no glowing couples in the ads, which struck me like running a campaign against school segregation while being afraid to show any minority kids with textbooks in their hands. But the pro-8 ads went straight for the gut, linking marriages like ours with the rape of children and compulsory sex ed for kindergarteners.

Postelection morning was bittersweet. Like most of our friends, we were overjoyed that change would finally come to Washington.

But the narrow passage of Proposition 8 tasted like sand in our slice of victory cake.

As a Buddhist, I vow to cultivate compassion for every sentient being, even those who are trying to legislate our love out of existence. I try to understand their fears about tinkering with an institution so fundamental to human happiness. I imagine that some of their sons and daughters are waiting patiently for the day they can finally be honest with their parents about who they really are.

The extraordinary truth about gay marriage is that it's completely ordinary. Keith and I wake up at dawn, and I make him a sandwich to take to school. He gets kids excited about the wonders of the universe for a living, and I try to do the same thing for adults in my science writing. In a universe in which loved ones and tall buildings can turn into ashes overnight, it's good to know where your garden is—whether it's a committed relationship, a daily sitting practice, or a handful of earth and seeds. And it's important to remember that *happily ever after* is getting shorter all the time.

The Joy of Mindful Cooking ◎))

Laura Fraser

More and more people these days are interested in mindful living—bringing the meditative mind into all aspects of their lives without necessarily adopting a new religion. This movement may have started in the kitchen of a Zen center in California, where Ed Brown, author of the classic Tassajara Cooking, *and his fellow cooks meditated, produced great food, and changed the way America eats. Laura Fraser thought she'd try her hand at mindful cooking, and went to the Tassajara experts for advice.*

Dinners at the Nevada Ranch, where Dale and Melissa Kent work as caretakers, are potluck. Whoever is visiting or living on the former dude ranch—now a private retreat, set up against the Eastern Sierras—shows up with a big pot of posole, fresh greens from the garden, handmade tortillas, or a peach crumble made with fruit picked from the orchard outside. The wide-open kitchen is infused with the cheerful spirit of its former owner, Maya, who passed away a couple of years ago at ninety; I can still see her kneading the sourdough bread she made in the quiet mornings, doing nothing else with her great intelligence and energy, at those moments, but kneading bread.

The ranch dinners are always fresh, and the various dishes made with love, but I've noticed, visiting over the years, that Dale and Melissa's contributions to the meals taste brighter and are presented more beautifully than, say, the goat cheese and crackers I plop onto a plate. Even their simplest dishes, mere vegetables cooked with some olive oil and salt, are somehow transformed; they're not just yummier, they're mysteriously more satisfying to the soul. Nor do the Kents ever seem frantic getting something to the table on time, fret about the result, or burn anything in their haste to finish cooking already. It's as if their food is seasoned with grace.

That cooking magic has something to do with the fact that they spent seven years at Tassajara Zen Mountain Center, the renowned Buddhist monastery in California's Ventana Wilderness, where Dale did a two-year stint as *tenzo,* head of the kitchen. Tassajara has a long lineage of great cooks and cookbooks, starting with Zen priest Edward Espe Brown and his *Tassajara Bread Book* (1970) and subsequent works and including Deborah Madison (who wrote *The Greens Cookbook* with Brown, along with her own books *The Savory Way, Vegetarian Cooking for Everyone,* and others), and Annie Somerville (*Fields of Greens* and *Everyday Greens*). Like these other Tassajara cooks, Dale and Melissa Kent don't just practice cooking; they've made cooking a practice, one that benefits not only what is on their plates and in their bellies but what is in their hearts.

The Kents now offer their next-generation Zen-inspired cookbook, *Tassajara Dinners and Desserts,* which sets down recent recipes from the monastery, along with their own thoughts about mindful cooking and words of wisdom from guest cooks who have passed through those gates. The recipes are simple, calling for improvisation, and focus on seasonal, organic, and local ingredients, as well as some ethnic and exotic ingredients that are more readily available now than they were at the time of earlier Zen cookbooks.

Each time I relished their meals, I wondered whether I could also learn to cook more mindfully—but without spending years in a monastery. My cooking is usually messy and distracted, except when I make soup, because you can't screw up soup, and something about chopping vegetables and tossing them in a pot restores my calm and equanimity. But I never know how anything else will turn out: when I made my great-grandmother's recipe for fig-filled cookies shaped like delicate sand dollars, for instance, the friend I was baking with observed that mine came out looking like "mud huts." My scattered haste in the kitchen is even dangerous: I once sliced off my entire index fingernail along with the onions. And let's not discuss what I have burned.

I had no idea how to begin to cook mindfully, or really what that meant. I had an image of slow-motion cooking, of a Zen monk taking an hour to slice one carrot, pausing to breathe, focusing on its texture, color, smell, and the miracle of its being alive, as if studying it on high-grade LSD. I pictured it as cooking in a trance, which struck me, given the knives and heat, as quite dangerous, too.

I asked Edward Brown, whose cookbooks are ragged in my kitchen from twenty years of thumbing through for simple, reassuring recipe ideas, about my notion of slow, mindful cooking. He told me that Zen monks like to eat on time like everyone else. "Some people think they're being mindful by working very slowly, but they're confusing being mindful with being quiet, still, and composed—which are different qualities," he said. "You can work extremely diligently and quickly and be mindful."

Mindfulness, he says, is more about simply being present when you cook, fully engaged with the food and your relationship to it, from the earth it was grown in to the table. It's being aware of the food with all your senses, and of how you transform it with your hands, knives, herbs, and heat—making it taste alive, nourishing yourself and those who eat your meals. "Your awareness can be in bringing the activity alive and giving it some energy, vitality, and exuberance," he said.

When you see Brown cook, as in the 2007 film about him, *How to Cook Your Life* (from the German director Doris Dörrie), he fairly sparkles with that vitality, passing energy from his body and hands to the bread dough, and vice versa. But I wondered how you accomplish that trick of mindfulness, of making your experience and the food you cook come alive, when the temptation in busy times is to put packaged meals into the microwave, carelessly throw together a sandwich while on the cell phone, or for special occasions, fearfully measure and rigidly follow a recipe, hoping it turns out to be perfect.

Being a Zen priest, Brown didn't offer me any easy answers, only a few ideas to chew on. "Mindfulness is much more about receiving your experience than dictating it," he told me. "Most people's habits of mind and activity, when it comes to cooking, are about making it come out the way it's *supposed* to, rather than receiving and appreciating it the way it is." The mindful focus is more on the kale in your hands—its curly leaves, earthy smell, and deepgreen color—than on the casserole you hope will come out of the oven crisp and browned at precisely seven o'clock.

Brown offered a quote from Zen master Tenkei about how to cook mindfully: "See with your eyes, smell with your nose, taste with your tongue." That sounds obvious, but cooks are often so used to going through the motions, so focused on a recipe, a habit, or the product of our efforts—not to mention a million other distractions—that we forget to stop and experience the food we're cooking. The nature of awareness, Brown says, is to resonate with the object of awareness; with cooking, it is responding to the food you choose in the market, wash, and place on the cutting board in the kitchen. It's establishing a connection to the food, a relationship with it. "You're waking up to the way things are," he says. "Smell, see, taste, touch. Start to notice." His simple recipes aren't exact instructions for cooking, but permission to experiment and a structure within which to explore a deeper sort of joy of cooking.

Brown's other instruction about mindful cooking is one he says is classic Zen: "When you wash the rice, wash the rice; when you stir the soup, stir the soup." Give your attention to what you're doing, rather than to the preoccupations and daydreams scampering through your mind. "This is what some people call reinhabiting your body—extending your consciousness into your feet and hands, finding the life and vitality in your body and activity, rather than going through motions so it's a chore and drudgery." With cooking, you can use your awareness to inhabit physical movements that may be new, he says—cutting, washing, examining, mixing, folding—until, with practice, there is an invigorating flow of energy in those physical experiences, a delight.

Such energy, focus, and wholehearted attention nourishes yourself and those you feed, Brown writes in the introduction to his new *Complete Tassajara Cookbook:* "Cooking is not just working on food, but working on yourself and other people."

Dale and Melissa Kent, who met at Tassajara in 1997, were both attracted to the monastery partly because of the cookbooks; the way to their hearts, they said, was through their stomachs. "I found *The Tassajara Bread Book* in a used bookstore and wrote to the address on the back," said Dale. A promising philosophy student, he confounded everyone in his life by finding work as a baker instead of going to graduate school. "I was following my breath while doing repetitive tasks, and feeling real peace," he said. "*The Tassajara Bread Book* described what I had been doing and encouraged me to pay attention, to treat pots and pans and knives as friends. Its poetry and sweetness spoke to me."

After two years at the monastery, Dale began to work in the kitchen. At Tassajara, monks work in silence, except for occasional functional speech ("What's burning?"). From the various tenzos he cooked with, Dale says, he learned different lessons—how to taste food and pay attention to the details of a dish, when to salt, how to be generous and fearless, how to plan and move quickly, how to be playful, and to be patient. He also learned how energy, intention, and mood affect what you cook. "If someone was angry and making the bread, they would turn out these angry little loaves of bread."

I wondered how cooking mindfully would be different outside the monastery, whether it would be more difficult to have a sense of spirituality in your own kitchen. Melissa, who was *ino,* or head of the meditation hall, told me that cooking is actually a reminder that the spiritual is always at hand. "When you cook mindfully, you're honoring an everyday activity as sacred, and an opportunity for peace," she said. "When people elevate time in the meditation hall above time doing the dishes, they're missing the point. There's nothing special about meditating in a monastery."

Annie Somerville, who was tenzo at Tassajara and has been chef at Greens Restaurant for twenty-eight years, says her experience at the monastery grounded her for cooking in the rest of her life. "It's the hidden storyline," she says. "All those years of Zen practice were great life training for experiencing all the things that have come my way." But her practice now is in the restaurant kitchen. "The reason I'm in the kitchen and not sitting in the *zendo* is that I like to run around," she says. Cooking, she says, is fully engaging and sharpens her sensory attention—she can see when pasta is done, smell when the vegetables are roasted, and know the onions are ready because they're translucent. That kind of attention can be freeing for home cooks, too, she says. "For a lot of people, cooking is a wonderful release from the stresses and strains of your daily life. It's an escape to get into the kitchen, to make food that is delicious and nurturing and beautiful, and to be involved in that process from beginning to end."

Deborah Madison, whose new cookbook is called *What We Eat When We Eat Alone,* cooked at the Zen Center in San Francisco, Tassajara, and Green Gulch for eighteen years; when she left she found that cooks could be as mindful in a chaotic atmosphere as in a silent one. "When I went from Zen Center to Chez Panisse, there was opera playing, and people coming through saying hello to each other, but the cooks were in some ways even more focused than in a Zen Center kitchen." Mindfulness, she says, is about intention and focus, and isn't dependent on externalities in the kitchen, including silence.

Madison, who lives in New Mexico, says she no longer even consciously thinks of her cooking as a spiritual practice. "I don't use those words," she says. "But when I go into the kitchen to cook, I enjoy a calmness and the connection I feel with food I've grown myself or that comes from a rancher down the road. There's a shift in me when I cook with that kind of food, and I always recognize it when I see it in other people's food—there's a brightness, cleanness, and energy."

Madison doesn't use the word "mindful" about cooking much, either. "It can sound scoldy, like 'Pay attention!'" But the benefits of awareness in the kitchen are clear to her. "Whenever you're doing something with awareness, it's a two-way street; things talk back to you. In the kitchen you get a lot of immediate feedback, and consequences to your actions. You have sharp, hot things, you check your e-mail and your turnips are burned, you cut yourself, or you have wonderful tastes." Cooking, she says, is a wonderful opportunity to observe—the food, yourself, and the magic that can happen between the two.

"People feel so frazzled about their lives, and being in the kitchen, putting dinner on the table, even if it's simple steamed vegetables, is a way to step into another world and out of that chaos," she says.

Dale and Melissa and I decided to make dinner together so I could learn something not only about how to follow their recipes but also about their practice of mindfulness in the kitchen. It was a chilly winter day in Nevada, snow barely sticking to the ground. I have little experience with formal spiritual practice—Vipassana meditation and a little yoga—and so was worried I couldn't cook alongside a couple of Zen pros without revealing myself as a slob, both spiritually and as a cook. But Melissa told me to relax: we were just going to make some pizza.

We started by cleaning all the counters and washing our hands, which had a ritual feeling to it. "You lay everything out very carefully that you're going to use for the meal," Dale said. "Before you pick up a knife, you stand and feel your feet on the ground and take a few deep breaths, bring your attention into your hands and to what's on the cutting board." We turned off the music to focus on the cooking, though they often cook with music on.

We began by dissolving yeast into water, which sounds simple. But Dale's yeast started to bubble alive, and mine did not. He'd said the water should be body temperature, and in my impatience I'd tossed the yeast into hot water without feeling how warm it (or my body) actually was. I started over. When my yeast began to bubble in the water, too, I added flour and salt. I measured from Dale's recipe into my bowl, while he just threw the ingredients into his, telling me to respond more to what I saw in the bowl than to the exact measurements he had written in his book. He showed me how to fold the ingredients together gently so that the proteins in the flour would stay long and pliable, until we had what he calls a "shaggy mass," which was slightly sticky to the fingers. He turned his dough out onto the floured counter, and it bounced around in his hands as if it were alive. Mine needed coaxing. Dale told me to be careful to keep all my dough together, not some on my hands or the side of the bowl, because they didn't like to be separated. It sounded like he was speaking about little creatures. Dale turned his ball of dough into an olive-oiled bowl.

"You go!" he told it. Then he looked at me a little sheepishly. "Some people would say you pray over the dough. It's about the power of intention."

"You go!" I said to my dough.

The dough rose, we gently spread it out, nice and elastic, and topped it with what we had at hand. The pizza turned out crusty and flavorful, one sprinkled with onion confit and oozing Gorgonzola, another with tomatoes, anchovies, and olives. Somehow, after having worked with the dough and noticed its texture and its response to my fingers, I found that the pizza tasted better.

Two days later, I tried making pizza myself. It was my birthday, and I have a tradition, borrowed from the Italians, of offering a meal to my friends on that day. So I invited thirty or forty people over and began preparing that morning. I had just absorbed all this good advice from Zen master cooks, so I felt pretty invincible. I was looking forward to having some relaxed time to enjoy the twin benefits of mindful cooking that Melissa had described, of combining peaceful space with yourself with cooking healthy, delicious food and nourishing your friends.

I began by preparing all the ingredients carefully and putting them into pretty little bowls for later on. I kept in mind what Annie Somerville had suggested about doing things ahead of time to make the experience more enjoyable. "Break a dish down into its elements," she said. "Then when the time comes, it's easy, because you're ready. Everything is in the prep work."

So for a couple of hours I shredded mozzarella cheese, stirred a simple tomato sauce, tore arugula, sliced anchovies and prosciutto (the Tassajara cookbooks are vegetarian, but I am not), and assembled all the other pizza toppings. My kitchen was calm and orderly, and I felt a tremendous sense of well-being, especially given that I was a year older that day, and already in my late forties.

Then I started in on the dough. I felt my skin temperature, felt the water, and sprinkled the yeast in the bowl. It bubbled up just right. Then I realized that I hadn't actually written down the recipe for the dough. All I knew was flour, water, salt, olive oil in the pan. I called Dale: no answer, and no reply on Melissa's cell phone. No one answered e-mail. I tore through a bunch of recipe books, but none seemed to have the same recipe as the pizza dough I'd made with Dale. I opened Brown's *Tassajara Bread Book* for advice and got angry that he hadn't thought, in 1970, to include pizza: What? Pizza isn't bread? Then I grabbed his *Tassajara Recipe Book* and found this:

> The truth is you're already a cook.
> Nobody teaches you anything,
> But you can be touched, you can be awakened.
> Put down the book and start asking,
> "What have we here?"

So I took a deep breath and looked. I added flour and salt, and looked some more. I tried to create a shaggy mass. I felt how sticky the dough was. I oiled the bowls and put the dough somewhere warm, perhaps too warm, to rise.

It rose and rose. I cut it into quarters, made little balls, patted them around, placed them on greased cookie sheets, and they rose some more. I put them in the fridge to stop their promiscuous reproducing, and there they combined into one big, flat blob. The dough was sticky and exuberantly unruly. It was suddenly five o'clock, and my guests were coming at six. Maybe I could just serve them a lot of wine and olives, stick a few crackers on a plate with some cheese.

Then I picked up a ball of dough and added some flour. "It'll be all right," Dale said when my dough at the ranch had been too blobby. The dough seemed like it would be forgiving. So I worked the dough until it felt more like something you could make pizza out of. Then I greased some pans, spread it out, spun some around for an added Italian effect before laying it out to bake, and added toppings.

"You go," I said before I put it into the oven.

My friends arrived, and the kitchen was full. The pizza came out fine. It was not great; it didn't have a perfect crispy crust, it was a sad cousin to Dale's pizza, and it will take some practice. My friends, on the other hand, were wonderful. They threw themselves into sprinkling toppings onto crust, cutting the pies, checking the oven, and eating square after square of different pizzas. Full and content, they talked and laughed and sparkled and even cleaned up afterward as a gift to the cook. It seemed like magic, the way everyone loved that imperfect pizza party.

"The real magic," Brown writes in the introduction to his *Complete Tassajara Cookbook*, "is that you could grow kind, generous, and larger-hearted in the process of preparing food—because you give your heart to the activity. You are realizing yourself by realizing food. Instead of looking good, you are becoming you."

Joyful Wisdom

Yongey Mingyur Rinpoche

*All you have to do is look at a picture of Yongey Mingyur Rinpoche and
you'll know from his smile that he is a joyful man. He wasn't born that
way; in fact, he went through difficult times when he was young. His joy
comes from his practice as a young master of the Nyingma school of
Tibetan Buddhism, renowned for its profound teachings on mind called
Dzogchen. We may find it hard to believe in the midst of life's difficulties,
but such joy can be ours too.*

When I'm teaching in front of large groups, I often confront a rather
embarrassing problem. My throat gets dry as I talk, so I tend to drain
my glass of water pretty early on in the teaching session. Invariably,
people notice that my glass is empty and they very kindly refill it. As I
continue to speak, my throat gets dry, I drink the entire glass of water,
and sooner or later, someone refills my glass again. I go on talking or
answering questions, and again someone refills my glass.

After some time—usually before the teaching period is scheduled to end—I become aware of a rather uncomfortable feeling, and
a thought crosses my mind: *Oh dear, there's an hour left for this
session and I have to pee.*

I talk a little bit more, answer some questions, and glance at
my watch.

Now there's forty-five minutes left and I really have to pee.

Half an hour passes and the urge to pee really becomes intense. Someone raises his hand and asks, "What is the difference between pure awareness and conditioned awareness?"

The question goes to the heart of the Buddha's teaching about the third noble truth. Often translated as "the truth of cessation," this third insight into the nature of experience tells us that the various forms of suffering we experience can be brought to an end.

But by now I REALLY, REALLY have to pee.

So I tell him, "This is a great secret, which I'll tell you after a short break."

With all the dignity I can summon, I get up off the chair where I've been sitting, slowly pass through rows of people bowing, and finally get to a bathroom.

Now, peeing may not be anyone's idea of an enlightening experience, but I can tell you that once I empty my bladder, I recognize that the deep sense of relief I feel in that moment is a good analogy for the third noble truth: that relief was with me all the time as what you might call a basic condition. I just didn't recognize it because it was temporarily obscured by all that water. But afterwards, I was able to recognize it and appreciate it.

The Buddha referred to this dilemma with a somewhat more dignified analogy in which he compared this basic nature to the sun. Though it's always shining, the sun is often obscured by clouds. Yet we can only really see the clouds because the sun is illuminating them. In the same way, our basic nature is always present. It is, in fact, what allows us to discern even those things that obscure it: an insight that may be best understood by returning to the question raised just before I left for the bathroom.

Two Types of Awareness

The essence of every thought that arises is pristine awareness.
—Pengar Jamphel Sangpo, *Short Invocation of Vajradhara*, translated by Maria Montenegro

Actually there's no great secret to understanding the difference between pure awareness and conditioned awareness. They're both awareness, which might be roughly defined as a capacity to recognize, register, and in a sense, "catalog" every moment of experience. *Pure awareness* is like a ball of clear crystal—colorless in itself but capable of reflecting anything: your face, other people, walls, furniture. If you moved it around a little, maybe you'd see different parts of the room, and the size, shape, or position of the furniture might change. If you took it outside, you could see trees, birds, flowers—even the sky! Whatever appears, though, are only reflections. They don't really exist *inside* the ball, nor do they alter its essence in any way.

Now, suppose the crystal ball were wrapped in a piece of colored silk. Everything you saw reflected in it—whether you moved it around, carried it to different rooms, or took it outside—would be shaded to some degree by the color of the silk. That's a fairly accurate description of *conditioned awareness:* a perspective colored by ignorance, desire, aversion, and the host of other obscurations. Yet these colored reflections are simply reflections. They don't alter the nature of that which reflects them. The crystal ball is essentially colorless.

Similarly, pure awareness in itself is always clear, capable of reflecting anything, even misconceptions about itself as limited or conditioned. Just as the sun illuminates the clouds that obscure it, pure awareness enables us to experience natural suffering and the relentless drama of self-created suffering: me versus you, mine versus yours, this feeling versus that feeling, good versus bad, pleasant versus unpleasant, or a desperate longing for change versus an equally frantic hope for permanence.

The truth of cessation is often described as a final release from fixation, craving, or "thirst." However, while the term "cessation" seems to imply something different or better than our present experience, it is actually a matter of acknowledging the potential already inherent within us.

Cessation—or relief from suffering—is possible because awareness is fundamentally clear and unconditioned. Fear, shame, guilt, greed, competitiveness, and so on are simply veils, perspectives inherited and reinforced by our cultures, our families, and personal experience. Suffering recedes, according to the third noble truth, to the extent that we let go of the whole framework of grasping. We accomplish this, not by suppressing our desire, our aversions, our fixations, or trying to "think differently," but rather by turning our awareness inward, examining the thoughts, emotions, and sensations that trouble us, and beginning to notice them—and perhaps even appreciate them—as expressions of awareness itself. Simply put, the cause of the various diseases we experience is the cure. The mind that grasps is the mind that sets us free.

Buddhanature

> When you are living in darkness, why don't you look for the light?
> —*The Dhammapada*, translated by
> Eknath Easwaran

In order to explain this more clearly I have to cheat a little bit, bringing up a subject that the Buddha never explicitly mentioned in his teachings of the first turning of the wheel. But as a number of my teachers have admitted, this subject is implied in the first and second turnings. It isn't as if he was holding back on some great revelation that would only be passed on to the best and brightest of his students. Rather, like a responsible teacher, he focused first of all on teaching basic principles before moving on to more advanced subjects. Ask any elementary school teacher about the practicality of teaching calculus to children who haven't yet mastered the basics of addition, subtraction, division, or multiplication.

The subject is *buddhanature*—which doesn't refer to the behavior or attitude of someone who walks around in colored robes, begging for food! *Buddha* is a Sanskrit term that might be roughly translated as "one who is awake." As a formal title, it usually refers to Siddhartha Gautama, the young man who achieved enlightenment twenty-five hundred years ago in Bodh Gaya.

Buddhanature, however, is not a formal title. It's not a character-istic exclusive to the historical Buddha or to Buddhist practitioners. It's not something created or imagined. It's the heart or essence inher-ent in all living beings: an unlimited potential to do, see, hear, or ex-perience anything. Because of buddhanature we can learn, we can grow, we can change. We can become buddhas in our own right.

Buddhanature can't be described in terms of relative concepts. It has to be experienced directly, and direct experience is impossi-ble to define in words. Imagine looking at a place so vast that it surpasses our ability to describe it—the Grand Canyon, for exam-ple. You could say that it's big, that the stone walls on either side are sort of red, and that the air is dry and smells faintly like cedar. But no matter how well you describe it, your description can't re-ally encompass the experience of being in the presence of some-thing so vast. Or you could try describing the view from the observatory of the Taipei 101, one of the world's tallest buildings, hailed as one of the "seven wonders of the modern world." You could talk about the panorama, the way the cars and people below look like ants, or your own breathlessness at standing so high above the ground. But it still wouldn't communicate the depth and breadth of your experience.

Though buddhanature defies description, the Buddha did pro-vide some clues in the way of signposts or maps that can help direct us toward that supremely inexpressible experience. One of the ways in which he described it was in terms of three qualities: boundless wisdom, which is the capacity to *know* anything and everything—past, present, and future; infinite capability, which consists of an un-limited power to raise ourselves and other beings from any condition of suffering; and immeasurable loving-kindness and compassion, a limitless sense of relatedness to all creatures, an open-heartedness toward others that serves as a motivation to create the conditions that enable all beings to flourish.

Undoubtedly, there are many people who fervently believe in the Buddha's description and the possibility that, through study and practice, they can realize a direct experience of unlimited wisdom, capability, and compassion. There are probably many others who think it's just a bunch of nonsense.

Oddly enough, in many of the sutras, the Buddha seems to have enjoyed engaging in conversation with the people who doubted what he had to say. He was, after all, only one of many teachers traveling across India in the fourth century B.C.E.—a situation similar to the one in which we find ourselves at present, in which radio, TV channels, and the Internet are flooded by teachers and teachings of various persuasions. Unlike many of his contemporaries, however, the Buddha didn't try to convince people that the method through which he found release from suffering was the only true method. A common theme running through many of the sutras could be summarized in modern terms as, "This is just what I did and this is what I recognized. Don't believe anything I say because I say so. Try it out for yourselves."

He didn't actively discourage people from considering what he'd learned and how he learned it. Rather, in his teachings on buddhanature, he presented his listeners with a kind of thought experiment, inviting them to discover within their own experience the ways in which aspects of buddhanature emerge from time to time in our daily lives. He presented this experiment in terms of an analogy of a house in which a lamp has been lit and the shades or shutters have been drawn. The house represents the seemingly solid perspective of physical, mental, and emotional conditioning. The lamp represents our buddhanature. No matter how tightly the shades and shutters are drawn, inevitably a bit of the light from inside the house shines through.

Inside, the light from the lamp provides the clarity to distinguish between, say, a chair, a bed, or a carpet. As it peeks through the shades or shutters we may experience the light of wisdom sometimes as intuition, what some people describe as a "gut level" feeling about a person, situation, or event.

Loving-kindness and compassion shine through the shutters in those moments when we spontaneously give aid or comfort to someone, not out of self-interest or thinking we might get something in return, but just because it seems the right thing to do. It may be something as simple as offering people a shoulder to cry on when they're in pain or helping someone cross the street, or it may involve a longer-term commitment, like sitting by the bedside of someone ill or dying. We've all heard, too, of extreme instances in which someone, without even thinking about the risk to his or her own life, jumps into a river to save a stranger who is drowning.

Capability often manifests in the way in which we survive difficult events. For example, a long-time Buddhist practitioner I met recently had invested heavily in the stock market back in the 1990s, and when the market fell later in the decade, he lost everything. Many of his friends and partners had also lost a great deal of money, and some of them went a little crazy. Some lost confidence in themselves and their ability to make decisions; some fell into deep depression; others, like the people who lost money during the stock market crash of 1929, jumped out of windows. But he didn't lose his mind, his confidence, or fall into depression. Slowly, slowly, he began investing again and built up a new, solid financial base.

Seeing his apparent calm in the face of such a terrific downturn of events, a number of his friends and associates asked him how he was able to retain his equanimity. "Well," he replied, "I got all this money from the stock market, then it went back to the stock market, and now it's coming back. Conditions change, but I'm still here. I can make decisions. So maybe I was living in a big house one year and sleeping on a friend's couch the next, but that doesn't change the fact that I can choose how to think about myself and all the stuff happening around me. I consider myself very fortunate, in fact. Some people aren't capable of choosing and some people don't recognize that they can choose. I guess I'm lucky because I fall into the category of people who are able to recognize their capacity for choice."

I've heard similar remarks from people who are coping with chronic illness, either in themselves, their parents, their children, other family members, or friends. One man I met recently in North America, for instance, spoke at length about maintaining his job and his relationship with his wife and children while continuing to visit his father who was suffering from Alzheimer's disease. "Of course it's hard to balance all these things," he said. "But it's what I do. I don't see any other way."

Such a simple statement, but how refreshing! Though he'd never attended a Buddhist teaching before, had never studied the literature, and didn't necessarily identify himself as Buddhist, his description of his life and the way he approached it represented a spontaneous expression of all three aspects of buddhanature: the wisdom to see the depth and breadth of his situation, the capability to choose how to interpret and act on what he saw, and the spontaneous attitude of loving-kindness and compassion.

As I listened to him, it occurred to me that these three characteristics of buddhanature can be summed up in a single word: courage—specifically the courage to *be,* just as we are, right here, right now, with all our doubts and uncertainties. Facing experience directly opens us to the possibility of recognizing that whatever we experience—love, loneliness, hate, jealousy, joy, greed, grief, and so on—is, in essence, an expression of the fundamentally unlimited potential of our buddhanature.

This principle is implied in the "positive prognosis" of the third noble truth. Whatever discomfort we feel—subtle, intense, or somewhere in between—subsides to the degree that we cut through our fixation upon a very limited, conditioned, and conditional view of ourselves and begin to identify with the capability to experience anything at all. Eventually, it's possible to come to rest in buddhanature itself—the way, for instance, a bird might rest in coming home to its nest. At that point, suffering ends. There is nothing to fear, nothing to resist. Not even death can trouble you.

JOYFUL WISDOM

You will succeed if you persevere; and you will find a joy in overcoming obstacles.
—HELEN KELLER

Within our perceived weaknesses and imperfections lies the key to realizing our true strength. By facing our disturbing emotions and the problems that occur in our lives, we discover an experience of well-being that extends outward as well as inward. Had I not faced the panic and anxiety I felt through most of my youth, I would not be in the position I find myself today. I would never have found the courage or the strength to get on a plane, travel around the world, and sit before an audience of strangers passing on the wisdom I'd learned not only through my own experience, but the experiences of the truly great masters who were my guides and teachers.

We're all buddhas. We just don't recognize it. We are confined in many ways to a limited view of ourselves and the world around us through cultural conditioning, family upbringing, personal experience, and the basic biological predisposition toward making distinctions and measuring present experience and future hopes and fears against a neuronal warehouse of memories.

Once you commit yourself to developing an awareness of your buddhanature, you'll inevitably start to see changes in your day-to-day experience. Things that used to trouble you gradually lose their power to upset you. You'll become intuitively wiser, more relaxed, and more openhearted. You'll begin to recognize obstacles as opportunities for further growth. And as your illusory sense of limitation and vulnerability gradually fades away, you'll discover deep within yourself the true grandeur of who and what you are.

Best of all, as you start to see your own potential, you'll also begin to recognize it in everyone around you. Buddhanature is not a special quality available to a privileged few. The true mark of recognizing your buddhanature is to realize how ordinary it really is—the ability to see that every living creature shares it, though not everyone recognizes it in him- or herself. So instead of closing your heart to people who yell at you or act in some other harmful way, you find yourself becoming more open. You recognize that they aren't "jerks," but are people who, like you, want to be happy and peaceful. They're only acting like jerks because they haven't recognized their true nature and are overwhelmed by sensations of vulnerability and fear.

Your practice can begin with the simple aspiration to do better, to approach all of your activities with a greater sense of awareness and insight, and to open your heart more deeply toward others.

Motivation is the single most important factor in determining whether your experience is conditioned by suffering or by peace. Wisdom and compassion actually develop at the same pace. The more attentive you become, the easier you'll find it to be compassionate. And the more you open your heart to others, the wiser and more attentive you become in all your activities.

At any given moment, you can choose to follow the chain of thoughts, emotions, and sensations that reinforce a perception of yourself as vulnerable and limited—or you can remember that your true nature is pure, unconditioned, and incapable of being harmed. You can remain in the sleep of ignorance or remember that you are and always have been awake. Either way, you're still expressing the unlimited nature of your true being. Ignorance, vulnerability, fear, anger, and desire are expressions of the infinite potential of your buddhanature. There's nothing inherently wrong or right with making such choices. The fruit of Buddhist practice is simply the recognition that these and other mental afflictions are nothing more or less than choices available to us because our real nature is infinite in scope.

We choose ignorance because we can. We choose awareness because we can. Samsara and nirvana are simply different points of view based on the choices we make in how to examine and understand our experience. There's nothing magical about nirvana and nothing bad or wrong about samsara. If you're determined to think of yourself as limited, fearful, vulnerable, or scarred by past experience, know only that you have chosen to do so. The opportunity to experience yourself differently is always available.

In essence, the Buddhist path offers a choice between familiarity and practicality. There is, without question, a certain comfort and stability in maintaining familiar patterns of thought and behavior. Stepping outside that zone of comfort and familiarity necessarily involves moving into a realm of unfamiliar experience that may seem really scary, an uncomfortable in-between realm. You don't know whether to go back to what was familiar but frightening or to forge ahead toward what may be frightening simply because it's unfamiliar.

In a sense, the uncertainty surrounding the choice to recognize your full potential is similar to what several of my students have told me about ending an abusive relationship: there's a certain reluctance or sense of failure associated with letting go of the relationship. The primary difference between severing an abusive relationship and entering the path of Buddhist practice is that when you enter the path of Buddhist practice you're ending an abusive relationship with yourself. When you choose to recognize your true potential, you gradually begin to find yourself belittling yourself less frequently, your opinion of yourself becomes more positive and wholesome, and your sense of confidence and sheer joy at being alive increases. At the same time, you begin to recognize that everyone around you has the same potential, whether they know it or not. Instead of dealing with them as threats or adversaries, you'll find yourself able to recognize and empathize with their fear and unhappiness. You'll spontaneously respond to them in ways that emphasize solutions rather than problems.

Ultimately, joyful wisdom comes down to choosing between the discomfort of becoming aware of your mental afflictions and the discomfort of being ruled by them. I can't promise you that it will always be pleasant simply to rest in the awareness of your thoughts, feelings, and sensations—and to recognize them as interactive creations of your own mind and body. In fact, I can pretty much guarantee that looking at yourself this way will be, at times, extremely unpleasant.

But the same can be said about beginning anything new, whether it's going to the gym, starting a job, or beginning a diet. The first few months are always difficult. It's hard to learn all the skills you need to master a job; it's hard to motivate yourself to exercise; and it's hard to eat healthfully every day. But after a while the difficulties subside; you start to feel a sense of pleasure or accomplishment, and your entire sense of self begins to change.

Meditation works the same way. For the first few days you might feel very good, but after a week or so, practice becomes a trial. You can't find the time, sitting is uncomfortable, you can't focus, or you just get tired. You hit a wall, as runners do when they try to add an extra half mile to their exercise. The body says, "I can't," while the mind says, "I should." Neither voice is particularly pleasant; in fact, they're both a bit demanding.

Buddhism is often referred to as the "middle way" because it offers a third option. If you just can't focus on a sound or a candle flame for one second longer, then by all means stop. Otherwise, meditation becomes a chore. You'll end up thinking, "Oh no, it's 7:15. I have to sit down and cultivate awareness." No one ever progresses that way. On the other hand, if you think you could go on for another minute or two, then go on. You may be surprised by what you learn. You might discover a particular thought or feeling behind your resistance that you didn't want to acknowledge. Or you may simply find that you can actually rest your mind longer than you thought you could. That discovery alone can give you greater confidence in yourself.

But the best part of all is that no matter how long you practice, or what method you use, every technique of Buddhist meditation ultimately generates compassion. Whenever you look at your mind, you can't help but recognize your similarity to those around you. When you see your own desire to be happy, you can't avoid seeing the same desire in others. And when you look clearly at your own fear, anger, or aversion, you can't help but see that everyone around you feels the same fear, anger, and aversion. This is wisdom—not in the sense of book learning, but in the awakening of the heart, the recognition of our connection to others, and the road to joy.

Smile at Fear ⤜⟫

Carolyn Rose Gimian

*The late Chögyam Trungpa Rinpoche was unique among Buddhist
teachers in emphasizing fear as a central cause of our spiritual problems.
Fear undermines our natural confidence. It stops us from experiencing
life fully. It traps us in a small world. The antidote, as Carolyn Rose
Gimian—Trungpa Rinpoche's brilliant editor—explains, is the teachings
of a fearless lineage.*

Spiritually speaking, I come from an eccentric family. The patri-
arch of my family was the Indian *mahasiddha* Tilopa who, while
spiritually accomplished, was not motivated by worldly success. He
held humble jobs: grinding sesame seeds into oil during the day, and
at night, procuring clients for a prostitute. Later in life, having attained the supreme realization of the Vajrayana, he became a wandering yogi, known to feast on fish entrails left by fisherman down
by the lake. At least, that's the story passed down to me, told with a
great deal of family pride.

His spiritual son, Naropa, was a renowned scholar at the greatest Indian university of his era, Nalanda. After realizing that he
didn't understand the inner meaning of the texts he was studying,
he left the university to study with Tilopa. Naropa was subjected to
a series of difficult trials by his teacher, such as jumping off buildings
or lying in leech-infested water. Eventually, he attained complete,

stainless enlightenment when Tilopa whapped him across the cheek with his sandal.

The next forefather, Marpa, owned a farm in Tibet and was married with children. From time to time, he traveled to India to study the dharma. There he found Naropa. Marpa had brought a bag of gold dust to make offerings to the teachers he encountered. When Naropa demanded the whole bag, Marpa didn't want to part with it, but he gave in. At that point, Naropa scattered the gold dust into the air, singing: "Gold, gold, what is gold to me? The whole world is gold to me." This was the beginning of Marpa's training with Naropa, which led to his ultimate liberation.

The next spiritual son, Milarepa, studied black magic and sent a hailstorm to destroy the farm of his aunt and uncle, who had made him and his mother into servants, but the vengeance did not fundamentally satisfy him. Eventually he found Marpa, who asked him to construct a series of buildings in exchange for receiving the teachings. Milarepa had to carry large boulders and shove them into place by himself, but Marpa would show up, often drunk, and ask Milarepa just what in the name of heaven he was doing. Ordered to dismantle the edifice, he would have to put up another somewhere else. Finally, when Mila was completely broken down and close to suicide, Marpa give him formal initiation. Mila eventually left to pursue meditation in solitude, spending the remainder of his life in caves, surviving mainly on nettles (to the point of developing a green glow). Milarepa sang to anyone who came by his cave, leaving thousands of songs of realization for us to contemplate.

These are some of the early forefathers of the Karma Kagyu school of Vajrayana Buddhism, a lineage that has continued in this manner down to the present day. It is now led by Ogyen Trinley Dorje, the Seventeenth Karmapa, who had to make a dangerous escape from Tibet in order to receive thorough training and education. These life stories of the great figures of the Kagyu lineage show us what extreme human beings they were. The wisdom that comes from this family tree is *extreme* wisdom, and it may be just what is needed for the current situation.

This article is not intended to make you long for the "fish-entrails diet." Nor does it prescribe the "sandal-whap facial," the "throw your money in the air" freeing-therapy, or the "if you build it, you will tear it down" theory of insight. Rather, it asks: What helpful insights can we glean from the teachings of people like these? Why would we turn to such people now?

Because they were all *fearless*. They were not intimidated by external difficulties. In fact, they approached their lives with spontaneity, humor, and a sparkling sense of dignity and decorum that were completely independent of outside circumstances. They were not preoccupied with themselves or their problems. They were concerned about others; in fact, they embodied compassion, either ruthless or gentle depending on what was called for. And they were very, very wise, in the ways of the world, the ways of the heart, and the ways of the spirit.

In tough times, we need wisdom that is not dependent on conditions. When things are falling apart, we need wisdom that is not propped up. The basis for this wisdom is freedom—freedom from confusion, freedom from fear, and interestingly enough, freedom from extreme views. Extreme views in this context means eternalism and nihilism, the belief in either existence or nonexistence as ultimate reality or saving grace. The origin of this wisdom is simplicity, or nonattachment, which is a bit less threatening than calling it "riding on the razor's edge," which might also apply.

Tilopa, Naropa, Marpa, Mila, and all their descendants exemplified the freedom of profound simplicity or naturalness of mind, which can adapt to and transform any external circumstance. Their lifestyles might look extremely unconventional to us, perhaps even unspiritual, but in fact these were people completely at ease in their world, having nothing more to attain and nothing more to give up.

How can we, as beginners on the path, relate to this way of being? To follow their example does not mean mimicking their behavior. Rather than trying to imitate or adopt something external, which will never be a thoroughly satisfying solution, we need to emulate their inner practice and, ultimately, their state of mind.

This may seem like a tall order, but to begin, at least, it is not that complicated. In the beginning, we need simply to examine what's taking place; we need to familiarize ourselves with ourselves. As long as we are in a state of panic, it is very difficult to actually see what is happening to us, to others, or to the world altogether. So in the beginning, developing simplicity means making friends with our fear. When the situation in the world around us inspires panic, we may regard that panic as something unusual or extraordinary. But actually, we are panicked all the time. Fear is already an old friend.

However, fear is so ingrained in us, as anxiety and denial, that we generally don't recognize it. We try to suppress our awareness of it. But in extreme times, this becomes harder to do. To keep ourselves from feeling panicked, we have to build a much denser wall of denial and self-deception, which we construct from the building blocks that the Buddhist teachings call the three poisons: passion, aggression, and ignorance.

On the other hand, we could take the approach that an extreme time is an opportunity as well as an obstacle. We could even celebrate and encourage the chance to bring fear to the surface, into the open. We could welcome our fear for the opportunity it brings us to develop fearlessness. Fear is not the enemy, unless we allow it to become that. Instead, fear can be conquered. But that requires that when we see fear, we smile—an image imparted to me by my teacher, Chögyam Trungpa Rinpoche.

What does it mean to smile at fear? To begin with, it means to relax with our fear, by allowing ourselves to be fully with ourselves. One way to cultivate this relaxation is through the practice of meditation. In the Buddhist tradition, the practice of sitting meditation has two elements: simplicity, or peacefulness, and insight, or clarity. The application of mindfulness allows us to stop the world from spinning, by stopping the spinning of our own minds. This is the essence of the simplicity or peacefulness of *shamatha*. Then we can see the confusion. We can shine the light of *vipashyana*, or clear seeing, on confusion, and that brings the clarity of seeing things as they are. When we begin to see the situation as it is, and when we begin to see our own minds clearly, we defuse the panic.

From the experience we have in meditation, we also may begin to see how we can relax on the spot in the midst of the most difficult experiences in our lives. We begin to see that it is possible to be there in a simple and open way. What are we afraid of all the time? Often, it is the unknown. If we are willing to simply witness what is there, although it might in fact be devastating, it also turns out to be more benign, more manageable, and more ordinary and transparent than we expected. This is where we begin to discover the quality of freedom, in the emptiness of our freak-out, which allows us to remain vulnerable.

The Buddha himself set the example for us. Here was an extreme human being if ever there was one. Having left the comfort of his father's palace and his own regal life, he tried every method he encountered to achieve liberation. Having practiced intense asceticism and arduous disciplines for a number of years, he realized that struggle was not the path to enlightenment. And this, I think, is when he began to smile at fear.

Make no mistake. The closer the Buddha got to enlightenment, the more forceful and insistent were the obstacles he encountered. We sometimes seem to approach the experience of enlightenment as though it were like a long drowsy soak in a warm perfumed bath. After our nap, we will arise as the Awakened One. The stories of the Buddha's enlightenment instead describe how the greatest obstacles, or *maras*, appeared to the Buddha the night before he attained enlightenment. Meeting their challenge required vigilance, or openness, rather than somnolence. As the Buddha sat in meditation beneath the bodhi tree, Mara sent his daughters in the guise of beautiful women to seduce the Buddha; he sent his troops of warriors to attack the Buddha. The Buddha manifested as the victorious one, *vijaya*, or the fearless one, the warrior of nonaggression. He remained unmoved by passion and aggression. He chose instead to be awake. Mara's arrows then became a rain of flowers.

In our own lives, it is difficult to be open yet unmoved by extreme situations, but we too, like the Buddha, have the choice to be wakeful. Whether it is the crash of the financial markets, the death of a loved one, the experience of chemotherapy, the failure of a relationship, or the violence of an angry mob—whatever the difficulties, they can be the bearers of good news, or at the very least, real news. That's quite an outrageous thing to say, but it is truly the message of people like the Kagyu lineage forefathers, who lived in the ground of reality beyond pain and pleasure, good and bad. This is not suggesting that the worse things get, the better it is; nor that we shouldn't have sympathy and feel compassion for our own and others' difficulties. However, unless we can make friends with what occurs in our life, we are simply subject to circumstances and controlled by them. Often, the worst—whatever it is—has already happened by the time we realize the need to apply these teachings. In that sense, we have no choice. We can't take our life back. It is not a rehearsal.

When circumstances bring our emotions to a sharp point, at that point both confusion and wakefulness emerge from the same ground. If we are willing to practice in that groundless ground, that too is smiling at our fear. In the Kagyu tradition, this is also called practicing in the place where rock meets bone. I always thought this phrase referred to the meditator's bony behind sitting on the bare rock of a meditation cave, but I learned recently that it refers to crushing bones for soup with a heavy rock mallet. That sense of crushing or breaking through our confusion and hesitation is also an expression of opening everything up, letting everything go, exposing the innermost marrow of the situation. It is about our ultimate vulnerability.

I can't offer you a finite list of things to do, nor can I tell you exactly how you can smile at fear. I'm working with turning up the edges of my mouth when I feel anxious. The advice I give myself is: Don't avoid the opportunity to grin back at fear. And if you can dive into that empty feeling in the pit of your stomach, well, that would be excellent! We each have to find our own inner grin.

The time where rock meets bone turns out to be the time we are always living in, although we don't always acknowledge that raw mark of our existence. To do so is to meet the moment where neither past nor future exist and where we cannot hold on to the present for security. In that moment, the closing bell of the stock market is no different from the bell that calls us to the shrine room. In that moment, our dharmic ancestors will all applaud our fearless smile.

Seeking Peace: Chronicles of the Worst Buddhist in the World

Mary Pipher

It takes courage to fully acknowledge and experience our pain, shame, and self-doubt, but only in that way can we experience spiritual progress, for denial is a permanent stop sign on the path. Mary Pipher, the author of the best-seller Raising Ophelia, *found such courage as she began her practice of meditation. You'll see that she is far from the worst Buddhist in the world.*

Despair is the subjective state we experience when our inner and outer resources are insufficient to cope with the situation at hand. At core it involves a breakdown in our trust of ourselves and the universe. It is a 911 call from deep within, warning us that we must make changes if we are to survive psychically.

Of course, my understanding of despair is more theoretical. Many of my family members have battled addictions and struggled with emotional disorders. Both my parents and my husband's parents died slow, painful deaths. I've worked for thirty years as a therapist, listening to people share their darkest and saddest stories, and I have interviewed refugees about Kosovo, Sierra Leone, and

Afghanistan. I feel qualified to write about what humans do with despair. I think all of us are qualified.

While I can't compare myself to Job, my anguish has carried me to many dark and lonely places. My suffering helps me connect to others who are coping with much darker scenarios. As I write this today, a young teacher I know lies in a nearby hospital dying of cancer. Most likely, someone reading this has lost a child in Iraq or is married to a person with Alzheimer's. Other readers stagger under money and health worries. Some are fighting foreclosure, prejudice, or uncaring employers, while others are holding on to their sanity for dear life. I am no Job, but the world is full of people suffering as he did. For many people, facing the day requires extraordinary courage and self-discipline.

Most of the time we humans keep our suffering to ourselves. We are polite people who don't want to inflict our burdens on others. We are proud people who don't want to be pitied. Some of the time we keep our despair from ourselves.

One of the saddest things about despair is our attempt to deny it. To move toward our pain requires us to buck a well-tuned system of defenses. We repress, somatize, rationalize, and avoid our own despair. Too often we give our deepest pain orders to march off a cliff, forgetting that this pain is our psyche's way of encouraging us to take it easy and offer ourselves some compassion.

We may banish despair from our consciousness, but it doesn't disappear. The stress hormones keep on pumping. Tightness in our chest, tension in our shoulders, and a feeling of heat on our faces— all of these are attempts by our bodies to urge us to pay attention. The body signals us constantly about our inner and outer situations. It is our personal GPS, and we ignore it at our peril.

Our biggest problems come from our cover-ups. While facing anguish is difficult, not facing it is even harder. Our daily headlines tell stories of deflected despair. The unemployed father is arrested for road rage. A bullied teenager shoots his classmates. Shame and humiliation have motivated many a terrorist. Bars and nightclubs are full of people who cannot face pain.

After a life of running from my own pain, I realized I couldn't do it any longer. Full of fear and uncertainty, I embarked on a journey of self-exploration. I wanted to stop inflicting pain on myself and, instead, find my strengths and my goodness. Especially at first, I trudged though a pretty hellish set of discoveries—that I was a mess, that I had glossed over my childhood suffering, and that I was emotionally tapped out with nothing left to give away.

I shouldn't have been surprised that when I first looked deeply into myself, I felt crummy. I knew from experience that therapy clients often feel worse before they feel better. In their beginning sessions, they discuss their traumas and they cry or rage. They flail at themselves or others for weakness. Only later do they begin to see positives and discover strengths. People who meditate often talk about feeling crazy or uniquely weird during their first sits. Many describe sobbing and falling apart as they face their fears and sorrows. The journey toward a more examined life nearly always begins with pain.

Certain parts of my past were "no-fly zones." I remembered only a few of the many times my father had been angry. When we lived in the trailer in Ozarks, Dad lost control a few times when he was punishing me. He didn't injure me physically, but his fury scared me. I had an almost dreamlike memory of a night in Beaver City when he threw a skillet across the kitchen toward my mother. Aunt Margaret told me about an incident at a lake when my cousin forgot to put the plug in the boat and it filled with water. My father was so angry that my uncles had to stop him from physically injuring my cousin. I was there, but I don't remember that.

Even if I could recall certain events, I felt no emotions about them. I could describe what happened, but I described it as if I were reading from a dictionary. My head remembered, but my body felt dead. One treatment for chronic pain is to literally freeze nerve endings with liquid nitrogen. I felt as if I had frozen the nerve endings that connected me to memories of my deepest sorrows. "No pain for me, thank you."

As I meditated on my childhood, I reexperienced some of these sorrows. I would recall a traumatic event and my stomach would ache. My jaw would clench. My heart would feel hard and cold. Sometimes I could cry; other times I felt as if I were locked in a block of ice. Afterward, I would be dazed for a few hours.

Gradually, I became more clear-eyed about my parents. I didn't love them less, but I did acknowledge that their actions had enormous consequences on the lives of my siblings and myself. Since I viewed myself as accountable, I had to hold my parents to some standards as well. This realization was incredibly painful. When I considered the effects of my parents' choices, I felt a stab of separation and disconnection. My chest hurt and my breathing became ragged. Still, I stayed with these feelings. Over time, I learned I could be more realistic about my parents' failings and still love them.

My discomfort with anger has always been pronounced. I have never been able to watch violent movies or television, or to read about domestic violence or child abuse. Sometimes I feel other people's pain in ways I do not feel my own. In Sunday school I had learned "Love thy neighbor as thyself," yet I was never really taught to love myself.

As I meditated about my past, I realized that I was seething with anger and that it was all directed toward myself. I was responsible for everything and to blame for everything. Whatever happened in my world, internally or externally, was my fault. Repeatedly I had failed to keep everyone content, and for that I condemned myself. This hanging judge was so much a part of me that, like breathing, I didn't notice until I slowed down and really paid attention. When I did, it alarmed me. I had always seen myself as loving and gentle. Who knew how filled with venom I had become?

I had made myself my own grand inquisitor. If I had a weird nightmare about a reptile or a house fire, I would tell myself it was because I was nutty. If I dropped an egg on the counter and broke it, I would tell myself I was clumsy and careless. Of course, I knew other people had nightmares or broke things from time to time. While I could exempt them from judgment, I could not absolve myself.

With practice, I became more mindful of the rules I had made for myself. For example, if I woke up in a sour and surly mood, I would give myself a hard time. I'd ask myself, "What is wrong with you?" As I learned to observe my thought sequences carefully, I had a realization so simple that it is embarrassing to share. I thought, "Who does wake up sunny every morning?" I gave myself permission to join my fellow humans who don't arise from their beds smiling.

When my father was deeply critical of someone, he said, "He's no damn good." I realized that, at core, that is what I believed about myself. I constantly questioned my own thoughts, feelings, and behavior. My answer to the "why" questions was always either "I'm no damn good" or "I'm screwed up."

Perhaps my core belief about myself was that I was not worthy. My deepest pain came from not seeing my own goodness. I felt so damn broken. I didn't trust myself just to be who I was. I felt I deserved my misery, even that I caused it. I could not see all the love and joy that I held within myself.

These ideas stemmed from my early years with absent parents. At the time, I couldn't blame them for being gone because I needed to love them. So instead, I blamed myself. Somehow I deserved to be lonely. I told myself that what I didn't get, I didn't need. By becoming the universal donor, I relinquished my rights to have needs.

Most of my life, I could dish out compassion, but I couldn't take it. I was extremely embarrassed by gifts or compliments. When people offered to help me, I almost always said, "No, I can handle it." "Don't worry about me." "No, I don't need any presents." "I like the leftovers." "I'll wear the hand-me-downs." Or, "I'll sit in the back middle seat." In my emerging life, I yearned to find ways to both accept love from others and extend it to myself.

Over time, through meditation, I acquired some ability to acknowledge whatever was happening. Sometimes I could smile at my intensity. I would have a thought sequence like this: I am aware of how hard it is to break through my own denial system. I feel heavy and I have goose bumps. I want to believe I am flawless and that the world is made of spun sugar. I don't believe it, though. My heart is racing. My mouth is dry. I am filled with flaws too awful to admit. What are my flaws? What can I confess to? I am often fearful and wary. I don't trust others as much as I think I should. I think I know everything. I think I know nothing. I am clumsy with others. I don't appreciate every moment to its fullest.

I would accept all those thoughts and then say a prayer for everyone who could turn drinking a cup of cider into a metaphysical event. All my life I had been told that I thought too much. I now learned to pray for humans who think too much. All things considered, we weren't such a bad lot.

Meditation helped me stay with my own experience and not censor or censure upsetting information. Instead of being utterly entangled in my thoughts and feelings, I learned to note them without judging them. I would even wait to pounce on a thought so that I could label it. Nothing slowed my thinking down more rapidly than that. I am just stubborn that way.

I read of a Buddhist teacher who developed Alzheimer's. He had retired from teaching because his memory was unreliable, but he made one exception for a reunion of his former students. When he walked onto the stage, he forgot everything, even where he was and why. However, he was a skilled Buddhist and he simply began sharing his feelings with the crowd. He said, "I am anxious. I feel stupid. I feel scared and dumb. I am worried that I am wasting everyone's time. I am fearful. I am embarrassing myself." After a few minutes of this, he remembered his talk and proceeded without apology. The students were deeply moved, not only by his wise teachings, but also by how he handled his failings.

There is a Buddhist saying, "No resistance, no demons." I worked to stop resisting my pain. I tried to look at myself with more curiosity and less judgment. I invited all my thoughts to the table and welcomed them like long-awaited guests. As I watched them come and go, I could sometimes see beneath my layers of pain, my desperately self-protective ego, and my habitual ways of viewing the world. Sometimes I felt connected to something light and spacious.

Of course, it wasn't always that way. Some days I never escaped the Mary that I had been all my life. I berated myself for not breathing properly or for not noticing a sensation in just the right way, whatever that meant. I wanted to connect with wisdom and instead found contempt for myself. I wanted to feel humility, but often I felt self-humiliation.

Recognizing the immensity of my self-judgment was progress. It was impossible to solve a problem that I didn't recognize existed. I learned to count the number of times I criticized myself during my half-hour meditations. Sometimes the number was as high as a hundred. Still, I was counting, not just judging. I began to cut myself some slack. A Buddhist friend told me that he had outgrown the need to judge himself and that he had found peace in simply being kinder to himself. His simple statement gave me hope.

I conducted a simple psychological exercise. I drew a picture of myself. I looked worn and worried with waves of dark energy emanating from my forehead, but I had a smile on my face and wide curious eyes. Then I sketched another of my biggest problems. I showed myself carrying a heavy bag filled with guilt, shame, self-loathing, and dread. I was so weighed down by this bag I could barely walk. Finally, I drew another of myself with my biggest problems solved. Birds had carried away my huge pack of sorrows and I was dancing with abandon and joy.

Slowly, I learned how to lift my heavy burden off my shoulders. One morning, I noticed this thought sequence: I woke up feeling happy and physically relaxed. Within ten seconds, I began to feel guilty because I was enjoying lying in bed. I asked myself, "Am I lazy?" Then I felt guilty because I hadn't gotten out of bed. "Am I depressed?" I wondered. Then I felt guilty because I thought I should get up. I asked myself, "Am I driven?" Finally, I felt neurotic because I had so many thoughts and couldn't simply enjoy lying in bed. I asked myself, "Am I salvageable?"

When I castigated myself this way, I followed Thich Nhat Hanh's example and told myself, "Darling, I love you just the way you are." I realized I was simply committing the crime of being human. When

I thought of something I was ashamed of, such as "I am mad at Jim," I would pray for all the wives who had ever felt mad at their husbands. When I felt irritated with myself for doing something stupid, I would say a prayer for all the other people on Earth who had made a silly mistake. That would make me smile and lighten up.

Instead of dividing my actions into good and bad ones, I studied what behaviors caused what results. I paid more attention to karma, or the fact that actions have consequences. If I was focused and cautious, I did less harm. When I thought carefully before I spoke, my words had a better effect. If I allowed myself time to rest in the late afternoon, I would be more cheerful at dinner. When I could put aside my own neediness and be present for another person, she benefited from my attention.

Paradoxically, as I embraced my basic goodness, I could be more honest about my shortcomings. When I had treated myself harshly, I had needed to deny my very real flaws and mistakes to avoid my own self-judgments. As a hanging judge whose every transgression merited the death penalty, I couldn't afford to see the effects of my behavior on others. Now I could face facts. I could admit that I had spoken too quickly or been unreasonable. After all, don't all of us make these mistakes?

I developed mantras to help with self-acceptance. "I forgive myself for losing perspective, for being fearful, for being overconfident and for lacking confidence. I forgive myself for being ungrateful and for chiding myself for not feeling gratitude every moment of my day. I forgive myself for the thoughtless remark, the inattentive moment, the careless gesture, and the undelivered gift." "Forgiven, forgiven, forgiven. I am forgiven."

Although with others, I was not a demanding person, I had sent myself a different quality of message. I developed new ways of dealing with myself. The first time I noticed I had changed was when I accidentally spilled tomato juice on our light gray rug. My internal dialogue began with my habitual responses: "You are stupid, careless, clumsy, and awful," but suddenly I asked myself, "How mad would you be at a friend who did this?" I smiled and told myself, "Accidents happen. Let yourself off the hook."

I practiced what the Dalai Lama calls "inner disarmament." Of course, I still had judgments, but I tried to accept even my judgments without judgment. At a glacial pace, I moved beyond repression and self-criticism to something more skillful. I discovered the difference between recoiling from feelings and opening to them. I trained myself to be more curious than fearful. Sometimes I even felt compassion for myself as I struggled.

Taking the Leap

Pema Chödrön

Perhaps you've seen those paintings of the wrathful deities of Vajrayana Buddhism. They are a manifestation of fierce compassion, because sometimes that's what we need. People rightly love the American Buddhist nun and teacher Pema Chödrön for her warmth and gentleness, but I think of her as one of those fiercely compassionate deities. Her message is loving but tough: we can't hide, we can't fool ourselves, and all our tricks only make things worse. It's called truth. She's faced it herself, and we need to, too.

Before we can know what natural warmth really is, often we must experience loss. We go along for years moving through our days, propelled by habit, taking life pretty much for granted. Then we or someone dear to us has an accident or gets seriously ill, and it's as if blinders have been removed from our eyes. We see the meaninglessness of so much of what we do and the emptiness of so much we cling to.

When my mother died and I was asked to go through her personal belongings, this awareness hit me hard. She had kept boxes of papers and trinkets that she treasured, things that she held on to through her many moves to smaller and smaller accommodations. They had represented security and comfort for her, and she had been unable to let them go. Now they were just boxes of stuff, things that held no meaning and represented no comfort or security to anyone. For me these were just empty objects, yet she had clung to them. Seeing this made me sad, and also thoughtful. After that I could never look at my own treasured objects in the same way. I had seen that things themselves are just what they are, neither precious nor worthless, and that all the labels, all our views and opinions about them, are arbitrary.

This was an experience of uncovering basic warmth. The loss of my mother and the pain of seeing so clearly how we impose judgments and values, prejudices, likes and dislikes, onto the world, made me feel great compassion for our shared human predicament. I remember explaining to myself that the whole world consisted of people just like me who were making much ado about nothing and suffering from it tremendously.

When my second marriage fell apart, I tasted the rawness of grief, the utter groundlessness of sorrow, and all the protective shields I had always managed to keep in place fell to pieces. To my surprise, along with the pain, I also felt an uncontrived tenderness for other people. I remember the complete openness and gentleness I felt for those I met briefly in the post office or at the grocery store. I found myself approaching the people I encountered as just like me—fully alive, fully capable of meanness and kindness, of stumbling and falling down and of standing up again. I'd never before experienced that much intimacy with unknown people. I could look into the eyes of store clerks and car mechanics, beggars and children, and feel our sameness. Somehow when my heart broke, the qualities of natural warmth, qualities like kindness and empathy and appreciation, just spontaneously emerged.

People say it was like that in New York City for a few weeks after September 11. When the world as they'd known it fell apart, a whole city full of people reached out to one another, took care of one another, and had no trouble looking into one another's eyes.

It is fairly common for crisis and pain to connect people with their capacity to love and care about one another. It is also common that this openness and compassion fades rather quickly, and that people then become afraid and far more guarded and closed than they ever were before. The question, then, is not only how to uncover our fundamental tenderness and warmth but also how to abide there with the fragile, often bittersweet vulnerability. How can we relax and open to the uncertainty of it?

The first time I met Dzigar Kongtrül, who is now my teacher, he spoke to me about the importance of pain. He had been living and teaching in North America for more than ten years and had come to realize that his students took the teachings and practices he gave them at a superficial level until they experienced pain in a way they couldn't shake. The Buddhist teachings were just a pastime, something to dabble in or use for relaxation, but when their lives fell apart, the teachings and practices became as essential as food or medicine.

The natural warmth that emerges when we experience pain includes all the heart qualities: love, compassion, gratitude, tenderness in any form. It also includes loneliness, sorrow, and the shakiness of fear. Before these vulnerable feelings harden, before the storylines kick in, these generally unwanted feelings are pregnant with kindness, with openness and caring. These feelings that we've become so accomplished at avoiding can soften us, can transform us. The openheartedness of natural warmth is sometimes pleasant, sometimes unpleasant—as "I want, I like," and as the opposite. The practice is to train in not automatically fleeing from uncomfortable tenderness when it arises. With time we can embrace it just as we would the comfortable tenderness of lovingkindness and genuine appreciation.

A person does something that brings up unwanted feelings, and what happens? Do we open or close? Usually we involuntarily shut down, yet without a storyline to escalate our discomfort we still have easy access to our genuine heart. Right at this point we can recognize that we are closing, allow a gap, and leave room for change to happen. In Jill Bolte Taylor's book *My Stroke of Insight,* she points to scientific evidence showing that the life span of any particular emotion is only one and a half minutes. After that we have to revive the emotion and get it going again.

Our usual process is that we automatically do revive it by feeding it with an internal conversation about how another person is the source of our discomfort. Maybe we strike out at them or at someone else—all because we don't want to go near the unpleasantness of what we're feeling. This is a very ancient habit. It allows our natural warmth to be so obscured that people like you and me, who have the capacity for empathy and understanding, get so clouded that we can harm each other. When we hate those who activate our fears or insecurities, those who bring up unwanted feelings, and see them as the sole cause of our discomfort, then we can dehumanize them, belittle them, and abuse them.

Understanding this, I've been highly motivated to make a practice of doing the opposite. I don't always succeed, but year by year I become more familiar and at home with dropping the storyline and trusting that I have the capacity to stay present and receptive to other beings. Suppose you and I spent the rest of our lives doing this? Suppose we spent some time every day bringing the unknown people that we see into focus, and actually taking an interest in them? We could look at their faces, notice their clothes, look at their hands. There are so many chances to do this, particularly if we live in a large town or in a city. There are panhandlers that we rush by because their predicament makes us uncomfortable; there are the multitudes of people we pass on streets and sit next to on buses and in waiting rooms. The relationship becomes more intimate when someone packs up our groceries or takes our blood pressure or comes to our house to fix a leaking pipe. Then there are the people who sit next to us on airplanes. Suppose you had been on one of the planes that went down on September 11. Your fellow passengers would have been very important people in your life.

It can become a daily practice to humanize the people that we pass on the street. When I do this, unknown people become very real for me. They come into focus as living beings who have joys and sorrows just like mine, as people who have parents and neighbors and friends and enemies, just like me. I also begin to have a heightened awareness of my own fears and judgments and prejudices that pop up out of nowhere about these ordinary people that I've never even met. I've gained insight into my sameness with all these people, as well as insight into what obscures this understanding and causes me to feel separate. By increasing our awareness of our strength as well as our confusion, this practice uncovers natural warmth and brings us closer to the world around us.

When we go in the other direction, when we remain self-absorbed, when we are unconscious about what we are feeling and blindly bite the hook, we wind up with rigid judgments and fixed opinions that are throbbing with *shenpa,* a Tibetan word usually translated as "attachment," but more generally describing the energy that hooks us into our habitual patterns. This is a setup for closing down to anyone who threatens us. To take a common example, how do you feel about people who smoke? I haven't found too many people, either smokers or nonsmokers, who are shenpa-free on this topic. I was once in a restaurant in Boulder, Colorado, when a woman from Europe who didn't realize you couldn't smoke inside, lit up. The restaurant was noisy, bustling with conversation and laughter, and then she lit her cigarette. The sound of the match striking caused the whole place to stop. You could hear yourself breathe, and the righteous indignation in the room was palpable.

I don't think it would have gone over very well with the crowd if I had tried to point out that in many places in the world smoking isn't viewed negatively and that their shenpa-filled value judgments, not this smoker, were the real cause of their discomfort.

When we see difficult circumstances as a chance to grow in bravery and wisdom, in patience and kindness, when we become more conscious of being hooked and we don't escalate it, then our personal distress can connect us with the discomfort and unhappiness of others. What we usually consider a problem becomes the source of empathy. Recently a man told me that he devotes his life to trying to help sex offenders because he knows what it's like to be them. As a teenager he sexually abused a little girl. Another example is a woman I met who said that as a child she had hated her brother so violently that she thought of ways to kill him every day. This now allows her to work compassionately with juveniles who are in prison for murder. She can work with them as her equals because she knows what it's like to stand in their shoes.

The Buddha taught that among the most predictable human sufferings are sickness and old age. Now that I'm in my seventies I understand this at a gut level. Recently I watched a movie about a mean-spirited seventy-five-year-old woman whose health was failing and whose family didn't like her. The only kindness in her life came from her devoted border collie. For the first time in my life I identified with the old lady rather than her children. This was a major shift: a whole new world of understanding, a new area of sympathy and kindness, had suddenly been revealed to me.

This can be the value of our personal suffering. We can understand firsthand that we are all in the same boat and that the only thing that makes any sense is to care for one another.

When we feel dread, when we feel discomfort of any kind, it can connect us at the heart with all the other people feeling dread and discomfort. We can pause and touch into dread. We can touch the bitterness of rejection and the rawness of being slighted. Whether we are at home or in a public spot or caught in a traffic jam or walking into a movie, we can stop and look at the other people there and realize that in pain and in joy they are just like us. Just like us they don't want to feel physical pain or insecurity or rejection. Just like us they want to feel respected and physically comfortable.

When you touch your sorrow or fear, your anger or jealousy, you are touching everybody's jealousy, you are knowing everybody's fear or sorrow. You wake up in the middle of the night with an anxiety attack and when you can fully experience the taste and smell of it, you are sharing the anxiety and fear of all humanity and all animals as well. Instead of your distress becoming all about you, it can become your link with everyone all over the world who is in the same predicament. The stories are different, the causes are different, but the experience is the same. For each of us sorrow has exactly the same taste; for each of us rage and jealousy, envy and addictive craving have exactly the same taste. And so it is with gratitude and kindness. There can be two zillion bowls of sugar, but they all have the same taste.

Whatever pleasure or discomfort, happiness or misery you are experiencing, you can look at other people and say to yourself, "Just like me they don't want to feel this kind of pain." Or, "Just like me they appreciate feeling this kind of contentment."

When things fall apart and we can't get the pieces back together, when we lose something dear to us, when the whole thing is just not working and we don't know what to do, this is the time when the natural warmth of tenderness, the warmth of empathy and kindness, are just waiting to be uncovered, just waiting to be embraced. This is our chance to come out of our self-protecting bubble and to realize that we are never alone. This is our chance to finally understand that wherever we go, everyone we meet is essentially just like us. Our own suffering, if we turn toward it, can open us to a loving relationship with the world.

Hard Times, Simple Times

Norman Fischer

*The recent sudden death of his best friend was a shock and deep blow to
the poet and Zen teacher Norman Fischer. The intensity of his reaction
and how he worked with it through his Buddhist practice led to this extraordinary contemplation on loss as a path to deeper love and realization.
Loss has infinite variations but is at heart a shared human experience. All
of us need the wisdom Fischer offers.*

One day in January, feeling expansive and cheerfully open to being
interrupted, I answered the phone in my study. Sherril was on the
line. "Alan just died in Baltimore," she said. "Can you come over
right now?"

Alan is Sherril's husband and my closest friend. We'd known
each other forty years, since our days as students at the University of
Iowa Writers' Workshop, through years of Zen practice, through
Alan's becoming a rabbi and my ordination as a Zen priest, through
our establishing a Jewish meditation center together, through retreats, teaching sessions, workshops, marriages, divorces, children,
grandchildren. We had shared so much for so long that we took
each other's presence in the world as basic.

I got in the car and drove to San Francisco in a daze—a daze I may never recover from.

Our first response to loss, difficulty, or pain is *not* surrendering to what has happened. It seems so negative, so wrong, and we don't want to give in to it. Yet we can't help thinking and feeling differently, and it is the thinking and the feeling—so unpleasant and painful—that is the real cause of our suffering. These days many of us experience troubled thinking and feeling because times are tough. So many are losing jobs, savings, homes, expectations. And if we are not losing these things ourselves, we are receiving at close range the suffering of others who are losing them, and we are reading and hearing about all this in the media and on the Web, which daily depict the effects of economic anxiety all over the world. We are all breathing in the atmosphere of fear and loss.

In one of our last conversations, Alan shared with me an odd and funny teaching about death. He had a sense of humor, and his spiritual teachings were often odd and funny, sometimes even ridiculous, which made their profundity all the more pungent. This teaching involved his fountain pen collection, which was extensive, and worth a lot of money. He had sold several thousand dollars' worth of pens to a man he'd contacted online. Before payment was mailed, the man, some years younger than Alan, suddenly died. Since there was no good record of the transaction, the attorney who was handling the estate for the widow said he would not pay. Alan could have hired his own attorney to recover the money, but it wasn't worth the trouble and expense, so he ate the loss. "But I didn't mind," he said, "because I learned something that I should have known and thought I knew but actually I didn't know: when you're dead you can't do anything." He told me this with great earnestness. As if it had actually never occurred to him before that when you're dead you can't do anything anymore.

In a memorial retreat we held a few days after Alan's death, a retreat full of love and sorrow, I repeated this story. I said that since Alan was now dead and couldn't do anything, we would now have to do something because we were still alive. What that something was,

I didn't know. I only knew that somehow, in the face of a great loss, one does something different than one would otherwise have done. So this is what I learned (with Alan's help) about the meaning of loss: that love rushes into the absence that is loss, and that love brings inspired action. If we are able to give ourselves to the loss, to move toward it rather than away in an effort to escape or deny or distract or obscure, our wounded hearts become full, and out of that fullness we will do things differently and we will do different things.

The Tibetan Buddhist master Chögyam Trungpa talks about a soft spot, a raw spot, a wounded spot on the body or in the heart. A spot that is painful and sore. A spot that may emerge in the face of a loss. We hate such spots, so we try to prevent them. And if we can't prevent them we try to cover them up, so we won't absentmindedly rub them or pour hot or cold water on them. A sore spot is no fun. Yet it is valuable. Trungpa Rinpoche calls the sore spot embryonic compassion, potential compassion. Our loss, our wound, is precious to us because it can wake us up to love, and to loving action.

When sudden loss or trouble occurs, we feel shock and bewilderment, as I did when Alan died. We wonder: what just happened? For so long we expected things to be as they have been, had taken this as much for granted as the air we breathe. And suddenly it is not so. Maybe tomorrow, we think, we will wake up to discover that this devastating change was all just a temporary mistake and that things are back to normal. (After Alan's death I had some dreams that he hadn't actually died, that it had all been some sort of correctable slipup.) After the shock passes, fear and despair arrive. We are anxious about our uncertain future, over which we have so little control. It's easy to fall into the paralysis of despair, caroming back to our childish default position of feeling completely vulnerable and unprepared in a harsh and hostile world. This fearful feeling of self-diminishment may darken our view to such an extent that we find ourselves wondering whether we are worthwhile people, whether we're capable of surviving in this tough world, whether we deserve to survive, whether our lives matter, whether there is any point in trying to do anything at all.

This is what it feels like when the raw spot is rubbed. The sense of loss, the despair, the fear, is terrible and we hate it, but it is exactly what we need. It is the embryo of compassion stirring to be born. Birth is painful. All too many people in times like these just don't have the heart to do spiritual practice. But these are the best times for practice, because motivation is so clear. Practice is not simply a lifestyle choice or a refinement. There is no choice. It's a matter of survival. The tremendous benefit of simple meditation practice is most salient in these moments. Having exhausted all avenues of activity that might change your outward circumstances, and given up on other means of finding inner relief for your raging or sinking mind, there is nothing better to do than to sit down on a chair or cushion and just be present with your situation. There you sit, feeling your body. You try to sit up straight, with some basic human dignity. You notice you are breathing. You also notice that troubling thoughts and feelings are present in the mind. You are not here to make them go away or to cover them up with pleasant and encouraging spiritual slogans. There they are, all your demons, your repetitive negative themes. Your mind is (to borrow a phrase from the poet Michael Palmer) a museum of negativity. And you are sitting there quietly breathing inside that museum. There is nothing else to do. You can't fix anything—the situation is beyond that. Gradually it dawns on you that these dark thoughts and anxious feelings are just that—thinking, feeling. They are exhibits in the museum of negativity, but not necessarily realities of the outside world. This simple insight—that thoughts and feelings are thoughts and feelings—is slight, but it makes all the difference. You continue to sit, continue to pay attention to body and breath, and you label everything else, "thinking, thinking; feeling, feeling." Eventually you are able to pick up your coat from the coat check and walk out of the museum into the sunlight.

Confronting, accepting, being with negative thinking and feeling, knowing that they are not the whole of reality and not you, is the most fruitful and beneficial of all spiritual practices—better even than experiencing bliss or Oneness. You can practice it on the meditation cushion in the simple way I have described, but you can also practice it in other ways.

Journaling practice can be a big help. Keep a small notebook handy during the day and jot down an arresting word or phrase when you read or hear one. From time to time look at these words or phrases (they need not be uplifting or even sensible; they can be quite odd or random) and select the ones that attract you. These become your list of journaling prompts. When you have time, sit down with your notebook (doing this in a disciplined way, at a certain time each day, is best), choose a prompt, and write rapidly and spontaneously for ten to fifteen minutes, pen never leaving the paper, whatever comes to mind, no matter how nonsensical or irrelevant it may seem. In this way you empty out your swirling mind. You curate your own exhibition of negativity. It can be quite entertaining and even instructive.

Another way to reorient yourself with your thoughts and feelings is to share them with others. If you are feeling fear or despair these days, you can be sure that you are not alone in this. No doubt many of your friends and family members are feeling this as well. Rather than ignoring your anxieties—which tend to proliferate like mushrooms in the dark room of your closeted mind—or complaining obsessively about them to everyone you meet, which also increases the misery, you can undertake the spiritual discipline of speaking to others.

Taking a topic or a prompt from your notebook, or cueing off something you've read or written, or simply distilling what you have been thinking or feeling into a coherent thought, you can speak to one or more people in a structured way. Bring a few friends together. Divide yourselves into groups of three or four. After five minutes of silence to collect your thoughts, have each person speak as spontaneously as possible for five to seven minutes on the chosen topic. The others just listen, no questions, no comments. If it seems useful, one person can give feedback to the speaker. Not advice (it is a much better practice if advice and commentary are outlawed), but simply reviewing for the speaker, in your own words, what you have heard him or her say. Listening to what you have said repeated back to you in another's voice can be extremely illuminating. And forgetting about your own trouble long enough to actually listen to another is a great relief. It is likely to cause you to feel sympathy, even love. There is no better medicine than thinking of others, even if for only five minutes.

Working with these practices, you'll get a grip on the kinds of thinking and feeling that arise when conditions are difficult. The goal is not to make the thoughts and feelings go away: when there is loss or trouble, it is normal to feel sorrow, fear, despair, confusion, discouragement, and so on. These feelings connect us to others, who feel them as we do, so we don't want to eliminate them. But it would be good to have some perspective—and occasional relief—so these thoughts don't get the best of us and become full-blown demons pushing us around.

Having considered some extensions of meditation practice, let's return to the basic practice. When you sit, noticing the breath and the body on the chair or cushion, noticing the thoughts and feelings in the mind and heart and perhaps also the sounds in the room and the stillness, something else also begins to come into view. You notice the most fundamental of all facts: you are alive. You are a living, breathing, embodied, human being. You can actually feel this—feel the feeling of being alive. You can rest in this basic feeling, the nature of life, of consciousness, the underlying basis of everything you will ever experience—even the negativity. Sitting there with this basic feeling of being alive, you will feel gratitude. After all, you didn't ask for this; you didn't earn it. It is just there, a gift to you. It won't last forever, but for now, in this moment, here it is, perfect, complete. And you are sharing it with everything else that exists in this stark, basic, and beautiful way. Whatever your problems and challenges, you *are*, you exist in this bright world with others, with trees, sky, water, stars, sun, and moon. If you sit there long enough and regularly enough you will feel this, even in your darkest moments.

And based on this experience, you will reflect differently on your life. What is really important? How much do your expectations and social constructs really matter? What really counts? What is the bottom line for a human life?

To be alive. Well, you are alive.

To love others and be loved by others. Well, you do love, and it is within your power to love more deeply. And if you do, it is guaranteed that others will respond to you with more love.

To be kind to others and to receive kindness is also within your power, regardless of expectations, losses, and circumstances.

You need to eat every day, it is true. You need a good place to sleep at night. You need some sort of work to do, but probably you have these things, and if you do you can offer them to others. Once you overcome the sting and virulence of your naturally arising negativity, and return to the feeling of being alive, you will think more clearly about what matters more and what matters less in your life.

You will see that regardless of your conditions you can participate in what matters most. You will see that in the big picture of things, you have what you need and there is plenty to be grateful for—and plenty to do based on this gratitude. You may not have as many impressive appointments to keep as you did when you were busy with your high-powered job. But you have more time to keep up with friends and family—to call and say hello, how did your day go, happy birthday, happy anniversary, happy holiday, and oh yes, I love you and am glad you are in my life.

You may not be able to afford the fancy gourmet meal or the person who comes in to clean the house, but you can prepare with great care some steamed greens with olive oil and lemon and find someone you love to eat it with, and clean up the house yourself, noticing, maybe for the first time, how good the workmanship is on this dining room chair as you dust and polish its legs. Living more slowly and simply—although this may not be what you wanted or expected—may not turn out to be so bad after all.

My own personal reference point for material happiness is a memory I have of my days at the Tassajara Zen monastery, where I lived for five years when I was young. Tassajara is in a narrow mountain canyon that can get pretty cold in the winter months, when very little sun gets in. Our rooms in those days were unheated, so the cold really mattered.

I remember winter mornings standing at a certain spot in the center of the compound, where the first rays of the day's warm sunlight would come. So far, no material luxury I have encountered surpasses this, and I feel it again every time I feel the sun's warmth. Hard times are painful, and no rational person would ever think to intentionally bring them on. Quite the contrary, ordinary human day-to-day life is mostly about trying to avoid the financial, health, romantic, and psychological disasters that seem to be lurking around every corner. So we do not valorize or seek out what is hard or unpleasant. Yet disasters are inevitable in a human lifetime, and it is highly impractical not to welcome them when they come.

Hard times remind us of what's important, what's basic, beautiful, and worthwhile, about being alive. The worst of times bring out the best in us. Abundance and an excess of success and good fortune inevitably bring complications and elaborations that fill our lives with more discrimination and choice. We like this, and seek it, but the truth is it reduces joy. We are less appreciative of what we have. Our critical capacities grow very acute, and we are always somewhat skeptical of whatever excellence we are currently enjoying, ready to reject it in a moment, as soon as something we recognize as superior comes along, whether it's a new phone or a new spouse. When there's less, there's more appreciation, more openness to wonder and joy, more capacity to soften critical judgment and simply celebrate what happens to be there, even if it is not the best—even if it is not so good. It *is,* and there's a virtue merely in that. The sun in the morning and the moon at night.

I remember my good friend Gil, like Alan also gone now, who went to India to relieve the misery of poverty-stricken villagers by offering them the expert eye care he had been so well trained to deliver. He was shocked to gradually realize that these destitute, ill-schooled villagers were happier and wiser than he and his prosperous, well-educated friends in San Francisco. This is when Gil began his spiritual practice.

In retrospect we can see that the last fifty years or so of ever-increasing prosperity and opportunity have been based on an enthusiastic, exuberant, and naive lust for material goods—as if the goods themselves, and not our satisfaction in them, were the source of our happiness. That lust so raised the bar on what we expect to possess—the houses, cars, vacations, gadgets, information—that we have lost all sense of proportion and have forgotten almost entirely how our ancestors lived and how most of the world still lives. The various economic bubbles produced by that exuberance have proved to be much shakier than they had seemed when we were in the midst of them.

Most experts on the economy predict a slow period of at least a year, to be followed, inevitably, by a return to the upward-reaching growth economy we have come to feel is as reliable as a law of nature. But suppose they are not correct. Suppose we are reaching limits on a limited planet, and that we are in for a very long period of reduced circumstances. What if in the future we won't have top-notch medical care, high-performance cars, automatic houses, and abundant energy? Such an eventuality might cause such a crisis of despair due to dashed expectations that it might usher in a terrible period of the sort of dystopian nightmares we've seen in movies or novels, with chaos and violence everywhere. Or it could bring the opposite—more happiness, more sharing, more wisdom, bigger hearts. More people growing gardens, cooking food, working on farms, taking care of others. A slower, more heartfelt and realistic style of living, and a move toward dying at home surrounded by friends and spiritual supporters rather than in high-tech hospitals hooked into alienating machines run by busy professionals.

This probably won't be the case; the economists are probably right that things will return to what we have come to call normal after a while, maybe after only a year or two. But even so, it would be a healthy exercise to visualize and celebrate this simpler, sparer life—and maybe even to live it.

No Self, No Problem

Anam Thubten

Here's a teaching that gets right to Buddhism's core insight: that we suffer because we believe we have a self. Of course we do exist at the common sense level—that can't be denied—but we do not exist as a permanent, ongoing, unified self. Trying to maintain that illusion is the source of great struggle, insecurity, and suffering, and letting go of it is liberation. The Tibetan teacher Anam Thubten describes this profound truth simply and beautifully, and shows how we can get there directly.

There are quite a few ideas about what it takes to realize enlightenment. Some people say it takes a long time to awaken and some people say it takes a very short time to awaken. Some people say there are ten miles between us and enlightenment and some people say there are a billion miles between us and enlightenment. Sometimes it is hard to decide which one is the correct perspective.

What is liberation? What is awakening? Actually, if we are searching for awakening as a moral reward or as an idealized utopian realm, then enlightenment is like chasing after a rainbow. We can chase a rainbow but we can never catch it. Perhaps one of the main hindrances keeping us from having a direct experience of enlightenment is our preconceived notion of what enlightenment is. So we have to give up every idea we have of what enlightenment is.

Sometimes that can be a little bit uncomfortable, especially if we have very high hopes about enlightenment. When we are asked to give up every idea we have about enlightenment, we sometimes feel that we are losing everything, even our beloved illusion, enlightenment. How merciless and coldhearted. But the ultimate truth, or emptiness, is the destruction of all illusions and that includes the illusion of enlightenment.

When we meditate, when we sit and simply pay attention to our breath, we begin to see that there is an "I," a self, who is searching for enlightenment and liberation from suffering. But if we keep paying attention to our breath and body sensations, then eventually all of those ideas, concepts, and illusions begin to dissipate one after another and truth reveals itself. It's like watching a mountain that is covered by clouds. In the beginning we don't see the mountain because it is covered by heavy clouds. But if we keep watching, then, as the clouds dissolve, the mountain begins to emerge and eventually, when all of the clouds are gone, the mountain that was always there appears.

In the same way, when we pay attention to our breath, body sensations, and to the awareness that arises, then all the illusions, suffering, confusion, sorrow, and personal issues, all of this begins to dissipate. We see that all of these experiences are born of delusion. This is the sense of "I." "I am real. I am truly existent." Everything is gone except this "I," this sense of self. Then, when we continue meditating, the sense of self also goes away. When we just keep meditating, when we just remain in that present awareness and observe, then the self dissolves too. When the self dissolves there is just pure awareness. When the self completely collapses, there is this inexpressible, simple yet profound and ecstatic, compassionate awareness. Nobody is there. "I" is completely nonexistent in that place. There is no separation between samsara, bad circumstances, and nirvana, good circumstances, and there is nobody pursuing the path or chasing after enlightenment. In that moment we realize the essence of the Buddha's teaching.

I'll tell you a bit of my personal story. When I first went to the monastery I had many fantasies. I thought that it was going to be a journey full of visions, revelations, and angels with flowers descending upon me. Then one of the first prayers that we learned was called the *Heart Sutra*. The *Heart Sutra* can be very dry to those who haven't realized its true meaning. It is not like some of those beautiful, ecstatic, mystical verses. The line goes, "There's no nose. There's no mouth. There's no tongue. There's no sound, no smell, no taste, no touch." Anyway, we kept reciting the *Heart Sutra* every day until we had completely memorized it. More than memorizing it, we were able to recite it so fast it was unbelievable. Then one day many years after memorizing and reciting the *Heart Sutra*, I finally came close to a sense of affinity with the meaning of the *Heart Sutra* and the meaning of this notion that there is nothing there in the ultimate sense. There is not even the nothingness. This truth is the great emptiness. Having even a glimpse of that understanding can be very transformative for the rest of our life.

The very essence of all spiritual teaching is about dissolving attachment to the self, and about dissolving every attachment to form, sound, smell, taste, touch, good and bad ideas, and all concepts. It is about dropping all attachment without exception. In Buddhism we often say that one has to be a renunciant in order to bring about awakening or complete liberation in one lifetime. When we say "renunciant" we are not really speaking about becoming monks or nuns officially or externally but more about becoming monks or nuns internally. The ultimate way of becoming a renunciant is by giving up attachment internally, attachment to everything, not just attachment to samsara and the things that we don't like. We give up attachment to nirvana and the things that we love too, because when we are attached to nirvana that is just another way of lingering. It's another way of sustaining this flimsy ego. Therefore, we have to give up attachment to nirvana and to every form of ego because ego takes all kinds of forms. Sometimes ego can even take the form of spiritual phenomena.

Believe it or not, we often use the spiritual or religious path to construct ego identity, even when this is not conscious at the time. That is not a surprise, since the function of neurosis is to suppress awareness of reality. Fear, pride, exclusion, even bigotry—not only are they far from being dissolved, rather they're being well maintained. This is what we've been doing for thousands of years, since the dawn of civilization, and it is still one of our favorite behaviors, not in any one particular circle, but in every religious tradition. This may continue indefinitely on a large scale, since we're still evolving. Buddha realized that we cannot be liberated as long as we are holding on to any form of neurosis. Before him, in Indian culture, neurotic patterns were able to leak into the sacred teachings and scriptures. Things such as the caste system and discrimination based on gender were considered normal. Buddha was the first to invite untouchables and women into his congregation, which caused lots of controversy and created opposition.

People always ask me what it means to be Buddhist. My reply is, "It means being nobody." The true spiritual path is not about becoming. It is about *not* becoming. When we let go of this futile effort to be or become somebody, freedom and enlightenment take care of themselves. We see that we are inherently divine already and we are enchanted to see how effortlessly liberation unfolds.

Ultimately we must dissolve all of the defense mechanisms of our ego. This includes the spiritual ones too, because sometimes ego manifests in different forms, in camouflage. Therefore, true liberation requires the complete renunciation and transcendence of our ego, the self. We might think, "This is the same old message, this idea about eradicating attachment to the self. I've heard it many times. More than that, I have failed at it many times. Actually I came here looking for a different solution. I still want enlightenment but I want a different method." Ego says, "I still want enlightenment but without this whole business about eradicating self-attachment. I will do anything except that. Please give me a break. Let's bargain a little."

Ego likes to bargain, to have an argument with the truth. "Ask me to do anything. I will jump off a cliff. I will restrain my sexual impulses. I will do anything. But don't ask me to do this. I can't do this because if I do I will die into the great unknowable truth." Once again, we start wiggling around this last assignment of dissolving the self or melting into what is. Actually there is no way to bargain with the truth, emptiness. Whatever we call it—truth, emptiness—dissolving into it is the only way. And the more we realize the truth, the more we realize that there isn't any other way.

The only way we can bring about perfect, total awakening, right now in this moment, is by dissolving the self on the spot. But there are two ways to do that: a painful and an ecstatic way of transcending. The ecstatic way is known as the path of bliss. The reason that we call it the path of bliss is because it involves an effortless way to go beyond the self. How do we dissolve the self blissfully? When we try to wage a war as a means of eradicating ego's empire we won't be very successful in the end.

As spiritual practitioners, especially as Buddhists, we have been declaring war on the ego and blaming it for all of our problems and confusions. Ego is our scapegoat. We blame everything on our ego as if it were a separate entity. We have a war with ego and sometimes we feel that we are winning the war and sometimes we feel that ego is winning the war. Sometimes the very self that is fighting ego is actually ego and that's even trickier. But sometimes we can just look directly into our consciousness and ask, "Who is fighting against ego?" Often everything collapses right there. Therefore, the path of bliss is really not about declaring war on the ego in order to get rid of anything we see as a stumbling block on the road to our imagined final destination. Rather it is about allowing the self to dissolve spontaneously by giving up nothing and going nowhere.

How do we do that? There are many, many ways. But in the end, it turns out that these many ways are ultimately the same. Sometimes we just rest and that is all that we need to do. In Buddhist teachings, meditation is defined as the art of resting. When we rest, we pay attention to our breath. We pay attention to our body sensations. At first we see a huge empire of concepts and ideas, but if we keep paying attention to that present awareness, that peace and serenity, then the empire of ego, that big castle of self-illusion, begins to disappear. In that moment, "I" is gone and what is revealed is pure awareness. It appears spontaneously, just like the mountain appeared when the clouds dissolved. Just like that, our true nature shows itself. In that place, there is no self and there is no other. We know this experientially, not conceptually. We know it directly and without any doubt. We know who we are. We know our true nature, right there, with complete confidence. It's extraordinary when we glimpse that.

Sometimes when we sit and pay attention to our breath, ego tries to jeopardize our path. Ego tells us, "Well this is too simple. You are getting nowhere. There is nothing special happening here. There are no fireworks. This is not going to lead anywhere." Ego is trying to seduce us into chasing some beautiful exotic illusion. But if we just surrender and remain in that present awareness, paying attention to our breath, then amazingly the self dies. There is no longer a self who says, "I don't like what is going on. I don't like this ordinary moment. I don't like just sitting here paying attention to breath." The "I" who doesn't like what is unfolding is completely gone and that is all that matters in the ultimate sense.

When self dissolves, everything is already awakened. Trees are awakened, rocks are awakened, birds are enlightened, and the clouds in the sky are enlightened. When the Buddha had this moment of complete realization, he discovered that this whole universe is already enlightened. More than that, he realized that every particle on the ground is enlightened. He saw that every particle is a Buddha paradise. In each particle there are billions and trillions of Buddha paradises. In each of those particles there are billions of buddhas residing. This whole universe becomes suddenly enlightened and perfect just as it is.

That does not mean that we are going to be completely lost in some kind of spiritual trance, losing our common sense, driving through red lights, wearing socks on our head, and so forth. Of course ego will tell us not to completely surrender our ordinary, self-grasping mind because there will be retribution. Ego is always trying to warn us not to be completely awake. A little bit awake is OK but not completely awake. Ego has many ways to convince us not to become totally awake. Sometimes it will give us treats by letting us get intoxicated by spiritual highs masquerading as true awakening. Other times it will strike us with terrors of doubt and despair, throwing us into a darkness that negates all aspiration. The hindrances to inner awakening can be so subtle they are almost unperceivable and usually they sneak through the back door. Many spiritual traditions teach us that we cannot be free in this lifetime. But even if they teach us that it is possible, they make it sound like it is some kind of a super attainment unlikely for us to reach. Some even go to the extreme of saying that it can only be achieved by surrendering to an outer authority. As long as we believe those rumors, we're not going anywhere but in circles. Our practice won't amount to anything more than a dog chasing his tail.

As meditators we can relate to those situations. When we have been practicing meditation for a long time, we know many moments when we have experienced extraordinary transformations and awakening inside. But part of us really doesn't want to completely renounce our attachment to suffering. We don't want to fully dissolve into that great truth, emptiness.

Part of us wants to hold on to that last attachment. We want to awake a little but not completely. It's convenient for ego not to awaken completely but this is the only way to liberation. Sooner or later we have to completely awaken. That means that we have to completely dissolve into that great emptiness, the ultimate truth of nothingness, without holding on to anything, not even enlightenment, not even confusion about liberation or truth. We have to let go of all of it. How do we do it? When we try to get rid of it, it doesn't work. It backfires because who is trying to get rid of it? There is nobody there in the ultimate sense. So this is about melting; this is about dissolving the self, and when we know how to dissolve the self, then liberation becomes effortless. It is like drinking nectar rather than working hard. In general, this is a way of dissolving the self ecstatically and without any struggle, without any resistance. Devotion plays a very important role.

When we pray, what we are doing is invoking the spirit of devotion. Devotion is about no longer resisting anything. We are no longer trying to hold the composure of this illusory entity, ego or self. Self is always collapsing and dissolving in each and every moment. It dissolves if we leave it as it is because it's not real from the very beginning. It's already unreal. It's already collapsing. When we try to construct and maintain the illusion of self, then we suffer quite a lot. We experience insecurity and madness because we are trying to uphold something that is already falling apart. Self is already falling apart. Suffering is already falling apart. And who is it that works so hard twenty-four hours a day trying to keep samsara together while complaining about it at the same time? Who is that person?

There is a bit of a dichotomy here. It's confusing too because we come to the spiritual path with a lot of enthusiasm and determination. We are complaining about samsara, our misery, and we are looking desperately for liberation. At the same time, we must remember that samsara is already falling apart. We may wonder how that can be. I have been stuck in it for many lifetimes. This vicious cycle is not falling apart on its own. The question is actually, "Who is the self? Who is the one who is trying to maintain that samsara?" Samsara is really very high maintenance. It costs lots of headaches and heartaches to maintain. Who is this self trying to construct samsara? Who is that person? Well, actually they don't exist.

A while ago I was giving a weekend meditation retreat and a middle-aged lady approached me during one of the breaks. "Are you asking us to die?" I answered, "Absolutely!" while joining my palms and bowing toward her in reverence. "You got the message, that's it. There is nothing more to learn." When I looked up, I saw her face lighting up in a beautiful smile. No doubt she knew the way to liberation at that moment. One has to allow this illusory self to die again and again.

This death is deeper than physical death. This death allows all of our anguish to dissolve forever. It is not the end of something. It is the beginning of a life where the flower of love and intelligence blossoms. One of my friends used to tell me that the only way that one can be a true spiritual teacher is to give up every idea that one is a teacher. He is absolutely right. You have to renounce the idea, "I am a Dharma teacher." He used to tell me that when we are able to completely transcend and cut through even that idea, then we can be great Dharma teachers. So what he was basically talking about is dissolving the attachment to any identification. Imagine that we have a very strong belief in our identity or role in society. Imagine that you are a boss or a CEO.

Imagine that you are considered a beautiful woman or that you believe you are a young person. Imagine that you are heavily identified with one of those illusions of who you are. See how much suffering and anxiety you can go through just trying to secure and maintain that identity. Many people want to be the boss, a leader in this conventional world. Many people want to be elected mayor or president because then that becomes their identity. And many people inflict much pain and suffering on other people in order to sustain that identity.

Throughout history leaders have sometimes served as amazing archetypes or models demonstrating how destructive and dangerous ego identity can be. Millions of people have lost their lives and suffered greatly because of people fighting over a position. What is a position? It is unreal. It's illusory. Attachment to any identity can be very violent and destructive. This is the very makeup of samsara. Therefore, the essence of all spiritual paths is about dissolving everything here and now without waiting. And again, how do we dissolve that self ecstatically? We are just present, paying attention to the breath, and then the self begins to dissolve. This sounds so simple.

We may think, "I have paid attention to my breath many times and never had any revelations." But that is the past talking, trying to trap us in that old pattern again. This time be aware and let go of that thought too. Sometimes we must pray. When our heart is completely taken over and seized by the force of devotion, then self does not have any power to maintain its composure. Ego just dies right there on the spot, without dismantling the self into tiny pieces and investigating whether they are real or not. There is no time for analytical meditation. There is no time to prepare to transcend the self.

Self is gone the moment our heart is completely taken over by the spirit of devotion.

When we meditate I encourage all of us to have the attitude that we are meditating to dissolve the self. That's why we meditate. Hold this perspective in your awareness and let your dualistic mind dissolve for at least a half hour, or at least for ten minutes every day. When you allow yourself to witness that unexpected glimpse of the truth, where the self is dissolved, it's like drinking nectar. It's inexpressible. We often use the word "bliss" to describe that state. "Bliss" is a good word but it can be misunderstood. The bliss that I am speaking about has nothing to do with ordinary bliss. It's not like the bliss of having great food or other sensual pleasure. This is nonconceptual bliss that is not based on emotions but is based on awareness. We often say that realizing the true nature of who we are is like drinking the nectar of ultimate bliss. The more we drink, the more we are going to be addicted, which is very good.

It is not enough to drink that nectar once or twice. We have to learn how to drink the nectar of great bliss from the dissolution of self many times. It is not enough to simply remember having the experience some time ago. In the beginning we should drink this nectar of bliss at least three times every day. That's the assignment for everybody who is looking for liberation. Then as time goes by, we drink many times, hundreds of times every day. Eventually we drink a thousand times every day. After a while we drink in each and every moment, when we are asleep, when we are awake, when we are talking, when we are meditating, when we are playing music, when we are fighting with people. We drink that nectar of bliss all the time. This is called "complete total awakening" and this is our goal. This is our intention and our highest aspiration.

I remember a very short quote from a Buddhist teacher: "No self, no problem." It is really short but true and very effective too. There is always struggle in our lives either consciously or unconsciously. Many people in the world are going through struggles with social injustice, violence, and war. Even in the most prosperous countries, which are in some ways more fortunate because they enjoy many material comforts, people are suffering. Some people feel that they don't have enough money or that they are not beautiful or intelligent enough. They don't have an ideal relationship or they are worried because they are not enlightened. Many people suffer because of anger, hatred, and judgment. All these problems spring from the mistaken notion of what and who we are. This idea of "self," "me," and "mine" is the source of our inner struggle. It is like an author creating relentless agony in our consciousness.

When we go beyond the self then we go beyond everything. We go beyond every form of struggle that we encounter in life. For example, when I meditate, if I am not really ready to melt the self, then I am struggling. My ego is struggling. "Well, I want to be enlightened. I want to have that bliss that he is talking about right now. I want to feel good. I want to have rapture but it's not there. Time is running out. I want to transcend self but it is not working very well. That's why I am kind of frustrated. I am struggling."

So this kind of struggle is pervading almost every aspect of life. There are times when we are on the meditation cushion, where we are looking very holy, perfectly spiritual, and we are feeling blissed out. But sometimes we are so ordinary. We are talking on the phone, shouting loudly. We are quite angry at someone. It is amazing how many roles we go through in everyday life. When we sit on the meditation cushion we are very holy. But when we are driving our car in traffic, talking on the phone, and somebody cuts in front of us, we become very reactionary. We may even start cursing. We don't look at all like the guy who was sitting peacefully in meditation a few hours ago. The idea is that there is always struggle. There is always struggle in different forms. There is struggle when we are meditating and there is struggle when we are not meditating, as long as the self is being perceived as real. When the self goes away, then we are already in paradise and there is nothing to do. There isn't anything to do and there isn't anything to acquire. So this should be our mantra for the rest of our life: *No self, no problem.* Keep this in mind: *No self, no problem.*

I know that in our deepest heart each of us has strong faith, real longing, and undying aspiration to go beyond the self. But at the same time there is a way that we also might allow ego to buy time. Ego is very afraid of its complete demise, so it tries all kinds of methods and strategies to buy time and postpone. If it cannot do anything else, at least it can always postpone. So it keeps postponing and postponing complete liberation. Therefore, we always have to be mindful about that and pray to remove all hindrances from our path. The hindrances on the path are actually ego's resistance to complete liberation. That is the ultimate hindrance. So we pray to go beyond all the hindrances and obstacles that ego casts on us, so that we can be awakened as soon as possible and so that everybody else can be awakened as soon as possible too. We must realize that the wisdom that lies within each of us can transcend all hindrances. That requires an act of empowering ourselves. Let yourself be a peaceful warrior. We are all born peaceful warriors. There is nothing to fight against outside. The peaceful warrior is the spiritual hero who conquers inner adversaries by the force of pure consciousness.

The Art of Awareness

Dzigar Kongtrül Rinpoche

*Dzigar Kongtrül Rinpoche is a modern Tibetan lama. He is married, lives
in Colorado, uses the Internet as a teaching tool, and is an avid painter.
This is on one hand an essay on painting and the creative process, but on
the other a traditional and powerful Dzogchen teaching on riding mind's
energy and play.*

My interest in Western art has a lot to do with my own meditation
practice. Though Buddhist meditation and abstract art may seem
like an odd combination, the practice of meditation and the practice
of abstract painting are actually complementary.

As Buddhists, we are taught that the natural state of mind is
pristine and enlightened in itself. To embody this view of the natural
state, first we need to work with our mind through discipline. In our
meditation practice, sometimes we are present with this experience
of the natural state and sometimes we are not. When something
pleasant arises, we often grasp at it, and when something unpleasant
comes, we may reject it. Our discipline is to transcend these grasping and rejection tendencies that cause us so much suffering.

Over time, as we feel more self-confident and secure in our
practice of meditation—and in our understanding of the true nature of mind pointed out by our teacher—we will see that the true
nature is pristine and stainless. In the traditional analogy of the

ocean and its waves, it is said that however large or small the waves, all are essentially made of the element of water and cannot be separated from the ocean. Similarly, in the view of meditation, all our thoughts and various feelings arise out of the natural state of mind and are ultimately made out of the same "material." That material is empty awareness itself. If we do not succumb to habits and insecurities, or preconceptions about meditation and how our mind should be, we can then recognize that everything that arises is simply a manifestation of this very nature. Any expressions that arise from this enlightened nature can be understood as enlightened expressions when we do not approach them through the habits of acceptance and rejection.

Realizing this, we can begin to experience relaxation, as well as a lessening of judgments and reactivity. We experience more openness and acceptance. Slowly, and naturally, we begin to see the world as pure—not as in "pure" versus "ugly," but pure in the sense of seeing the perfection of its existence. This existence is not determined according to some concept or idea of the way it should be; it simply has come to exist naturally. Its beauty is found in it being just the way it is. The world has found its own shape, form, and color. All of it arises out of the nature of mind.

We understand that the nature of mind is not simply a void. If it were, it could not produce anything. Rather, this nature must have tremendous vitality to give birth to all of the things we experience in the mind and in the world. Part of the meditation practice shown to me by my teachers His Holiness Dilgo Khyentse Rinpoche, Tulku Urgyen Rinpoche, and Nyoshul Khen Rinpoche was to be able to trust this vitality, without becoming dualistic in my view or experience. I've been a meditator since I was fourteen and this has been my passion. That's about thirty years now.

I believe we can view art as a form of contemplative meditation. I don't see it as separate from meditation practice in any way. However, since art making involves being actively engaged with the physical body, the emotions, and the mind, in contrast to resting in the nature of mind without moving, we could consider art to be a form of meditative conduct. In Vajrayana Buddhism, "conduct" refers to activity that supports our meditation practice and view. If the conduct were something separate from what we're trying to accomplish in meditation, then it wouldn't have much place in the life of a meditator. It would be something altogether different.

I began to paint nine years ago. Many years before, when I studied with Khyentse Rinpoche, I met Yahne Le Toumelin, the mother of the Buddhist monk and author Matthieu Ricard, who was the late Khyentse Rinpoche's translator and student. I knew she was a painter but I did not know what kind. When I visited France for the first time, I had a chance to meet her privately in her studio while she was painting. Her painting process looked freeing, nonconceptual, and expressive. It seemed very much like a process of trying to go beyond the restrictions of her own judgments—a very fearless expression. It was fearless in the sense of not remaining stuck with hopes, and in terms of getting beyond all attachments, overcoming rejections and insecurities. I thought, "Oh, this would be an excellent modern-day conduct to support meditation practice. This could be something I could learn from her to enhance my meditation and view of the practice of Dzogchen."

That's how I made a connection with painting. Yahne offered to teach me, and a few years later I started studying with her. As she instructed me, she was very free with the expression that was surfacing out of the mixture of turpentine and paint on the canvas or paper. Whenever there was any sense of becoming stuck with hopes or fears, she simply went beyond it. Sometimes she did so with great fearlessness.

In this way, art has become part of my practice. As I follow the approach Yahne showed me, I find that, because of the discipline of meditation, I can remove myself from the work and allow it to have its own life. When the work becomes a natural process in this way, there is a deep feeling of satisfaction. The satisfaction comes in knowing that the evolution of the painting on the outside reflects how resolved I feel on the inside through the discipline of relinquishing all attachment. The moment I stop painting is when the "outside" and the "inside" coincide in this way. That is, when the painting itself reflects a natural, uncontrived awareness.

As part of this discipline, it's important to be nonjudgmental, and instead cultivate an attitude of acceptance in which we attribute the work to our natural creativity. This creativity is the birthright of all beings, and we all long to express it in different forms and different ways. When it is expressed, there is a tremendous sense of joy, and a great feeling of well-being blossoms in the mind. When this is present in an artist's mind, I believe that a transference of consciousness occurs through the art itself. When we view this art, we can comprehend the emotions and the state of mind of the artist, and feel touched by it, even though we are not directly seeing the artist at work and are not able to see exactly what the artist went through. From that point of view, the art produced out of natural creativity is an offering to the observer, rather than a statement of our ego's own splendor.

Without art, I think the world would feel far too serious, too pragmatic, and very humorless. Such great beauty is brought into the world by artists, whether they are musicians, dancers, writers, poets, or painters. This world has been made greater by artists and by the creativity of the mind of the artist, which stems directly from the true nature of mind itself. My point is that when an artist is able to step out of the way—to not stand between the true nature of mind and the work that is being produced—the work of art itself becomes enriched and the offering made to the world thereby becomes more significant.

The world might think of an artist as great and acknowledge him or her as distinct or important. Nevertheless, the artist continuously has to step out of the way and not obstruct the nature of mind that is in the work as it is being produced. So, ultimately, we could say that any "greatness" is simply the manifesting of our innate natural vitality. Furthermore, in regard to this natural vitality, there is really no difference between someone who is labeled as an artist and someone who is not. All have the same nature and the same natural vitality, and that natural vitality is always creating. It is creating thoughts, emotions, our life, and the world that each of us inhabits. The universe is being created moment to moment out of the true nature of mind. Creating art is part of that very same process that takes place all the time on a larger scale. From that perspective, we really cannot be dualistic about our own creation versus someone else's creation, or about being an artist or not. We can appreciate all that is being created out of the true nature of mind and its natural vitality. When we come to understand how the nature of mind is vast and its vitality so pervasive and inspiring, we transcend all of the dualism between "my" work and "their" work. All artists, I think, have to appreciate the natural vitality of other artists' work.

Regardless of whether we are interested in expressing ourselves artistically, from the perspective of the Buddha's teachings we are always creating our world. The universe cannot be said to exist objectively on its own without our subjective mind to apprehend it. You cannot separate the two or speak of one without the other. In this sense, our life is created by our thoughts, feelings, and perceptions; and all of those thoughts and feelings are in essence being created by our natural vitality and our natural state of mind. If we look at it in this way, art can be seen as anything that arises from the true nature of mind, hand-in-hand with any conduct that promotes that expression. Anything that is in conflict with this natural vitality—that tries to freeze or grasp it—will create entanglement in the insecurities of the ego, causing misunderstanding of what the true nature of mind is, and fostering the ego's desire to secure something for itself.

These tendencies pose a challenge to creating something wholesome. Even if someone is able to produce something that becomes widely acclaimed and appreciated, they will suffer from this "me" and "mine" problem. All of that attachment and grasping, aggression and rejection, will hinder rather than liberate the artist. We could come to a point where our own work suffocates us, like the silkworm that creates a cocoon and expires inside. However, through the meditation practice of transcendental mind that acknowledges mind's true nature and natural vitality, all artists could create works that are beneficial to themselves and to others.

We all have an ego, and even when we want to, we cannot get rid of it easily. The ego and its attachments, aversions, and insecurities are naturally going to arise continually. However, whether you submit to them or move through them, whether you put them in charge or trust your natural ability to create—this is up to you. It's going to be difficult to create without moving through these things, but if you have self-confidence and repeatedly make it through attachments and fears, eventually you reach a place where you really trust yourself and allow yourself to become freely expressive. At that point, if you just "let it flow," the work becomes stainless. For instance, I paint over and over and over on the same canvas. Even though I can create an image in the first round, painting it over and over makes me move through many emotions and ego-contrivances. No matter how the painting ends up looking, it contains the blessing of what I have moved through. The first painting, even though it may be beautiful, does not have as much of a blessing as the end result of moving through and letting go of attachments. So I try to move through as much as possible. This is a big part of the discipline I suggest we try to cultivate as artists.

I would like to make a humble request to all who are artists to trust your true nature, trust your natural vitality, and fearlessly let go of the ego's insecurities. Simply embody self-confidence in the true nature of mind and its natural vitality and become accepting of all that is created naturally with such freedom. Then any form of art created in this way will not have to be divorced from your meditation practice. It could actually become the most supportive conduct for your practice. Regardless of whether you are a meditator or not, if your discipline is to move through your ego contrivance—trusting your creativity and remaining aware of it in the work, and then just allowing the process to take place—this itself is meditation. It makes no difference whether you have a separate meditation discipline. This is true for any form of art.

I consider teaching Buddhism to be an art form as well, yet teachings are conceptual. You think things through as you present various points. If you allow your thought process to flow naturally and creatively without any hindrance from ego or ego-contrivance, then your thought process can be the same as with abstract expressionist painting. Again, this thought process is the production of the true nature of mind, and allowing that natural process to take place without getting in the way is the same discipline—just go with the story you are writing or the music you are composing. Whether it is conceptual or nonconceptual it has to flow, and the flow has to come very genuinely out of your creative mind and not from nitpicking. This creative mind can be trusted to be there in your natural state, ready to express itself. Removing the hindrances of ego-contrivance—by moving through the ego-emotions as quickly as possible—is what is required.

Many people have told me that they used to be artists, but since they became Buddhist meditators they have let go of their art. They thought it too frivolous a pursuit, not supportive of their spiritual path and the practice of meditation. I think that is absolutely wrong. I think art can be the most supportive part of what one does in life with meditation practice. Art enriches the practice, and in the end, meditation practice and art become united. This is the goal of all practitioners: what we practice in meditation becomes our life. Life and our meditation practice become united to the point that there is not much difference between meditation sessions and post-meditation. Post-meditation becomes part of the same discipline as in-meditation, and with that there is a great sense of deep satisfaction.

Otherwise, we can have a connection to art and a longing to be an artist and yet see this as a conflict with our connection to meditation practice and our longing to be a meditator. Seeing it as a conflict, we might think we have to drop one and pick up the other, and in this way we lose something that is very important, enriching, and mutually supportive. In this case something important is not being understood or appreciated or taken onto the path. If we follow this route, even though we may become a good meditator, at the end of life we might feel that we had forsaken a part of our own deep longing or passion.

There is no reason to see a conflict between art and meditation practice. See them as supportive of one another. Both have connections, passions, fulfillment, and joy which, together, make us whole. This wholeness of being is the true accomplishment of a full life.

By Song, Not Album

Hannah Tennant-Moore

Honesty and love are the hallmarks of the best Buddhist writing, and this story has both. It's honest because Hannah Tennant-Moore writes sincerely and fully about her own difficulties, and doesn't sugarcoat her father's problems either. And yet the love of a father for his troubled daughter, and the daughter for her very human father, shine through this moving story.

My dad flew to Paris to rescue me, armed with music and marijuana. I was in France to study the language as part of my college major. Before that I'd spent a few months at a Buddhist monastery in India, where I'd experienced for the first time since childhood what it was like to be happy every day, to enjoy waking up each morning.

That feeling had disappeared as soon as I got to Paris. I spent most of my first month there trying to find sunlight. I was staying in a maid's garret room on the sixth floor of a creaky red boarding-house in the sixth *arrondissement*. The room was just big enough for a desk—really a plywood board on four sticks—and a twin bed. The only window was a small skylight. Anytime I thought I saw a ray of sun peeking through the overcast January sky, I would climb onto the desk and squeeze my head and shoulders into the skylight, turning my face up and hoping for a bit of warmth to fall on it. Sometimes I ended up tumbling to the floor, surrounded by the books, papers, and CDs that had been on my desk. Then I would leave to buy a few chocolate croissants down the street, or a cheap bottle of wine, which I would drink in the park with the winos and pigeons, the rain slowly soaking through my sweater. When I wasn't doing that, I was crying in phone booths or riding on buses and staring out the window. One day on the bus I sat in front of a little girl wearing a pink raincoat. We were riding by the Seine, and the girl asked her mother, "Est-ce qu'il y a des dauphins la, Maman?"

"Non, it n'y a pas de dauphins."

I thought that if she'd been my daughter, I would have answered, "Yes, perhaps there are some dolphins in the Seine." I remembered all the lies my father had told me when I was growing up, to make the world seem prettier than it was. It wasn't until I'd gotten older that I'd realized those fabrications were one of his many strategies for dealing with the pain of his daily life. He and I had both known long bouts of depression. It was at that moment that I decided to call him. I got off the bus near the Bastille and found a phone booth.

"I can't do it by myself anymore," I said as soon as my dad picked up the phone. "Is there any chance you could come visit me?"

I didn't have to explain to my father the nature of the weight that had fallen upon me as soon as I'd landed in Paris. It was not just culture shock or feeling lonely in a foreign country. Dad, who frequently had trouble getting out of bed in the morning, immediately recognized the deadness in my voice, and he started shopping for an airline ticket.

He also phoned my mother, who suggested I speak with a psychiatrist. I agreed, if for no other reason than I simply wanted to be able to sleep: in bed at night I would imagine myself chained naked to a table, being whipped; instead of counting sheep, I would count the lashes striking my body. The images soothed me. From a phone booth on the Boulevard Montparnasse I gave an American doctor the answers I knew he needed to prescribe me some relief: "No, I cannot remember the last time I enjoyed something. Yes, I would much rather be dead." He prescribed Celexa, and my dad brought a large bottle of the pills with him to France.

My father resisted treating his depression with prescription drugs. I had always done the same, in part because my father's sadness had seemed noble to me when I was growing up, an indication of his compassion, his sensitivity to the pain in the world. During high school, when friends turned mean and history class painted a bleak picture of humanity and I got my heart broken for the first time, I clung to my father's melancholic interpretation of life. My conversations with him felt truer than any interactions with my peers. Subconsciously I believed that taking antidepressants would mean acknowledging that the world was not better for the tears we shed over the news and the cruelty we encountered. Taking medication would have meant accepting that all our tears had been for naught. It took me a long time to learn that being miserable does not alleviate the world's misery.

I was lying on my lumpy bed in Paris with my eyes fixed on the ceiling when my dad called to tell me his plane had landed. He would rent a car and come pick me up. I had to find the boardinghouse address on a napkin to give it to him. When he saw me outside on the sidewalk, thinner than normal and with puffy red eyes, he grabbed his CD case. As I dropped into the passenger seat, he handed me his music and said, "Your choice."

I told him to take me out of the city. He followed signs that said *Toutes Directions:* all directions leading out of Paris. I had avoided talking for weeks, but now the words came out of me fast and sharp, like daggers I didn't know I'd swallowed. I spoke so quickly—about the man who'd spit in my face in the street, the waiter who'd kicked me out of a restaurant because I'd wanted my salad without anchovies, the bombs that kept falling on Baghdad—that I was soon out of breath.

My dad told me I was hyperventilating. "Maybe it would be best if we just listened to music for a while," he said. I chose sweet, familiar songs—Eva Cassidy and Nancy Griffith and Joni Mitchell—and I wanted it loud. My dad was more than happy to oblige.

There was a period in my elementary-school years when my dad and I listened to nothing but Billy Joel. His *Greatest Hits* was the soundtrack for the long drives when Dad took my sister and me to water parks or beaches or trailheads. Pat, our stepmom, didn't like hiking or amusement parks, so my sister and I got our dad all to ourselves on these outings. I liked when it got dark on the way home but the music was still loud, the two of us singing along to "Uptown Girl." My dad's face would become serious and quiet when "Piano Man" came on. My sister used to ask us to turn it down. She didn't understand how we could listen to the same songs over and over.

One time Dad planned a real vacation, just for the three of us. And even though he left his bag on one flight and our return tickets on the next, we made it to Arizona, rented an RV, and began to drive. We kept the minifridge stocked with ice cream and fudge. My sister and I made Pillsbury cinnamon rolls in the oven while our dad drove eighty on the open desert roads, singing along loudly to the Talking Heads. When we were too tired to find a campground at night, we parked illegally in supermarket lots. We went hiking in New Mexico and plunged into icy rivers in Colorado. My sister took a few pictures—she was the only one who'd brought a camera—and now she has a framed photo on her desk of my father and me grinning on top of some mountain, our arms around each other's shoulders, hair falling into our eyes.

When I think of my father on that trip—his reckless lust for life as he charged up a mountain or down a dirt road—I remember what an old boyfriend of mine used to call me: a "hyper-appreciator."

"You love the world too much," he said.

"Sometimes," I answered.

After a while Dad lowered the volume on the rental-car CD player. "I forgot to ask if you had a pipe. We'll have to buy one. I brought a little bud of grass for us." I didn't say anything. This was not the first time he had smuggled marijuana on an international flight.

"I know your mom and sister would think this was so irresponsible—coming to see you when you're depressed and bringing drugs," he said. "But I think my role should partly be to distract you. Sometimes you just need to get away from yourself."

I agreed, perhaps too energetically. I had decided long before that I would be the only person in my father's life who refused to see his unconventional choices as mistakes.

My dad put on a new CD of antiwar songs by a Vietnam vet from Texas. He told me to listen to the words; he thought I would appreciate their anger. I looked out the window and tried to listen. After three songs he stopped the CD.

"It sounds to me like maybe what you're going through is a loss of self," he said quietly. "Maybe from all your meditating in India. Like a loss of the ego. So you have nothing to hold on to."

Normally I dismissed my father's abstract Buddhist explanations for what seemed to me a very specific pain. But now I found myself reaching for my journal and reading aloud for Dad a few sentences I had written that morning after jerking awake at 5 A.M. from a wine-drunk sleep fully clothed, contacts dried to my eyes, the desk light glaring in my face. "That was the worst feeling I can ever remember having," I had scrawled in tiny letters. "As if I had disappeared. No more me." What my father had said seemed to fit so well with what I'd written that it woke me up a bit: the possibility of connection, someone responding to my state of mind with an idea that resembled one of my own.

My father was encouraged. He told me I could not be truly depressed if I still wrote in a journal. He thought I was doing great. I closed my eyes and felt the flicker in my chest die out. "Let's put on some Tom Petty," I said.

Only once in my life has my father asked me to turn down my music: Four friends were spending the night at my house to welcome summer's arrival. This was during the years when my mother had lost her job and was suing my father and his wealthy new wife. My sister had moved out of our mom's house, vowing to live with our dad until the lawsuit had ended, while I continued to travel back and forth between my parents' houses. I was thirteen and concerned exclusively with my friends. My dad did not like my music during those years: "Anger without beauty," he called it. But he listened to it with me anyway, chauffeuring me from one social gathering to another.

At the sleepover my friends and I listened to the band Live on my boom box as loud as it would go and took turns doing impressions of girls we didn't like. One friend had brought some NoDoz pills she'd stolen from the supermarket. We were going to stay up all night, no matter what.

When my dad came into my room at three in the morning, I started yelling before he did. We weren't doing anything wrong, I said. He told me to turn down the music; he and Pat couldn't sleep. I said I could do whatever I wanted, and he said I had better turn down the fucking music. I told him to stop acting like an asshole. He put his hands around my neck and tightened his fingers briefly, then let go. As he stormed away, I told him to fuck off and yelled that I was going to live with Mom and never see him again. I heard the front door slam shut.

The next day my stepmother did not know where Dad had gone. After my friends left, I walked to my mom's house. In the afternoon I called Pat, who tried not to sound worried and said it wasn't my fault. Late that night she called to tell me he had come home. I stayed with my mom for a couple of weeks and played my music so loud my ears wouldn't stop ringing.

The summer I turned nineteen, my dad drove from Vermont to Washington, D.C., to pick me up from a friend's townhouse where I'd been staying for two months. It hadn't been a particularly hard summer for either my dad or me: I had been working at a day-care center and swimming; my dad had been gardening and teaching yoga; we had both been smoking a lot of pot. But we hadn't kept in touch, and in the car there was a blunt sadness between us, because of nothing, which made me think it was because of everything.

We made a deal for the drive back to Vermont: music by song, not album. The passenger was responsible for switching CDs between every song. We went through Lucinda Williams, Bob Dylan, Belle and Sebastian, PJ Harvey, Van Morrison. The tension lifted, and we rolled the windows down and gulped summer air and sang our way through Maryland, Delaware, New Jersey. We spoke only when we stopped for meals, and then only to tell jokes. We stayed to the right so others could pass.

My dad drove about ten hours that first day we were together in France. At ten o'clock we found a motel in a small town. Every house was locked and shuttered. We ate in the motel's restaurant, and when the waitress took our order, I pretended I didn't know French and let my dad do the talking. That night I couldn't sleep and lay awake with my head shoved under the pillow and my heart pounding. My dad woke up once; he must have thought I was sleeping, because I heard him sighing and making soft crying noises, a cross between a little boy's whimper and an old man's weeping. Then he went to the bathroom.

After he came back to bed, I told him, "Dad, I can't sleep."

He was quiet for a while before he said, "It just hit me, the pain you're going through."

Depression is rarely described as "pain." It's most often considered a series of losses—of appetite, of enjoyment, of motivation—while the acute hurt that replaces what's lost goes unspoken. My father's instinctive choice of words was the reason I needed him, and no one else, with me in France.

Dad and I talked through the night, lying on our backs in our parallel twin beds. I remember few of the actual words we spoke, but I recall their cadence—short, quiet sentences with long pauses between—because it suited my mood so well. I could be myself with him, never having to fake sanity or explain how I felt.

When the first light of dawn came through the curtains, Dad reached over and turned off the alarm clock. I said I thought maybe I could sleep for a while. He started to tell me about a new folk CD he'd brought to play for me. "It's full of suffering, but it's not hopeless," he said. "When I heard it, I thought, *This is for Hannah.*"

After we checked out of the motel at noon, we bought a pipe at a tobacconist's and smoked pot in the rental car, bickering about whether to listen to jazz or rock. I guess he'd forgotten about the new folk CD he wanted me to hear. Once, after he'd passed me the pipe, I waited for a few seconds before I took a hit, and he said, "Don't waste it, babe, don't waste it," snapping his fingers lightly. That *babe* struck me as glaringly unparental, far from the father I wanted at that time. I did not need a friend, a flawed equal searching like me for a way out, but someone older and stronger to help me make sense of things. I looked out at the French countryside while profundities shot from my father's mouth: all his ideas on how to live a good life (if only he could make himself follow them) and theories on everything from coffee to the war. I decided then that, no matter how much I wanted to, I would never smoke pot with him again.

The next time my dad reached for the wooden pipe between our seats, I asked him not to smoke.

"Why not?" he asked, struggling to sound calm.

"Because then I can't talk to you," I answered. It was one of the few times I'd let my father know that he'd disappointed me.

We were quiet for many miles, both of us staring fixedly at the road. "Well, if you're not going to talk anyway," Dad said, and he lit a bowl with a motel matchbook, steering with his elbows.

My parents divorced when I was two, and my dad moved from Vermont to Massachusetts. My sister and I spent every weekend with him for two years, staying with my mom in Vermont during the week. Bedtime every Friday night was a ride in Dad's car between Brattleboro and Newton. We listened to one Raffi tape after another. I remember the first time I heard the song "Five Little Ducks Went Out One Day." When the little ducks set out to go "far away" from their mother, my thumb went straight into my mouth. By the time the mother duck went, *"Quack, quack, quack,"* and no little ducks came paddling back, my round face was covered in tears. Dad must have noticed in the rearview mirror, because he sang along loudly with the last line, "The mother duck went, Quack, quack, quack, and all of the little ducks came back!" But by then it was too late. He pulled over and lifted me out of my car seat. "It's OK," he said. "They all came back. The ducks are with their mommy now. They all came back." But my sister remembers that he was crying too.

My dad's father—a preacher and a drunk—left when my father was three. He took off in the middle of the night and wasn't heard from again until thirty years later, when my dad's aunt called to tell him his father was dying. He had a month to live, maybe less, and he wanted to see his son before he died; he had thought of Dad often throughout the years, she said, even though he'd been too much of a coward to contact him. Would my father like directions to the hospital? "No thanks," Dad said, and hung up the phone.

When my mother told me that story recently, I was struck by the difference between my struggle with depression and my father's. I grew up with a father who was around, who listened. In high school, when I had the same dead look in my eyes too many days in a row, Dad noticed and set up an appointment for me with a therapist. After several sessions the therapist asked me, "Do you think it's possible that your depression is your way of loving your father?"

There may be truth to this, but it's also true that my father's love is all that has prevented me from feeling unbearably alone during the darkest periods of my life. When I think back on my time in Paris, I remember a constant cosmic dread so pervasive that I'm unsure I would have survived it had I not had someone to call who would fully understand what I was going through.

The last night my dad was in France, we went to a Bach concert at the Church of Saint-Julien-le-Pauvre in Paris. "I'm assuming you don't want any grass?" my father asked before we left his hotel room. I said no, and he didn't bring any.

We sat in the front row and smiled for two hours. When it was over, we were the last ones to stop clapping. Walking around Notre Dame afterward, my dad confessed that he had not wanted to come to Paris when I'd first asked him. He'd been so sad himself for the previous few months that he'd doubted he could help me. He was just tired of every day being so hard, he said.

"But it's OK that we both help each other?" he asked. "That's OK, right?"

His blue eyes and freckled cheeks looked so fragile, so like my own, that I had to look away before I spoke. "Yes, of course, Dad. Of course."

Care Taking

Elizabeth Brownrigg

When age and dementia undo her friend Julia, Elizabeth Brownrigg discovers that true compassion sometimes means setting boundaries. Helping another doesn't mean hurting yourself, and when that's happening, no one benefits. But it's a hard lesson to accept when all we want to do is help.

On a cold, rainy afternoon I sorted through Julia's papers. There were hundreds of letters without envelopes or return addresses. So many friends had written so many heartfelt messages over the years. Where were they now? Julia wandered by the lakeshore calling for them.

There were old photo albums that she'd kept as a way to remember her life, only she couldn't recall where the pictures were taken or the names of the people in them. There were young lesbians in flannel shirts, groups of women sitting around and drinking, and some very intriguing shots of Julia standing naked in a forest. Going through the papers added so many dimensions to the person I'd come to regard only as a burden. The papers and photographs were going to the university archives. I kept a box of blank postcards for myself. They were the pictures of Julia's life and mind.

LES GUÉRILLÈRES

A drawing of a defiant woman merged with a bird. The postcard is an advertisement for Monique Wittig's book, which is described as "A delectable epic of sex warfare . . . an extraordinary leap of the imagination into the politics of oppression and revolt."

When I first met Julia in 1993, I was forty and she was seventy. She was colorful, unpredictable, a little abrasive, very smart. She had a long history of rebellion. In the 1970s, during the heyday of radical feminism, she'd left her position as a theater professor, founded a lesbian political journal, and traveled around the country with her much younger lover.

Her apartment was crowded with books and photographs and artwork—the gatherings of an interesting life well spent. On the wall, an artist friend had hung a cardboard snake made of these words: "The View after Seventy Is Breath-Taking." When Julia had a mastectomy a few years later, the last words were changed to "Breast-Taking."

She was at the center of our community. She wrote poetry and plays. She spent her evenings at the theater or the movies. She liked films that no one else cared for because the lighting reminded her of early French cinema or the staging was interesting. She saw the differences in the portrayals of men and women, how women are often naked and exposed objects but men never are.

She dressed with a sense of style: a black beret contrasting with her silver hair, a little bit of makeup, a colorful tie, flowing jackets. She walked as though she were striding across the stage. She was a mentor and a promise of what my old age might be.

As the years passed, Julia complained of her failing memory. She said, "I can't think clearly when it's cloudy." She didn't read long books anymore; she couldn't remember what had happened in the previous chapter. She spent her days in her dark apartment and tried to reconstitute her disintegrating past. I took her to doctors' appointments, resolved crises that usually concerned missing objects, and attempted to make sense of her checkbook.

On Fridays, we went out together. It was a little challenge for us both to find something new to do every week: seeing a play or an exhibit at the art museum, having lunch at a place we'd heard about. In keeping her world from shrinking, my world expanded; we showed each other the sights from our different perspectives.

She called me whenever she needed me; she called more and more often. She was slowly losing ground, especially on "cloudy days." But she could still drive, take care of herself and her cat, more or less keep up with the bills.

"I'll be eighty years old in August," Julia said. She mentioned it every time she saw me. I planned a big party for her. We invited all the people in her address book. Her godchildren traveled to North Carolina from Connecticut and California. The party was a slice of Julia's long life: an old friend sitting happily demented in a chair, former students, young neighbors, allies in the feminist struggle. When it was over, she said, "That was absolutely perfect."

The Snake with Two Hearts

An X-ray of a snake that has swallowed two lightbulbs. A shiny heart-shaped sticker is affixed to each bulb.

A month after the birthday party, Julia invited me to dinner. "You know what's wrong with you?" she suddenly spat out. "You're not a real feminist."

Her eyes were cold and glittering. She quizzed me about my past, dismissing every bit of evidence that I offered that, why, yes, I was a "real feminist," whatever that meant. She was enjoying herself. Clearly, she'd been planning this moment. I left as quickly as I could, not engaging, keeping up a veil of politeness.

Days later, Julia sent me a card saying that she merely wanted to "blow my cool."

"You'll forgive me, won't you?" she pleaded. "I don't want our friendship to change. I want it to be like it was."

We went to a piano recital. It was in the woods, at one of a collection of hand-built houses occupied by artists and musicians. On our drive through the countryside, Julia kept up a steady stream of complaints about how we were lost and how I didn't know what I was doing. After the recital, we went to a restaurant for dinner. Julia tried to pick a few more fights with me and, failing that, she lit into the waiter who didn't serve her quickly enough.

My friendship with her became like living with an alcoholic. I avoided restaurants. I was careful not to make any changes in scheduling and to arrive at the exact time that we'd planned—not that it made much difference. She misremembered the hour and chewed me out anyway. It was like tiptoeing through a minefield where someone kept moving the mines.

Julia could be a generous friend or the cruelest of enemies. I never knew which person I'd encounter. Over lunch one day, she thanked me for giving her the best seat. We had a real conversation, as two close friends might, about our complicated feelings for our mothers. Often, she offered me clothes, lamps, paintings, money, saying, "Take this, take this, you do so much for me. How can I pay you? Take this."

Or, her edge became a sword she wielded without warning, slicing me off at the knees. She was raging against the dying of the light and the rest of us still in the sunshine. Ultimately, there was something wrong with everyone. They were "ageist," or "shallow," or "materialistic," or "classist," or "too sensitive," or they "took advantage of people." With Julia, familiarity really did breed contempt.

I struggled with what I should do versus what I could do and what boundaries I should set. What was my obligation to my friends? Which friends would I do anything for and which friends would I only go so far for?

Dress Rehearsal

A dressing room filled with actors putting on makeup and donning costumes for the stage.

Julia considered moving to a retirement community, where she would have regular meals, safety, and some social contact. She decided and un-decided, signed the contract and ripped it up, agreed to a tour of places and then refused to go. Her goddaughter from Connecticut, her ex-lover from Canada, and local friends in North Carolina all searched for a place for her. Finally, with our help, she found an apartment and didn't change her mind. Over the month before the move, I packed her books, helped her get rid of things, and carried boxes over to her new apartment in the broiling August heat.

She fired me a week before the move. She accused me of stealing her will and threatened to call the police. She said she didn't trust me, that I was mad with power. My emotions during this bizarre exchange were curious—I felt my adrenaline pumping, of course, but I also felt a cold rage, almost an exhilaration. Hooray! Free at last!

Somehow, though, I had to orchestrate the move without Julia knowing of my involvement. I called the ex-lover to see if she could talk some sense into her. She remarked that her life had been subsumed by Julia's when they were together. We shared the experience of being the caretakers/enablers in an abusive relationship with the same person. Julia was who she has always been, only now dementia had unfettered her.

Eventually, Julia asked for my help because she couldn't manage the move by herself. Life pretended to go on. She forgot she was angry with me and that I might be angry with her.

Night Flight of Dread and Delight

A painting by Skunder Boghossian of owls and demons flying through the Ethiopian night.

Every morning I awoke in a foul mood and saw everything through a mesh of anger. If I hurried fast enough, the anger faded. I wanted my mind to be different; I wanted to just be in the world and be happy about that. Faintly, through my anger, I heard a beautiful day calling me. I could see it, but it was as though I were autistic. I knew it was pretty, but I didn't feel it.

I tried to explain Julia's taxes to her. She was mad at me for her loss of comprehension. I said nothing while she shouted. I left, my legs shaking with anger.

I had panic attacks whenever I approached her apartment. I panted; I couldn't get enough air. One day, after being blasted once again for neglecting her, I thought I heard a car door slam in my driveway. I thought it might be her. My physical reaction was sheer terror.

I could have made a horror movie out of this: Here cometh the embodiment of all my guilt and worst fears about my future. Here cometh my own rage, my own self-accusations. Here cometh a situation that is always on the verge of spinning out of control. No wonder old women are monsters in fairy tales. No wonder children are trapped by them. We cannot run away because we cannot in good conscience abandon our parents. Even if we do run away, they pursue us, because no matter what we do, it is not enough.

I wondered if meditation might release me from the clutches of my own mind. I signed up for a weekend meditation retreat.

The first thing I discovered was the startling depth of my self-hatred. During those two days of sitting and walking, sitting and walking, I glimpsed a bit of light on the far side of the enormous room of my mind, and then I pulled myself back because I needed to hang on to my thoughts, lest my true self come screaming out of the darkness. I was sure the other meditators in the room were staring at me and finding me lacking.

The most valuable lesson from that first long weekend was one of forgiveness; no matter how many times my thoughts carried me away, no matter how many times I failed, I could always return to the breath and begin again. There was only this moment, with its limitless possibilities.

Maybe the value of my experience with Julia would come from working through it. This was a complicated love, a love born of necessity. How could I survive that love?

Two Women, Disrobing

A series of photographs by Eadweard Muybridge, from his "Animal Locomotion" studies. A naked woman approaches another woman who is clothed in a Grecian robe. The first woman unwraps the robe from around the body of the second.

I was caught on the horns of compassion and rage. I saw Jack Kornfield's *A Path with Heart* on a bookstore shelf and wanted nothing to do with it. Compassion was my problem. Look what it had gotten me into. Why would I want to practice it anymore? I didn't understand what compassion was.

Compassion means caring for everyone, including yourself. It contains the irony of separating yourself from someone else even as you acknowledge that you are not separate. It means saying, "This is all I can do." In *The Places That Scare You,* Pema Chödrön says, "In order not to break our vow of compassion, we have to learn when to stop aggression and draw the line. There are times when the only way to bring down barriers is to set boundaries."

One day, I had a breakthrough with Julia. I went over to her apartment to work through her horrible finances. She wanted to be heard, like everyone else. So I let her talk. But I didn't confuse compassion with enabling. That was the tricky part for me: knowing that understanding how someone feels does not mean that I have to take care of them, or do everything for them, or even condone their behavior.

I felt so sad for Julia, with her constrained finances and her constrained life. She couldn't think straight or make any more money, and she knew it. During meditation, I contemplated compassion and understanding, detached from the conviction that I was responsible for fixing the misery. I could understand her fear and rage, without knowing what, if anything, I could do about it.

Julia called one evening with paranoid delusions about the retirement community management. She said they didn't think she was who she said she was. If one should ever doubt that thoughts aren't real, here's the proof. Julia's fears were reflecting off the walls of her skull as reality. "I'm angry" turned into "everyone is out to get me." "I don't know who I am anymore" became "they don't believe I am who I say I am."

I just listened and said I'd vouch for her if anyone questioned her identity.

FLIGHT RESEARCH #5

A photograph by Rosemary Laing. An Australian stuntwoman wearing a white wedding dress is suspended in flight against a bright blue sky.

Despite all this newly acquired wisdom, I was not really out of the woods. My flashes of compassion were overwhelmed by Julia's demands, the orchestrated crises, the angry phone calls.

Finally, I saw a therapist, who suggested there was a reason I'd chosen to be in this pickle. Here was an opportunity to understand my own part in the situation. The therapist suggested I stop being the caretaker; I'd done enough. Others had said they would help out, but since I'd assumed responsibility, they hadn't needed to. What did I want my role to be?

I steeled myself to talk with Julia. I even wrote what I was going to say on an index card. I told her that feeling responsible for her was very difficult for me and that it contributed to the tension between us. I could still help her with financial problems and medical appointments, but couldn't she think of other people to call on for other things? I mentioned a few names. She said she didn't like this person and didn't trust that person. I let that be her problem.

She said I didn't have to feel responsible, that other people were making me feel responsible. I let that one go.

We appeared to part on good terms and to have a new understanding. I felt immediately freed. I saw how much I'd contributed to the situation by acquiescing to the role of servant. I saw that, rather than stonily withdrawing, I could tell Julia what I was feeling.

Of course, Julia turned our conversation into a different story. She called her goddaughter, who in turn called me to ask if it was really true that I'd have nothing more to do with Julia, and that I had refused to help her out. Julia continued to spin fanciful tales of how I just wanted her money and I couldn't be trusted. My phone calls and visits were met with frosty silence.

During meditation, I contemplated change. Relationships change. They change the people involved in them. The people change, independent of the relationship. We arrive at a new understanding or reach an impasse. What endures?

The hardest thing of all is to change the dynamic you already have with someone else, especially if they're not willing participants in the change. Julia was perfectly pleased when I was in the servant role. Changing this had provoked her outrage. Dementia was her trump card. She interpreted my bid for independence as abandonment. She couldn't change, but I had to. It tore me up to pull away from her. It was an excruciating exercise in turning my back on someone else's pain/my own pain. But I had to step back in order for others to step in. Now other people were helping Julia.

Months later, I encountered a remnant of things past when Julia left a message asking me for help with her taxes. I lived through a thousand angry scenarios before I called her back. I was the shell-shocked veteran ready to hit the dirt at the sight of a trash bag fluttering by the side of the road. Sometimes it was only a trash bag; sometimes it was an IED.

This time, it was only a trash bag. Julia was amazingly sanguine about my filing her tax return. She wanted control, but she also wanted someone to take care of her problems.

The pendulum continued to swing, more slowly now that I saw her less often. She was pleased with me one time, angry the next. We enjoyed an evening at the theater. Then I returned from vacation to three increasingly furious phone messages: Julia said she had been outed as a lesbian and that she needed to leave the retirement community. Why was I ignoring her? She hung up on me when I called her back. Once again, I was left with the toxic detritus of her rage.

New England Fall Colors

Sunlight shines on brilliant orange trees along a country road.

Julia's goddaughter decided to move her up to Connecticut to be near her. I felt sad and relieved. This was what I wanted, and yet I wished I could have helped Julia the way I'd set out to do. The goddaughter said she couldn't bear to think of Julia fading away alone in North Carolina. It tortured both of us. You were damned if you helped her and damned if you didn't.

As the plans for the move progressed and it slowly became a reality, there was a seismic shift in my own psyche. From this new vantage point, the person who had taken responsibility for Julia's sorrows was a stranger, and clearly someone with boundary issues. I saw my place in our dynamic—how my stepping in, taking responsibility, trying to control a disaster—had given Julia someone to rebel against. The energy left my anger, like air escaping from a balloon.

On a fall day, we were driving past oaks and maples, gum trees and sycamores in shades of red and yellow. "That's what should happen to old people," Julia said. "We should turn different colors as we age. Wouldn't that be lovely?"

We saw Corneille's *The Illusion* at the local repertory theater. Julia didn't understand the plot but enjoyed the lighting and the staging. She still loved the look of the world, even though she couldn't understand what it was saying.

On our last day together, I took her to the airport. She fussed a bit about some object she'd lost. I started to reply and she said, "You don't have to take care of it."

At the waiting area next to the gate, it was nice to spend time with her, to chat about this and that. She remarked on the shapes of women's hairstyles as passengers walked past us. I watched her go through the gate, her silver hair a fading beacon.

THE HOUSE OF CLEOPATRA AT DELOS

A black-and-white photograph of white columns, the ruins of stone walls, and headless statues of women.

Only recently have I allowed myself to miss Julia and what I loved about her, all the qualities that were obscured by our difficulties.

What is loyalty? What is compassion? What is forgiveness? It's our suffering that unites us and divides us.

Now I have a vision: I am walking across a barren, windy landscape. In the far distance I can hear the crash of surf, but I can't see the ocean. At the top of a hill, I see the silhouettes of enormous old women, as still as stone. As I draw closer, I find that the silhouettes are really ruins, weather-worn and broken. The ruins cannot speak. The wind whistles through them as though it were saying something, but I can't make out what the wind wants to tell me. Maybe the wind will bring the old women's memories to me. Maybe it will blow them away.

Wonderland: The Zen of Alice

Daniel Doen Silberberg

Buddhist practice turns everything upside down. Existence becomes non-existence. Certainty becomes doubt. Mind becomes quiet. And life becomes joy. The Zen teacher Daniel Doen Silberberg calls this place Wonderland.

"Have you guessed the riddle yet?" the Hatter said, turning to Alice again.
"No, I give it up," Alice replied. "What's the answer?"
"I haven't the slightest idea," said the Hatter.
"Nor I," said the March Hare.

When my son Alex was about ten years old, he was very interested in the concept of "being right." It was spring and we were taking a walk. I started to tell him the names of the flowers. "This is a Red-Bearded Snake, and that is a Blue Mongoose." Eventually, he looked up at me and said, "You're making this up." I said, "No, I'm not." And he said, "Yes, you are." From that point onward, our conversations have been like playing very competitive Ping-Pong. Today we might have a discussion about which type of computer is best. For a couple of minutes Alex will say, "I think Macs are better," and I'll say, "Well, I don't see it that way." He'll say yes and I'll say no. Yes no, yes no, yes no. Then we switch, just to make the other one wrong. He says no, and I say yes. Now Alex is twenty-nine and I'm fifty-nine, and we still poke fun at our opinions in exactly the same way. This "yes no, yes no" is the essence of what goes on in *Alice in Wonderland*. In Alice's aboveground life, the rules are clear and everything has its proper place. At the beginning of the story, she is sitting on a riverbank with her sister, considering making a daisy chain. It's a perfectly normal day. Then she sees a white rabbit with a watch, she follows him, and soon she falls down a hole. A big hole.

After she falls, nothing she knew aboveground makes sense anymore. None of the rules are the same. She wanders around getting bigger and then smaller. She meets all kinds of characters who don't seem to be following rules at all, which causes quite a problem. They don't comply with her expectations or her understanding. They don't do anything she thinks is proper or right.

In time Alice goes to the Mad Hatter's tea party. Alice finds the Mad Hatter and his friends, the March Hare and the Dormouse, sitting at a long table under a tree. Mysteriously, they're all cramped together on one side of the table.

Alice asks if she can sit down.

"No room! No room!" they cried out when they saw Alice coming.

"There's plenty of room!" said Alice indignantly, and she sat down in a large armchair at one end of the table.

"Have some wine," the March Hare said in an encouraging tone.

Alice looked round the table, but there was nothing on it but tea. "I don't see any wine," she remarked.

"There isn't any," said the March Hare.

"Then it wasn't very civil of you to offer it," said Alice angrily.

"It wasn't very civil of you to sit down without being invited," said the March Hare.

Alice has her ideas of how things should be. The March Hare, the Mad Hatter, and the Dormouse see things completely differently. According to them, there really is no room at the table. According to Alice, there is plenty of room. In this same way, we come into our life and our practice with our own ideas of how it has to be. We erect the walls of our house and block the view of the sky.

Does Alice know what the Mad Hatter is talking about? How often are we willing to accept it when we don't know the answer to something? We'd rather know and be right than live in a state of wonder and uncertainty. When we get to the other shore, to what I am calling Wonderland, we may experience One Mind. One Mind is what we experience when we remove everything we know. The last thing to fall away is the idea of our separation from the world. Once that idea is gone, there is nothing left, and then you are on the other shore, in Wonderland, and experiencing One Mind. We can call it many things, but they are all ways to describe something we experience for ourselves when our thoughts become quiet and our minds concentrated for long enough.

"Do you mean that you think you can find out the answer to it?" said the March Hare.

"Exactly so," said Alice.

"Then you should say what you mean," the March Hare went on.

"I do," Alice hastily replied; "at least—at least I mean what I say—that's the same thing, you know."

"Not the same thing a bit!" said the Hatter. "Why, you might just as well say that 'I see what I eat' is the same as 'I eat what I see'!"

"You might as well say," added the March Hare, "that 'I like what I get' is the same thing as 'I get what I like'!"

Zen practice is the practice of liking what you get. We usually have a thin margin of acceptance; we like very little of what we get. We want something else. Maybe we want what we think we deserve or what we think everyone else has. We're convinced, along with Alice, that if everybody would just change his or her behavior, everything would be great. If only we lived somewhere else, if only we were younger, older, smarter, dumber, rounder, thinner, or sexier—if only all of that were true, life would be good.

We're told we're supposed to go a particular school, work at this kind of job, marry that person; this is the yellow brick road that leads to happiness. The only problem is: no one seems happy. Somehow the original plan, which was to understand exactly where you're going and what you're doing, isn't working. We're all stuck complaining that Wonderland isn't what we think it ought to be.

This same thing has happened to me. One experience I had early in my Zen practice still makes me laugh. It was 1980 and I was a student at Zen Mountain Monastery in upstate New York. Taizan Maezumi Roshi was abbot and the resident teacher was the late John Daido Loori. The monastery was relatively new and I was the head of administration as well as a senior student. My job was to keep everything running smoothly and ensure that the monastery flourished. I felt I was doing something noble and perhaps I was; however, I was also becoming righteous, irritable, and intolerant. One day Daido was walking though the monastery office where I was working. He sat down and I unloaded all my troubles and my complaints about the staff: this one was doing that, and that one wasn't doing this.

Daido asked if I remembered the first line of the verse we chanted each evening—the Four Vows.

"Yes," I said. "Sentient beings are numberless, I vow to save them." He said, "That's right. Now which sentient beings did you have in mind?"

And he chuckled as he watched my face.

Imagine what would happen if we gave up our ideas about how everything should be. What if we could peel away our constructed reality until we come to a place where a tree is just a tree, and not our idea of what a tree should be? "Tree" is just a word. "We're walking in a field" is just an idea. But the idea of "walking in a field" also has a lot of connotations—it could suggest I won't be able to walk someday. It could suggest life and death. Our words and ideas can be full of fear. Why don't we peel those away while we're at it?

How do we get to "One Mind"? Like Alice, our lives have us bumping into saints and sages who are pointing the way, if only we could see them.

When we engage in practices—sitting and walking meditation, and mindfulness in our daily lives—we gradually create an opening from which to see the events that occur. We add some breathing space—you might call it a hole—a place a white rabbit can pop out of. Practices create possibility. What appeared to be positive or negative experiences with people or events become opportunities for practice and the growth of understanding. We can learn to welcome our experience of our lives.

We often use our fears to maintain the illusion of safety. But that kind of safety closes down our lives. Here's a tool for getting closer to Wonderland:

Take a few moments to sit and breathe. Notice how often in a day you feel afraid or anxious. It may be helpful to keep a notebook and write down each time you experience this fear.

Each time it comes up, stop, sit, breathe, and notice.

It can be surprising to become aware of one's fears. It takes awareness and courage to open our eyes and say, "I really don't know what's going on. Bring on the awe. Bring on the eternal. Bring on that which I don't know." When we are open to the confusion and the craziness, we get little slivers of recognition.

. . . [S]aid the Hatter with a sigh: "it's always teatime, and we've no time to wash the things between whiles."

"Then you keep moving round, I suppose?" said Alice.

"Exactly so," said the Hatter, "as the things get used up."

That's why there's no room for Alice at the table. They have a perfect way of looking at things, and it works just as well as Alice's. It's always six o'clock; therefore, it's always teatime. They sit at the table and never put away the tea-things. They just keep moving to a new seat and another tea set; a new seat and another tea set; a new seat and another tea set. This is not so different from the way many of us handle our relationships.

In the beginning of my relationship with my wife, Caryn, I expected it to be like other relationships I'd had. Caryn is a quiet person and somehow that seemed like a problem to me. I wanted more interaction. At one point while on a long, relatively silent trip in a car, I got frustrated and she pointed out to me that quiet was her way. She asked me in a kindly way if I could just accept that. Finally, in that moment, I could. In the twenty-seven years since, the beauty of her quiet has supported our lives and practice.

I was able to see the magic that is Caryn instead of the preconceptions, resistance, and habitual patterns I was bringing to our relationship. This event has been like a bookmark in my life with her. I often return to it. It is also a practice, an ongoing way of developing my appreciation for our relationship and my relationship to others.

We are here today. A good number of us don't have to worry about where our next meal is coming from; and the weather is beautiful. If we can get a few things out of our way, then every day can be a good day; even a day when something bad happens. If we can really see this wonderful, mixed up life that we get to be in, with all of the suffering and pleasure, then we can accept that we are in Wonderland, and even possibly enjoy the trip. Most of us are like Alice, trying to get others to make sense (by our definition) and to do things that make us happy. Yet they won't. I know I need to remind myself of this daily: *The point of everybody else's life is not to make me happy.* What would your relationships be like if you accepted the people around you exactly as they are? There is nothing as transformative as being OK with everything. The craving to transform, to change, to make rules, to push people into shapes we like, isn't effective. It doesn't make us feel closer with our friends and family. Instead of trying to change others, maybe we can accept them as they are. Maybe we can even try to make *them* happy. They'd like that, since they likely think the point of everybody else's life is to make them happy!

When Alice wants to have a normal conversation with the Dormouse, she's quite sure it's time to start making sense.

"Once upon a time there were three little sisters," the Dormouse began, in a great hurry; "and their names were Elsie, Lacie, and Tillie; and they lived at the bottom of a well—"

"What did they live on?" asked Alice, who always took a great interest in questions of eating and drinking.

"They lived on treacle," said the Dormouse, after thinking a minute or two.

"They couldn't have done that, you know," Alice gently remarked. "They'd have been ill."

"So they were," said the Dormouse, "very ill."

"But they were in the well," Alice said to the Dormouse, not choosing to notice his last remark.

"Of course they were," said the Dormouse, "well in."

This answer so confused poor Alice that she let the Dormouse go on for some time without interrupting it.

"They were learning to draw," the Dormouse went on, yawning and rubbing its eyes, for it was getting very sleepy, "and they drew all manner of things—everything that begins with an M—"

"Why with an M?" said Alice.

"Why not?" said the March Hare.

Koans are a device used in Zen training. They are questions that need to be answered experientially, using insight, not intellect. They are usually drawn from the recording of conversations with the old Zen masters. The word *koan* translates roughly as "public case," like a law. It refers to something about which there is a level of common understanding.

Koans are questions that provide an opportunity to leave the intellect behind. They are like chances to fly. When done with the right spirit they provide a practice of forgetting the intellectual construct of self and joining the larger self the koan is pointing at. In time, life can become a koan practice in which we can learn to abandon our point of view and accept people and events that we might have resisted due to our conditioning, our story. Although koans are presented in many types of dialogues, or poetic phrases, the heart of koans is one question. What is the self? Who are you? Each koan is an opportunity to wake up to Wonderland.

In my own training, I've practiced with about 700 koans over a period of twenty-five years. Often there were additional challenges involved besides "seeing" the koan. We did koan study in a tiny room called the *dokusan* room. Very early in the morning an assistant would announce dokusan and everyone would run from the meditation hall to the dokusan line, elbowing and pushing for the privilege of getting in line and, hopefully, into the dokusan room for a one-on-one meeting with a teacher. The practice was even more challenging when Maezumi Roshi was in the dokusan room. I would finally make it through the line into the room only to hear Maezumi Roshi whisper, in his strong Japanese accent, words I could not decipher. I had to ask him to repeat himself over and over again. Outside the window, birds were singing, insects buzzing, water burbling. All these sounds mingled with Roshi and my koan. It was disorienting and magical. Perhaps Alice felt something similar on her way down the hole.

One of the koans asks the question, "The world is vast and wide. Why do we put on a seven-paneled robe (a traditional monk's robe) at the sound of a bell?"

This question could be translated as: *We are free. Why do we tie ourselves up?* But looking more deeply, the question might lead us to more questions. There are so many ways in which we're used to thinking about things, and so much we take for granted when we use language. The purpose of a koan is to wake us up from taking language—and the world around us—for granted.

What is the meaning of rain? Why do we walk in the woods? In Buddhism, we cultivate something called aimlessness, which is being and acting for the sole purpose of being or acting in that way, without further purpose, motive, or ambition. We put on the robe to put on the robe. We love simply to love.

The Dormouse had closed its eyes by this time, and was going off into a doze; but, on being pinched by the Hatter, it woke up again with a little shriek, and went on: "—that begins with an M, such as mousetraps, and the moon, and memory, and muchness—you know you say things are 'much of a muchness'—did you ever see such a thing as a drawing of a muchness?"

"Really, now that you ask me," said Alice, very much confused, "I don't think—"

Muchness is another word for a term we use in Buddhism: *suchness.* It means "things as they are," thus, before conceptual thought intrudes, separates, judges, and elaborates. For example, we see the white snow and we think we are purely seeing just snow, the "suchness" of the snow. But by naming it and putting it in the category "snow," where we already have a preconceived notion of what snow is, we are putting a filter over the thing itself, separating us from fully experiencing its "suchness." Mind creates all separation. Yet even the thing we call mind is just a word for what can't be grasped or put into a category of existence or nonexistence, large or small, collective or individual. Therefore, anybody's stupidity is just as good as anybody else's. Anybody's completely constructed view of reality is just as good as anybody else's—with one exception. If we create a reality that hurts other people, puts them on the outside, or makes them feel pain in any form, that view of reality creates an effect. That is what separates one reality from another: each perception bringing about a different consequence.

This is what is meant by *karma.* Karma is often explained either too magically or too simplistically. I like to think of it as simple cause and effect.

Cause and effect isn't something unique to individuals. A country, a time period, or an idea can all create cause and effect. In our own life we can clearly see that our actions toward others have a lot to do with what we get back from them. Showing sensitivity and kindness to others will not only please them, it will also transform us. The minute we stop believing that everything unpleasant that happens to us is someone else's fault, everything will change.

When I was a kid, I used to bounce a ball and chant: *A, my name is Alice and my husband's name is Abraham and we live in Alaska and we sell apples. B, my name is Barbara and my husband's name is Bob and we live in Bovina and we sell bubbles.* This children's game is a rehearsal for joining mainstream American society. We label ourselves: I am a doctor, a lawyer, a computer programmer, a mother, a father. What if none of that is who we really are? What if we were to get up in the morning without any preconceived notions of who we are?

We say in our practice that to realize the dharma is to forget the self. *Dharma* is a word that means "the teaching," or "the truth." It has different nuances of meaning in different contexts. We have a lineage, going all the way back to fifth-century China, of incredible teachers who would deliberately do to students what the Mad Hatter and his friends are doing to Alice—knock her out of her thinking mind. When you ask people to recall a time when they were happy, they often describe a time of being with friends, or hiking in nature, or swimming in the ocean, a time when they were in a state of mind beyond thinking.

In the movie *Serpico,* a New York City policeman meets a young woman and asks, "What are you?" And she says, "I'm an actress, a dancer, a writer, and a Buddhist." *B my name is Bob and I'm a Buddhist.* Don't be a Buddhist. If you're sure you're a Buddhist, then you're not looking at what else you might be in that moment. When Bodhidharma was asked who he was by the emperor of China, he answered, "I don't know." Bodhidharma is the legendary figure who brought Buddhism from India to China. It is said he lived to be 110 years old. He is known for meditating in a cave for many years. He was very brave and very truthful. He didn't just tell the truth; he sang it like a great soaring eagle.

Buddhism is not going to make us a Buddha. Nobody is going to make us a Buddha. We're already a Buddha. Buddha just means someone who is awakened. What do we have to do to be awakened? Wake up to the present moment.

Waking up to the present moment means stopping the relentless chatter of our associative minds. The sad part is that most of the chatter isn't very pleasant anyway; the chatter in our mind is often about fear, blame, anger, and all those wonderful things. The practice of stopping thoughts is one I often ask students to work on. I remember the first time I discovered I could do that. What a sense of freedom to realize that when I didn't know what else to do, when I didn't know the answer, I could simply stop. I could wake up. This experience was key to me wanting to practice. But it's hard to wake up when we have all these ideas. We need a reminder, a gentle shove. When we walk outside, the trees and the sun can be reminders to stop and wake up. If it snows, if the wind blows, these are also reminders. If there is someone in the house when you come home, and they smile at you, that is also a lovely reminder. We can begin to appreciate all the gifts that are pouring into our eyes and ears and that surround us at every moment.

I met my wife Caryn at Zen Mountain Monastery over thirty years ago. Eventually we moved into a place called Esopus House, which was deep in the country. The Northeast winters were very cold and Esopus House was small and drafty. The little woodstove didn't even keep the place heated through the night. Early every morning we would walk down the road for morning meditation. Across the road was the Esopus—the stream the house was named for. One particular morning, we opened the sliding doors to an incredible roar of water. Spring had come and the Esopus was surging free in the darkness of the morning. There was nothing in the world for us but that stream. Caryn and I looked at each other in awe; not here, there, or anywhere. We were out of our minds with wonder.

Suppose we are able to touch this Wonderland for a moment. Then we are, like Alice, brought back to the familiar world. What can we do? Let's say we have a moment where we're not resisting anything anymore. What are we going to do? Well, many of us then try to hold on to the One Mind. We might begin to tell others about it, try to persuade them of its truth. We might encourage them toward a seminar or a meditation class.

If we do any of that, we've lost Wonderland again. If we start thinking, "I know what's happening. I'm a Buddhist," we're grasping too tightly. The only way to hold on to the wonder of the moment is to let it go. We all feel we're in our particular lives without having chosen them. To consciously choose our human existence is a profound and beautiful practice. To be in touch with the wonder, we have to truly be wherever we find ourselves. The place of wonder can never be different from the place we're in.

The wonder of life is what we experience every day—washing our hands, breathing, taking a walk, working. There is no place to go other than here. Can we throw ourselves into that fully without understanding it? Do we have to know why we put on the seven-paneled robe?

When I was five or six and we were living in Danville, Illinois, my mother took me with her to visit a friend. She sat me down in a garden while she and her friend talked. I sat there for what seemed like an eternity looking around in wonder. I couldn't believe the colors and shapes; I looked inside the flowers and the colors changed. I was enthralled. That experience is still there when I allow it. It's there in the red rocks, in the sage, in my wife's face. The practice of restoring wonder, restoring awe, is the practice of Zen.

The Way of Mountains and Rivers 🌀

John Daido Loori, Roshi

The death of John Daido Loori, Roshi, in 2009 was a great loss for American Buddhism. At his Zen Mountain Monastery in upstate New York, Daido Roshi and his students developed a program of authentic Zen training for the West, while also doing impressive work in prison chaplaincy, environmental advocacy, media, and the arts. This teaching is on the Mountains and Rivers Sutra *by Dogen, founder of the Soto school of Zen and widely considered Zen's most important but difficult philosopher. Yet Daido Roshi in his commentary makes Dogen accessible and relevant to our lives on the planet today. The text beneath the ornament is from the first three sections of the* Mountains and Rivers Sutra; *the verse that begins each commentary is by Daido Roshi.*

❖   ❖   ❖

1.

These mountains and rivers of the present are the manifestation of the Way of the ancient sages. Each abides in its own dharma state, exhaustively fulfilling its virtues. Because they exist before the eon of emptiness, they are living in the present. Because they are the self before the appearance of any differences, they are free and unhindered in their actualization. Because the virtues of the mountain are high and broad, the spiritual power to ride the clouds is always entered through the mountains, and the capacity to follow the wind is ultimately liberated from the mountains.

Master Dayang Shanggai, addressing the assembly, said, "The blue mountains are constantly walking. The stone woman gives birth to a child in the night." The mountains lack none of their inherent virtues; therefore, they are constantly still and constantly walking. We should dedicate ourselves to a careful study of this virtue of walking. The walking of the mountains is no different than that of humans: do not doubt that the mountains walk simply because they may not appear to walk like humans.

These words of the ancient sage Dayang reveal the fundamental nature of walking. Therefore, we should thoroughly investigate his teaching on "constant walking."

COMMENTARY

Where can we put this gigantic body?
When clouds gather on the mountain,
thunder fills the valley.

Throughout the history of civilization, cultures the world over have regarded mountains as sacred places.

Religious pilgrimages and spiritual quests often lead seekers deep into the mountains. The Hindus and Jains travel to Mount Girnar; the saddhus to Mount Kailash. Spanish monks hike up to the summit of Mount Montserrat; Greek Orthodox priests live on Mount Athos. The Buddha ascended Vulture Peak, Jesus gave his

Sermon on the Mount, and Moses received the commandments on Mount Sinai. Muhammad was asked to recite the Qur'an in the cave of Hira on the mountain Jabal an-Nour. Chinese Buddhists have sought realization on the slopes of Mount Wutai. Dogen built his primary monastery, Eiheiji, deep in the mountains, preferring the unspoiled environment of forested hills, crags, and roaring streams to the high society of Kyoto.

In the same way, early on in my teaching career I was called to the mountains. It is there that Dogen's profound teachings contained in the *Mountains and Rivers Sutra* gradually became the guide for practice and training at Zen Mountain Monastery.

But what is the magic and attraction of the mountains? Is there something inherently special in them? If so, what is it?

When we look closely at the mountain we realize we're physically integrated with it. We drink the water that flows out of its springs. We grow our food in what millions of years ago was solid rock. Now it is our garden. We give to the mountain; the mountain gives to us. It becomes part of us. For this reason, it's difficult to say where the mountain ends and we begin.

Once, a friend came up to the Monastery from New York City and I took him on a tour of the grounds. We made our way up a hill bordered by a grove of eastern white pine, past a small pond and around a bend until we reached an open meadow with a magnificent view of the peak of Mount Tremper. My friend stopped dead in his tracks, and staring at the mountaintop he exclaimed:

"Oh, there's the mountain!"

"That's not the mountain," I replied.

My companion stared at me, perplexed.

"Then where is it?"

I said, "You're standing on it."

In fact, even to say "standing on" is extra. We are the mountain. There is no way that we can separate from it. This being the case, we should ask ourselves, what is the mountain? What are its contours? Where exactly is it?

❖ ❖ ❖

These mountains and rivers of the present are the manifestation of the Way of the ancient sages. Each abides in its own dharma state, exhaustively fulfilling its virtues. Because they exist before the eon of emptiness, they are living in the present. Because they are the self before the appearance of any differences, they are free and unhindered in their actualization.

In the opening sentence to the *Mountains and Rivers Sutra,* Dogen establishes the fact that mountains and rivers are expressing the teachings of the buddhas and ancient sages, just as a sutra does. In other words, this sutra is not *about* mountains and rivers; it is the mountains and rivers. Indeed, if we examine this teaching carefully, we'll see that all phenomena—audible, inaudible, tangible and intangible, conscious and unconscious—are constantly expressing the truth of the universe. A stand of oak saplings, a bed of river rocks, the autumn wind, are all ceaselessly manifesting the Way.

In this paragraph Dogen also says that because the mountains exist before the eon of emptiness—before the appearance of phenomena—they are present here and now. And it is because they live in the present that the self appears and is unhindered in all of its activities.

❖ ❖ ❖

Master Dayang Shanggai, addressing the assembly, said, "The blue mountains are constantly walking. The stone woman gives birth to a child in the night."

Blue mountains walking and a stone woman giving birth are both inconceivable events. In the context of the dharma, inconceivability points to the inherent emptiness or interdependent origination of all phenomena. Nothing is independent. Nothing has an absolute, own being. And yet, in the relative world, things do indeed exist. There's the child the stone woman gave birth to, there's you, me, and the ten thousand things. How do we reconcile this apparent contradiction?

There is an old Zen phrase that says, "When old man Zhang drinks wine, old man Li gets drunk." That is, what happens to you, happens to me. You and I are the same thing, yet I am not you and you are not me. What happens to a snapping turtle in the Catskills, happens to a businessman in Singapore. Yet a turtle is a turtle, a businessman is a businessman.

Whether or not we believe in our identity with all things—in our identity with the mountains and rivers—the fact is that it is the truth of our lives. Belief has nothing to do with it. Understanding has nothing to do with it. We have to realize it. And until we do—until we can clearly see this identity functioning in our lives—we will not truly grasp the effect we have on each other and on this great earth.

❖   ❖   ❖

2.

It is because the blue mountains are walking that they are constant. This walk is swifter than the wind. However, those in the mountains do not sense this, do not know it. To be "in the mountains" is the opening of flowers in the world. Those outside the mountains do not sense this, do not know this. Those without eyes to see the mountains do not sense, do not know, do not see, do not hear this truth.

They who doubt that the mountains walk do not yet understand their own walking. It is not that they do not walk, it's just that they do not yet understand, have not yet clarified, walking itself. If we are to understand our own walking we must also understand the walking of the blue mountains. The blue mountains are neither sentient nor insentient; the self is neither sentient nor insentient. Therefore, there should be no doubts about these blue mountains walking.

COMMENTARY

Endless blue mountains,
    free of even a particle of dust.
Boundless rivers of tumbling torrents,
    ceaselessly flowing.

The mountains' walking is an expression of activity in the world. It is because of the mountains' walking—because of their activity—that they are endless. They form a continuum that encompasses past, present, and future.

Dogen says, "It is because the blue mountains are walking that they are constant." We could also say that constant walking is the mountains' practice.

Old master Baoche of Mount Mayu was fanning himself. Seeing him, a monastic asked, "Master, the nature of wind is constant and there is no place it does not reach. Why must you still fan yourself?"

Mayu replied, "Although you understand that the nature of the wind is constant, you do not understand the meaning of its reaching everywhere."

The monastic persisted, "What is the meaning of its reaching everywhere?" Mayu just fanned himself. The monastic bowed with deep respect.

In this koan the monastic is asking, given our original perfection, why do we need to practice? In the early years of Dogen's training, this question was uppermost in his mind. It is what drove him to study exhaustively and to travel to China. It's a question that many of my students ask me: "Since I'm already enlightened, why do I have to do anything?" Because it is through practice that realization and actualization ultimately take place. It is through practice that we must see for ourselves how Mayu's fanning himself is not only the wind reaching everywhere, but the fan, Mayu, the monastic, and us reaching everywhere.

❖ ❖ ❖

To be "in the mountains" is the opening of flowers in the world. Those outside the mountains do not sense this, do not know this. Those without eyes to see the mountains do not sense, do not know, do not see, do not hear this truth.

"A flower opens and the world arises" is a line from a verse written by the Indian master Prajnatara. This phrase has also been translated as "opening within the world flowers," which means that mountains and the world are one reality. In Zen we use the expression: "In the marketplace, yet not having left the mountain; on the mountain, yet manifesting in the world." Nothing exists outside the mountains. Dogen refers to those "in the mountains" or "outside the mountains," but when he speaks of those "in the mountains," he is not discriminating between those "in the mountains" and the mountains themselves. He is in fact saying that the mountains are identical to those who are "in the mountains." "Those outside the mountains" are also the mountains themselves. The mountain reaches everywhere.

Then there is the line: "Those outside the mountains do not sense this, do not know this." We can understand this in one of two ways. Those outside the mountains are not aware of the mountains walking because they are the mountains. They no longer have a reference system with which to see or sense or hear the mountains. Another interpretation is that "those without eyes to see" are suffering from the blindness of ignorance.

In Buddhism there are five kinds of blindness. The first is what we call the blindness of ignorance or separation. The second, the blindness of one who denies the teachings of Buddhism. The third is the blindness of emptiness, where a person first perceives the absolute basis of reality. The fourth is the blindness of attaching to emptiness. The fifth is transcendental blindness, in which there is no distinction between seeing and not seeing.

In the midst of ignorance, we are convinced that we are separate from the mountain and from the rest of the world. We think the world is out there and we are here, contained in this bag of skin. The problem is that when we see ourselves as separate from the rest of the universe, we abdicate our responsibility for it. This is most evident in the way we treat the environment, what we commonly call nature.

In general, we have a very limited understanding of nature. We believe it's made up of phenomena in the physical world but does not include manufactured objects and human interaction. But the fact is that human beings are nature—just as much as a tree or a spider web or the Brooklyn Bridge is nature.

How can we discount our own role in creating the earth? We've altered this planet irreversibly. We've produced automobiles, factories, and aerosols. We've refined carbon-based fuels. We've created global warming. All of these are acts of nature—human nature.

Most of the disasters we face today are human created. Tsunamis and earthquakes kill tens of thousands, but our wars kill millions for profit. Yet we are blind to most of the killing. When we include the human element in our understanding of nature, we become conscious of the fact that we're responsible for the whole catastrophe. The question then becomes, what will we do about it? When will we do it? What are we waiting for?

❖   ❖   ❖

3.

We should realize that the blue mountains must be understood on the basis of many phenomenal realms. We must carefully investigate the walking of the blue mountains, as well as the walking of the self. And this investigation should include walking backward as well as backward walking. We should investigate the fact that since that very time before the appearance of any subtle sign, since the age of the King of Emptiness, walking both forward and backward has never stopped for a moment. If walking had ever rested, sages and wise ones would never have appeared; if walking were limited, these ancient teachings would never have reached the present. Walking forward has never ceased; walking backward has never ceased. Walking forward does not oppose walking backward, nor does walking backward oppose walking forward. This virtue is called "the mountain flowing," it is also called "the flowing mountain."

COMMENTARY

Though we may speak of it, it cannot be conveyed;
try to picture it, yet it cannot be seen.
When the universe collapses, "it" is indestructible.

Eighteenth-century zen master Tenkei Denson, who wrote a commentary on the *Mountains and Rivers Sutra*, suggests that Dogen's reference to "walking backward and backward walking" in this passage was actually a mistake, that Dogen really meant to say "walking backward and walking forward." Walking forward is activity, creation. Walking backward is stillness, extinction. Creation and extinction, or activity and stillness, are both characteristics of the blue mountain. When the mountain advances—when you're advancing—activity covers everything. When there is receding, stillness overtakes everything. There is nothing outside of it. But whether the correct translation is "backward walking" or "walking forward," the spirit of what Dogen is pointing to remains the same—whole body and mind stillness and activity.

We must keep in mind that even if we were able to establish without question Dogen's original intention in this or any other passage of the sutra, it would not make his teachings any more understandable or logical. Why? Because his teachings are not meant to be rationalized. They are not intended as an explanation; they're meant to point to the nature of reality.

As Dogen says, we must study the dharma exhaustively—which means we need to practice, realize, and actualize it. There's no other way to plumb its depths.

Once, when I was staying at my teacher Maezumi Roshi's house, I woke up late one night and saw a light in his study. I knocked on the door and heard Roshi's quiet, "Come in." I opened the door to find Roshi sitting at his desk, reading. "Roshi, it's three o'clock in the morning!" I said. "What are you reading?"

"Dogen," he replied.

"Dogen?!" I said, incredulous. He'd been studying Dogen for more than forty years.

He simply looked at me and laughed softly. "Yes, Dogen."

❖ ❖ ❖

We should investigate the fact that since that very time before the appearance of any subtle sign, since the age of the King of Emptiness, walking both forward and backward has never stopped for a moment.

Because all things are intrinsically empty, they lack self nature. To realize this emptiness, the absolute basis of reality, is to realize the first rank of Master Dongshan, "that very time before the appearance of any subtle sign."

The notion of emptiness, or *shunyata,* has become so convoluted in our language that it merits some clarification. First of all, the word "emptiness" is not even an accurate translation. We use the term in a way that implies that emptiness is the attribute of an object—like roundness. We say that a sphere is round, and simple observation will confirm this perception. Then we apply the same logic to emptiness, describing it as a quality of an object in the phenomenal world. But the emptiness of shunyata is not a thing. It's meant to oppose all views—including the view of emptiness. Shunyata is neither existent nor nonexistent.

When we say that an object is empty, this means that it is empty of independent existence or inherent characteristics. It is interdependent with everything. From a Mahayana Buddhist perspective, emptiness and interdependence are one and the same.

Samadhi, the falling away of body and mind, is usually a practitioner's first experience of emptiness. Samadhi is the state in which we relinquish all our passions and desires. Master Dazhu Huihai said: "Total relinquishment includes all ideas of duality, such as being and nonbeing, love and hate, pure and impure, concentration and distraction. In this, there is no thought of 'Now I see all duality as empty or now I have relinquished all of them.'"

In samadhi, all perspectives disappear. We become completely intimate with the breath, with a koan, with ourselves. *Zazen* becomes like a bottomless, clear pool.

Whether we are doing zazen or entering the mountains, intimacy is the basis of all of our practice. It is the basis of our lives. If we want to understand the mountain, we have to become the mountain. We have to let the mountain fill our whole body and mind.

A student asked Dongshan, "You always instruct us to follow the way of the birds. What is it to follow the way of the birds?" Dongshan answered, "You don't meet anyone."

What is it to follow the way of the birds, the way of the mountain, the way of the river? What is it to follow our own way? Before we can answer these questions, we must realize that fundamentally, there's not a single thing outside of this gigantic body. In the first rank we realize that our body and mind is the body and mind of the universe.

Master Dongshan's poem on this rank reads:

In the third watch of the night, before the moon appears,
No wonder when we meet, there is no recognition,
Still cherished in my heart is the beauty of the earlier days.

In the evening, before the moon shines there is complete darkness, complete emptiness. It's a state without form, without sound, and without smell. Every last fleck of cloud is wiped from the vast sky. This stage is where the first insight into the absolute basis of reality takes place. It is also the first step in realizing our intimacy with all things.

The Voice of the
Golden Goose ◯⟩⟩

Venerable Bhikkhu Bodhi

*Sometimes the political prescriptions of religious people can seem too general
to be helpful, but we should not confuse the general with the deep. The core
of the world's social and political problems is emotional, moral, and, yes,
spiritual, and if real progress is to be made, it must begin at those deep levels.
This essay by the Venerable Bhikkhu Bodhi, an American Buddhist monk
and scholar, explains the deep shift in our worldview required to
address the coming climate crisis.*

One of the Jataka stories, the *Palasa Jataka,* recounts a past life of
the Buddha when he was a golden goose living in the Himalayas.
The goose would regularly stop to rest in a large Judas tree, where he
befriended the resident deity of the tree. On one occasion a certain
bird, which had eaten the fruit of a banyan tree, perched in the Judas
tree and voided its excrement into a fork in its trunk. A seed of the
banyan fruit thereby germinated and began to grow into a small
banyan tree.

When the golden goose next visited the deity in the Judas tree,
the banyan had grown four inches and had bright red shoots and
green leaves. The royal goose told his friend: "Every tree on which a

banyan shoot springs up is destroyed by its growth. Don't allow this banyan to grow in the fork in your trunk or else it will destroy your home. Remove it immediately before it tears your dwelling limb from limb."

The Judas deity, however, demurred: "The shoot is small and harmless. It will provide shade and delightful tendrils." The goose insisted: "The shoot is dangerous; it will lead to your harm; as it grows bigger, it will push you off your tree and even destroy your home." When the Judas deity persisted in its decision, the goose understood it was futile to press its argument. It thus flew away and never returned.

As time went by, all happened as the golden goose had foretold. The banyan shoot sent down roots which wrapped around the trunk of its host and consumed its share of soil water and nutriment. The banyan grew bigger and stronger, until it split the Judas tree, which toppled to its death, bringing the deity's home down with it.

This ancient tale, originally intended as an allegory for the destructive power of evil, can be read as a parable for our present-day crisis of global warming. The banyan seed represents the use of carbon-based fuels, whose emissions of carbon dioxide are invisible, odorless, and, in small quantities, harmless. Just as the banyan shoot grew slowly and imperceptibly, so these fuels, diffused into the atmosphere, produce changes that are initially undetectable. But just as the mature banyan tree destroyed its host, unrestricted use of fossil fuels menaces the civilization that depends on them.

When coal was first used to transform water into steam and thereby drive a steam engine, no one could have foreseen that this marvelous invention marked the beginning of a trajectory that would one day even threaten the prospects for human life on Earth. Yet this is precisely the predicament that we currently face. Like the deity in the Judas tree, we have had sufficient warnings: many golden geese have cautioned us about the dangers of excessive carbon emissions. Already in June 1988 a scientific conference in Toronto on climate change concluded:

> Humanity is conducting an unintended, uncontrolled, globally pervasive experiment whose ultimate consequences could be second only to a global nuclear war . . . It is imperative to act now.

In the same month, James Hansen, director of NASA's Goddard Space Center, told Congress that it was virtually beyond doubt that burning fossil fuels was warming the Earth. He warned that if current trends continued the result would be more severe droughts and heat waves, but also heavier rains and more frequent floods.

Over the following two decades, successive American administrations failed to heed these warnings. The eight years of the Bush Administration were particularly disastrous for efforts to curb emissions. Despite uncanny climatic disasters, from drought in Australia to more intense hurricanes in the southern U.S. to relentless floods in Europe, despite the overwhelming testimony of unbiased scientists, the White House has offered only repeated prescriptions for failure. Administration officials have even muzzled government scientists and censored their warnings that global warming is indeed a consequence of the use of fossil fuels.

When he again appeared before Congress, on June 23, 2008—twenty years to the day after his initial testimony—Hansen stressed that time is running out:

> We have used up all slack in the schedule for actions needed to defuse the global warming time-bomb. The next president and Congress must define a course next year in which the United States exerts leadership commensurate with our responsibility for the present dangerous situation. Otherwise it will become impractical to constrain atmospheric carbon dioxide, the greenhouse gas produced in burning fossil fuels, to a level that prevents the climate system from passing tipping points that lead to disastrous climate changes that spiral dynamically out of humanity's control. Changes needed to preserve creation, the planet on which

civilization developed, are clear.... I argue that a path yielding energy independence and a healthier environment is, barely, still possible.

Hansen defined the precise targets we must meet to prevent warming from reaching catastrophic tipping points. The safe level of carbon dioxide in the atmosphere, he stressed, is no more than 350 ppm. What makes our current situation particularly ominous is that it is already 385 ppm and rising about 2 ppm per year. The prospects for the future, however, are not encouraging. Demands worldwide for electric power, cars, and meat (a major source of carbon pollution) are escalating. If higher carbon concentrations should push the average temperature of the planet 2°C above preindustrial levels, this could trigger the irreversible melting of the Greenland ice sheet, a process that has already started. The melted ice would cause a dramatic rise in sea levels of at least four to six feet (about two meters) by the end of the century, flooding the coastal belts of all continents and inundating all major coastal cities. Altered climate patterns would usher in severe droughts, resulting in crop failures, famine, and possible mass starvation. Desperate battles could erupt over dwindling supplies of food and other resources, and vast populations would migrate in search of food. If the mountain glaciers of the Himalayas, Andes, and Rockies disappear through climate warming around midcentury, the billions of people who depend on them for fresh water would be left dry and desolate. Violent conflict over vanishing sources of water could replace the "oil wars" of the present.

Reckless human activity not only contributes directly to global warming, but also triggers feedback processes that accelerate the buildup of greenhouse gases in the atmosphere. Three such feedback loops have already been instigated. There is progressive and self-generating loss of the "albedo effect," the benign reflection of sunlight back into space by white snow and ice. There is deforestation, which releases large quantities of carbon dioxide, removes a major "carbon sink," and by further raising temperatures, provokes more forest fires. A third feedback process involves prodigious frozen deposits of the highly potent greenhouse gas methane. These have begun to be released from Siberian (and Tibetan) permafrost, and even from below the Arctic Ocean seabed. They might create a giant positive feedback loop leading to more permafrost melting and methane release.

Such is the predicament that we face today: a planet in peril, moving ever closer to what energy expert Joseph Romm has called "hell and high water." What can we, as Buddhists, do to ameliorate the crisis of global warming and thereby avert the calamities that may follow if urgent, effective, and earnest action is not taken? Is our situation beyond redemption, or is there still room for hope?

As a spiritual teaching, Buddhism rests on two complementary pillars, wisdom and compassion, both of which can help us diagnose and address the dangers of climate breakdown. Through wisdom, we investigate a danger: see it as a whole, identify its underlying causation, and determine what can be done to remedy it at the causal level. Through compassion, our hearts feel the danger vividly and personally, and thereby expand to embrace all those exposed to harm: all who, like ourselves, are subject to suffering, who seek peace, well-being, and happiness.

Reflection on the broad consequences of runaway global warming enables us to see that this is not merely a problem of rules and regulations that can be solved by a simple technological fix. It is at base a deeply moral problem that challenges our humanity and ethical integrity. The fact that billions of human beings on this planet, as well as countless forms of nonhuman life, have to bear the brunt of the misery caused by the irresponsible behavior of a small number of nations—those that contribute most to global climate change—presents us with an ethical crisis that sears our conscience. This is particularly the case because the populations most likely to be hit hardest by the effects of global warming are those already living in poverty: the people of sub-Saharan Africa, where droughts will get worse; the inhabitants of Central and South Asia, where crop yield could drop by 30 percent; the populations whose island-nations would be swallowed by the sea; and the residents of the Asian mega-deltas, where billions will be in danger of floods. Additionally, if temperatures rise between 1.5–2.5° C, a quarter of all plant and animal species are at risk of extinction.

If we let our minds embrace all our fellow beings with loving-kindness, "as a mother does her only child" (Metta Sutta), we will feel a compelling sense of urgency swell up from our depths, rooted in a clear recognition of the perils that hang over innumerable beings, human and nonhuman, whether in this country or in other lands. And if we let our hearts be stirred by compassion, we will see that we have no choice but to act, and to act in ways that will truly make a difference. But effective action must be rooted in insight, in wisdom. Here the heuristic approach of Buddhism becomes pertinent. To resolve any problem effectively, it is necessary to see it whole and in its wider context.

As we grope for a solution to global warming, it is worth exploring the question: "What prevents the world community from adopting measures to curb carbon emissions rapidly and on the required scale?" If a fire breaks out in my house, I would quickly take any action necessary to extinguish it, even calling the fire department if it gets out of hand. Yet oddly, when our planetary house is aflame, we spend more time squabbling over who should extinguish the fire than we do actually pursuing ways to put it out. Those most responsible for setting the fire in the first place scheme and bargain to avoid making a full commitment to firefighting. The international protocols and agreements proposed to control carbon emissions, including the Kyoto Protocol, have been weak, limited, and flawed. In the U.S., proposals to Congress to impose mandatory limitations on carbon emissions and other controls on energy consumption have repeatedly failed to receive widespread support. The White House has consistently opposed regulating carbon emissions, contending it would cost too much and hurt economic growth.

Why is there this procrastination and denial, this reluctance to take the sweeping steps needed to save human civilization from almost certain calamity? Why has the compelling consensus of the international scientific community been punctured by the doubts of politicians who rely on the opinions of people outside the scientific community? Why do these deniers, at obvious risk to themselves and their children, sow seeds of skepticism among the general population?

A partial answer arises from an understanding of the strong grip that greed has upon the human heart, and when the people at the helms of the oil, coal, and gas companies—those most responsible for emissions—act in the grip of greed, we can see how immense is the resistance to effective controls on emissions. Economic power does not operate in a domain of its own but is intimately interwoven with political power, and in the U.S. the ties between the two are extremely hard to break. Through their lobbyists, the carbon energy companies have a substantial impact on the formulation of public policy, and the reluctance of politicians to press for stricter controls on carbon emissions is almost directly proportional to the contributions they receive from these industries. This is the hurdle we must clear if we hope to institute a sane environmental policy.

In the public sphere, ecology is locked in such a tense wrestling match with the economy that the relationship between the two seems to be one of inverse advantage. According to the dominant economic model, for an economy to thrive, it must become more productive, turning out a greater number of goods and services. Enhanced productivity involves increased use of energy, and since the energy comes from electricity (provided largely by coal plants), and goods must be transported (with oil-derived fuels), a successful economy almost inevitably results in higher carbon emissions. In the framework of our present economic model, placing restrictions on carbon emissions means limiting productivity, and a decline in activity entails economic losses that will spread throughout the entire economic order. Limits on productivity would usher in a recession, layoffs, lower wages, and reduced employee benefits. Within this framework, the one escape from this fate is increased production, which brings us back to square one.

While unmitigated greed certainly contributes to the resistance corporate leaders show to proposals to curb carbon emissions, greed alone is not a sufficient explanation. Buddhist psychology teaches that greed often coexists with a strong impulse to dominate and control, and this seems pertinent here. For the executives of the oil and coal industries, control over the mainsprings of the economy, its reservoirs of energy, confers the exhilaration of power, of knowing they can dominate national and international affairs. This intoxication with power is hard to relinquish, even though unrestrained use of these fuels endangers the planet, including the executives themselves and their descendents. Another motivating factor may be fear of stagnation, decline, or even collapse, if productivity is curtailed due to controls on carbon emissions. Such fear increases when, as recently, major financial institutions and automobile manufacturers totter at the edge of survival.

Another explanatory factor, most prominent among the general population, is delusion. Delusion screens from our minds the imminence of danger, giving us a foolhardy sense of invulnerability in the midst of insecurity. In our private lives, we unconsciously assume that we are immortal beings, exempt from old age, sickness, and death. Delusion also plants in us the assumption that our environment will always remain safe and secure. If hurricanes, droughts, and floods should strike, we persuade ourselves that they are only temporary displays of the moodiness of the weather and console ourselves that things will "return to normal." We resist acknowledging that our own behavior can be responsible for a potentially catastrophic and irreversible transformation of our climate. Such delusion, already entrenched in the human mind, is strongly reinforced when the energy corporations use their wealth and influence to spread disinformation and cast doubt on the truth and urgency of global warming.

Thus, in the U.S., denial of global warming and indifference toward its consequences stems from the potent mixture of corporate greed, the arrogance of power, fear of collapse, and stultifying delusion. In developing nations, in contrast, reluctance to counter global warming often springs from the sheer struggle for survival. These countries see enhanced economic activity as essential to their escape from poverty. Thus cuts in carbon emissions, in so far as they hamper economic productivity, appear to them as an unwelcome impediment to their aspirations for greater prosperity. From their perspective, environmental concerns are of limited importance; many in these countries even regard environmental issues as a peculiarly Western obsession. For the population of the developing world, the chief priority is to emerge from endemic poverty, and the road to this goal is economic development. A robust economy is one that constantly produces more goods and services, and thus necessarily consumes more energy. To compel such economies to impose caps on carbon emissions is, from their own point of view, to consign them to continued poverty, a bitter fate with which they are already too familiar.

Nevertheless, even the most "productive" economy cannot flourish on a planet beset by a torrent of environmental woes stemming from runaway climate change. Now that major ecological disasters have already started to manifest, our only chance to avert a catastrophic fate is to promptly adopt sweeping and comprehensive measures to reduce global warming. These must apply equally to both the developed and developing worlds.

Major changes are needed in both our personal conduct and our economies. While in our private lives we should certainly increase our environmental awareness and adopt as many small behaviors as possible that reduce our personal carbon footprint—for example, retrofitting windows, using compact fluorescent lightbulbs, turning off unused electric appliances, driving a fuel-efficient car, eating mainly vegetarian, keeping the thermostat low—it would be overly optimistic, even naive, to believe that merely reducing our personal share of carbon waste and encouraging others to do so will bring emissions down to the levels needed to avert future calamity. Global warming is a problem of truly global dimensions, intricately related to the gargantuan quantities of energy our economies devour to sustain forward movement and support the standards of living we have learned to expect. Hence there is no alternative to a wide-ranging plan that will dramatically transform the entire economy—our own and that of the world.

From a Buddhist perspective, a sane economy would be governed by the principle of sufficiency, which holds that the key to happiness is contentment rather than an abundance of goods. Our unquenchable compulsion to consume and enjoy is an expression of craving, the very thing the Buddha pinpointed as the root cause of suffering. In the dominant market-based model of the good life, the economy is governed by a "principle of commodification": whatever exists acquires its right to be because it is a potential commodity, something that can be transformed into a product to be marketed and sold. Such an economic model is dangerously beholden to a pervasive delusion, the tacit supposition that the economy functions in an inexhaustible, open-ended arena. To the contrary, the economy is a human field nested in the folds of the wider, more inclusive field of the biosphere. Because the biosphere is finite, fragile, and exhaustible, because it is delicate and vulnerable to damage, all economic activity occurring within its embrace must respect its finitude and fragility. The hubris of imagining the capacity for economic growth to be unbounded will eventually invite nemesis: the destruction of both the economy and the world community.

Our present economic model also presupposes that human beings are quasi-mechanistic systems driven by the repetitive cycle of desire, acquisition, and gratification. Hence the market treats people as essentially consumers, aiming to provoke in them ever-new desires to acquire and enjoy the commodities it turns out by sucking in and transforming the biosphere. A life revolving around production and consumption means people are persistently beset by insatiable craving, restlessness, and a chronic sense of lack: the ills of modernity. When viewed against this background, the crisis of global warming can be read as an object lesson on the limits of the prevailing paradigm of market economics. It points to the need to develop an alternative economic vision grounded in a more respectful conception of human nature. In place of the old model of market capitalism, in which the driving force of the economy is the exchange of money for goods and services, we need an economy governed by the principle of sufficiency: one which reveres the intrinsic beauty and value of the natural world; gives priority to the full development of the human person; promotes a wide sense of human community; and addresses the broad dynamics of what constitutes human happiness.

In brief, the crisis of global warming compels us to look far beyond the immediate exigencies that a changing climate itself portends and assigns us the task of forging a new vision of human life, one that can integrate our endeavor to achieve a satisfactory standard of living for people all across the planet with the need to actualize our highest potentials while cherishing the biosphere that nurtures and sustains our lives.

Why Buddhism Needs the West

David Loy

The West can certainly benefit from Buddhism, but David Loy believes the opposite is also true. While Buddhism offers the West profound wisdom and a path to spiritual liberation, the Western world offers political and social perspectives often lacking in Eastern traditions. Loy, one of Western Buddhism's most interesting thinkers, argues that the combination of Buddhist philosophy and modern political, economic, and social thought makes a complete package for human progress.

In an oft-cited statement, which might be apocryphal, the British historian Arnold Toynbee said, "The coming of Buddhism to the West may well prove to be the most important event of the twentieth century." Given the monumental social, political, and scientific changes of the last century, that claim seems pretty unlikely. But Toynbee may have noticed something the rest of us need to see: that the interaction between Buddhism and the West is crucial today, because each emphasizes something the other is missing. Whether or not Toynbee actually made this observation, the significance of the encounter may be nearly as great as his statement suggests.

For many Western convert Buddhists, the claim that Buddhism provides what the West lacks seems reasonable enough. They are, after all, converts. But I believe the opposite is also true: the West offers something just as important to Buddhism, something Buddhism needs if it is to fulfill its vision of human potential. In a way that neither seems to be aware of, Buddhism and the West need each other to complete themselves. To many partisans of either tradition, this idea may sound absurd or even insulting. Certainly it is challenging. Above all, however, it is hopeful.

In his 1969 book *Earth House Hold,* the Buddhist poet and essayist Gary Snyder wrote, "The mercy of the West has been social revolution; the mercy of the East has been individual insight into the basic self/void. We need both." Over the years, this observation has been quoted many times by those making the case for a more socially engaged Buddhism. The challenge is to better understand the relationship between the two: the mercy of the East and the mercy of the West.

What mercy does Buddhism offer the West? For those who read this book, answers to that question may already be apparent, but let's be precise. Buddhist teachings emphasize the basic connection between suffering (*dukkha*) and the absence of an abiding self (*anatta*). Why are we constantly dissatisfied? It's because our sense of self, being a delusion, is incapable of finding lasting satisfaction. We are unable to find happiness in our lives because we are haunted by a sense that "something's wrong," something we do not understand, and ego-driven attempts to resolve this just make things worse. According to Buddhism, the self, by its very (illusory) nature, *is* dukkha.

In contemporary terms, the sense of self is a psychosocial construct: psychological because it is a result of mental conditioning, and social because it develops in relation to others. Since "my" sense of self is composed of habitual ways of thinking, feeling, and acting, letting go of those mental habits (through a practice such as meditation) is like peeling the layers of an onion. Through practice, one eventually realizes directly the emptiness—the lack of self—at one's core. Awakening is recognizing that awareness is nondual: because "I" am not inside, the rest of the world is not "outside."

In the context of social ethics, this recognition implies that without individual transformation, social transformations are bound to be impaired. Why have so many revolutions and reform movements ended up replacing one gang of thugs with another? Because, many Buddhists will say, if we do not address our own greed, ill will, and delusion (the three unwholesome motivations, also known as the "three poisons"), our efforts to challenge them in their collective forms are likely to be useless—or worse. Certainly history provides us with many examples of tyrannical leaders emerging from movements whose initial goals were largely just.

But wait a moment . . . what does Buddhism have to do with political movements? Buddhism, so the response often goes, is a spiritual path for individuals, not a platform for social change. The problem with this way of thinking is that it is not always clear where one ends and the other begins. Buddhism is about ending dukkha by transforming the three poisons, yet those poisons are all the more toxic when they infect a ruler, who easily can—and often does—create widespread dukkha. As Buddhists, we need to consider how much suffering is perpetuated by social and political conditions as well as by individual tendencies.

We know that the historical Buddha applied his teachings to the social world with an insight and vigor unique for a religious figure of his time and place. In the earliest scriptures there are many instances in which the Buddha challenges prevailing social attitudes and advocates reform. Still, social analysis and criticism had a marginal role in the corpus of his teachings. The main thrust of the Buddha's teachings addressed the problem of individual suffering, and his thoughts about society were never elaborated in a similarly sophisticated or systematic way. As a result, after the Buddha passed away, the *sangha* (monastic community) for the most part adapted itself to the social forms and norms of Asian cultures. Buddhism has historically tended to passively accept, and sometimes actively support, social arrangements that now seem unjust.

In Asian Buddhist countries, for example, the monastic community has often relied on royal patronage. In these cultures, rulers were not only patrons and defenders of the sangha, they served as cultural ideals and living symbols of the social order, fulfilling a role that was necessary to maintain harmony between the state and the cosmos. In other words, their role was religious as well as political. The sangha generally accepted this view and, along with it, whatever injustices might be part of the social structure, for to challenge the order of society was to revolt against the order of the cosmos itself. What's more, such a state of affairs can be, and often has been, justified by a simplistic interpretation of Buddhism's doctrine of karma. The view that there is an infallible and precise cause-and-effect relationship between one's actions and one's fate implies that justice is already built into the way things happen. Karma has thus provided a rationalization for discrimination based on ethnicity, caste, class, birth handicaps, illness, and so forth. It has also justified the authority of those with political and economic power and the subordination of those who have neither.

By modern standards, this is an example of collective mystification. But such a way of viewing society is distinctly Western, rooted in ideas that originated in ancient Greece, particularly in Athens. The Greeks' understanding, which began to develop about the same time as Buddhism, was revolutionary in the way it challenged false ideas about society—in fact, just as revolutionary as the Buddha's challenge to delusive ideas about the self. It has been the norm in societies not exposed to these ideas to view their social structure as being in some way inevitable: as reflecting natural order or divine will. In the West, this way of thinking was challenged and eventually overthrown. The Greeks made a distinction between *nomos*—the "norms" or conventions of human society (including culture, technology, and so forth)—and *phusis*, the natural world.

The Greeks realized that, unlike nature, *whatever is social convention can be changed:* we can reorganize our own societies and in that way determine (or at least attempt to determine) our own destiny. Traditional societies didn't realize this distinction. Without our understanding of historical development, and therefore of future possibility, premodern peoples usually accepted their own social structures as inevitable, as something that was just as "natural" as their local ecosystems. When rulers were overthrown, new ones took their place at the top of the social pyramid, which was also a religious pyramid: kings were gods or godlike, because of the special role they played in maintaining harmony with the transcendent powers that kept the cosmos going.

We call the Greeks *humanists* because their great discovery challenged the religious worldview that supported the traditional social order; now humans would decide for themselves how to live. We in the modern world tend to take this insight and all it implies for granted, as foundational to our way of life and how we see the world. But in a way it was as pivotal as the Buddha's insight into the emptiness of the self. For just as the (sense of) self arises dependent on conditions, so too do the social and political arrangements under which we live. Self and society: both are impermanent, contingent, and therefore changeable.

An unusual set of cultural conditions encouraged this development in classical Greece. Homer's detached, ironical attitude toward the gods authorized no sacred book, proclaimed no dogma, and set up no powerful priesthood. Greek merchant fleets sparked a great colonizing movement that exposed the Greeks to very different cultures, which encouraged skepticism toward their own myths. Thales founded natural philosophy when he did not use gods to explain the world. Unlike Moses and Muhammad, Solon did not get his tables from a divine source when he gave Athens new laws. Greek drama reduced the gods' role by emphasizing human motivation and responsibility. Socrates' philosophical quest for wisdom did not depend upon them. With the help of some remarkable leaders, Athens was able to reorganize itself more or less peacefully. Solon broke the power of the aristocratic assembly by admitting the lower classes. Cleisthenes replaced the four traditional family-based tribes of Athens with ten districts, organized by one's area of residence. Pericles extended the access of humble citizens to public office. The result was a unique, although limited, experiment in direct democracy (women and slaves did not participate).

Not everyone liked democracy. Plato, for example, offered more elitist plans to restructure the Greek city-state in two of his dialogues, *The Republic* and *Laws*. But such alternative visions also presupposed the same basic distinction the Greeks had established between *phusis* and *nomos,* nature and social convention.

Virtually every social justice movement in modern times—the abolition of slavery, civil rights, feminism, workers' rights, anti-apartheid—is a consequence of this distinction. The various revolutions that for better and worse have recreated our modern world—English, American, French, Russian, Chinese, and so forth—all took for granted the understanding that if a political regime is unjust and oppressive it should be changed, because such systems are human constructs and can therefore be reconstructed.

But speaking of these revolutions also reminds us of the horrors of Stalin, Mao, Pol Pot, and others—revolutions that devolved into reigns of terror. Revolution, we have learned, does not necessarily imply mercy.

The Greek experiment with democracy failed for the same reasons that our modern experiment with democracy is in danger of failing. It is the reason I mentioned earlier: unless social reconstruction is accompanied by personal transformation, democracy merely liberates the ego-self. If I am still motivated by greed, ill will, and delusion, my freedom will be dangerous, to myself as well as to others. As long as the illusion of an individual self separate from others remains strong, democracy—despite the countless attempts that have been made to create systematic safeguards—can't help but provide opportunities for some individuals to take advantage of others.

Athenians became aware of this problem quite early. According to the sociologist Orlando Patterson, Greek individualism "was rooted in the Homeric tradition of personal fame and glory and was nourished by habitual competition, as much in art and athletics as in business, but everywhere off the battlefield with little team play." This individualism "was tempered by little sense of strictly moral responsibility, or in particular of altruism." It soon became obvious that "private appetites" were motivating people to corrupt the democratic process. Demosthenes lamented that politics had become the path to riches, for individuals no longer placed the state before themselves but viewed it as another way to promote their own personal advantage. Plato's distaste for democracy is explicit in *The Republic*, which argues that too much liberty encourages a lack of self-restraint that tends to yield to the strongest pressures of the moment—a recipe for social as well as psychological strife.

This sounds strikingly familiar, although today it's not so much private appetite as institutionalized greed that subverts the political process. We still distinguish between the economy and the government, but at top levels people easily move from corporate CEO to Cabinet position and back again, because they share the same self-serving vision: continuous economic growth is the most important thing of all, overshadowing all other social and ecological concerns. As Dan Hamburg concluded from his years in the U.S. Congress: "The real government of our country is economic, dominated by large corporations that charter the state to do their bidding. Fostering a secure environment in which corporations and their investors can flourish is the paramount objective of both [political] parties."

From a Buddhist perspective, it would be naive to expect social transformation to work without personal transformation. But the history of Buddhism shows us that the opposite is also true: although *buddhadharma* may focus on promoting individual awakening, it cannot avoid being affected by the social forces that work to keep us asleep and submissive. It is the mercy of the West that those social forces need no longer be mystified as natural and inevitable.

For modern Buddhists, the world shows us daily that our own awareness cannot thrive indifferent to what is happening to the awareness of others. As the old sociological paradox puts it, people create society, but society also creates people. Our economic and political systems are not spiritually neutral; they inculcate certain values and discourage others. As our awareness becomes more liberated, we become more aware of the suffering of others, and of the social forces that aggravate or decrease suffering. The bodhisattva path is not a personal sacrifice but a further stage of practice: if I am not separate from others, how can I be fully awakened unless they are too? Today our world calls out for new types of bodhisattvas, who look for ways to address suffering, dukkha, as it is institutionalized in our social and political lives.

Western attempts at collective social reconstruction have had limited success, because they have been compromised by ego-driven individual motivations. Buddhadharma, too, has had limited success, if the measure of its success is eliminating suffering and delusion, because until now Buddhism has not been able to challenge the delusion built into oppressive social hierarchies that mystify themselves as beneficial and necessary. Each has been limited because it lacked the other; their convergence in our times opens up fresh possibilities. Each might find in the other the perspective it needs to realize its own deepest promise.

Mindful Eating

Jan Chozen Bays

So much of our suffering is caused by habitual mental patterns, the mistakes and neuroses we fall into again and again, hurting ourselves and others. Meditation practice offers a variety of effective tools for recognizing and freeing ourselves from these destructive habits. A lot of us have bad habits revolving around food, and the Zen teacher and physician Jan Chozen Bays has developed a program to bring the power of mindfulness to our eating issues. It's these kinds of effective techniques that are attracting so many people to the concept of mindful living.

Our struggles with food can cause tremendous distress and suffering. Whether we have a tendency to overeat, undereat, or just feel conflicted about eating, the practice of mindfulness can help us to rediscover a healthy and joyful relationship to food. Mindful eating is an experience that engages all parts of us, our body, our heart, and our mind, in choosing, preparing, and eating food. It immerses us in the colors, textures, scents, tastes, and even sounds of drinking and eating. Mindfulness allows us to be curious and even playful as we investigate our responses to food and our inner cues to hunger and satisfaction.

Mindful eating is not directed by charts, tables, pyramids, or scales. It is not dictated by an expert. It is directed by your own inner experiences, moment by moment. Your experience is unique. Therefore you are the expert. In the process of learning to eat mindfully, we replace self-criticism with self-nurturing, anxiety with curiosity, and shame with respect for your own inner wisdom.

As an example, let's take a typical experience. On the way home from work Sally thinks with dread about the talk she needs to work on for a big conference. She has to get it done in the next few days to meet the deadline. Before starting to work on the speech, however, she decides to relax and watch a few minutes of TV when she gets home. She sits down with a bag of chips beside her chair. At first she eats only a few, but as the show gets more dramatic, she eats faster and faster. When the show ends she looks down and realizes that she's eaten the entire bag of chips. She scolds herself for wasting time and for eating junk food. "Too much salt and fat! No dinner for you!" Engrossed in the drama on the screen, covering up her anxiety about procrastinating, she ignored what was happening in her mind, heart, mouth, and stomach. She ate unconsciously. She ate to go unconscious. She goes to bed unnourished in body or heart and with her mind still anxious about the talk.

The next time this happens she decides to eat chips but to try eating them mindfully. First she checks in with her mind. She finds that her mind is worried about an article she promised to write. Her mind says that she needs to get started on it tonight. She checks in with her heart and finds that she is feeling a little lonely because her husband is out of town. She checks in with her stomach and body and discovers that she is both hungry and tired. She needs some nurturing. The only one at home to do it is herself.

She decides to treat herself to a small chip party. (Remember, mindful eating gives us permission to play with our food.) She takes twenty chips out of the bag and arranges them on a plate. She looks at their color and shape. She eats one chip, savoring its flavor. She pauses, then eats another. There is no judgment, no right or wrong. She is simply seeing the shades of tan and brown on each curved surface, tasting the tang of salt, hearing the crunch of each bite, feeling the crisp texture melt into softness. She ponders how these chips arrived on her plate, aware of the sun, the soil, the rain, the potato farmer, the workers at the chip factory, the delivery truck driver, the grocer who stocked the shelves and sold them to her.

With little pauses between each chip, it takes ten minutes for the chip party. When she finishes the chips, she checks in with her body to find out if any part of it is still hungry.

She finds that her mouth and cells are thirsty, so she gets a drink of orange juice. Her body is also saying it needs some protein and something green, so she makes a cheese omelet and a spinach salad. After eating she checks in again with her mind, body, and heart. The heart and body feel nourished but the mind is still tired. She decides to go to bed and work on the talk first thing in the morning, when the mind and body will be rested. She is still feeling lonely, although less so within the awareness of all the beings whose life energy brought her the chips, eggs, cheese, and greens. She decides to call her husband to say good night. She goes to bed with body, mind, and heart at ease and sleeps soundly.

Mindful eating is a way to rediscover one of the most pleasurable things we do as human beings. It also is a path to uncovering many wonderful activities that are going on right under our noses and within our own bodies. Mindful eating also has the unexpected benefit of helping us tap into our body's natural wisdom and our heart's natural capacity for openness and gratitude.

In the Zen tradition we practice bringing skillful attention, curiosity, and inquiry to all of our activities, including the activities of tasting and eating. The Zen teachings encourage us to explore the present moment fully, asking ourselves questions like:

Am I hungry?

Where do I feel hunger? What part of me is hungry?

What do I really crave?

What am I tasting just now?

These are very simple questions, but we seldom pose them.

Mindfulness Is the Best Flavoring

As I write this I am eating a lemon tart that a friend gave to me. He knows how much I love lemon tarts, and he occasionally brings them to me from a special bakery. After writing for a few hours I am ready to reward myself with a tart. The first bite is delicious. Creamy, sweet-sour, melting. When I take the second bite, I begin to think about what to write next. The flavor in my mouth decreases. I take another bite and get up to sharpen a pencil. As I walk, I notice that I am chewing, but there is almost no lemon flavor in this third bite. I sit down, get to work, and wait a few minutes.

Then I take a fourth bite, fully focused on the smells, tastes, and touch sensations in my mouth. Delicious, again! I discover, all over again (I'm a slow learner) that the only way to keep that "first bite" experience, to honor the gift my friend gave me, is to eat slowly, with long pauses between bites. If I do anything else while I'm eating, if I talk, walk, write, or even think, the flavor diminishes or disappears. The life is drained from my beautiful tart. I could be eating the cardboard box.

Here's the humorous part. I stopped tasting the lemon tart because I was thinking. What was I thinking about? Mindful eating! Discovering that, I have to grin. To be a human being is both pitiful and funny.

Why can't I think, walk, and be fully aware of the taste of the tart at the same time? I can't do all these things at once because the mind has two distinct functions, thinking and awareness. When the thinking function is turned up, the awareness function is turned down. When the thinking function is going full throttle, we can eat an entire meal, an entire cake, an entire carton of ice cream, and not taste more than a bite or two. When we don't taste what we eat, we can end up stuffed to the gills but feeling completely unsatisfied. This is because the mind and mouth weren't present, weren't tasting or enjoying, as we ate. The stomach became full but the mind and mouth were unfulfilled and continued calling for us to eat.

If we don't feel satisfied, we'll begin to look around for something more or something different to eat. Everyone has had the experience of roaming the kitchen, opening cupboards and doors, looking vainly for something, anything, to satisfy. The only thing that will cure this, a fundamental kind of hunger, is to sit down and be, even for a few minutes, wholly present.

If we eat and stay connected with our own experience and with the people who grew and cooked the food, who served the food, and who eat alongside us, we will feel most satisfied, even with a meager meal. This is the gift of mindful eating, to restore our sense of satisfaction no matter what we are or are not eating.

COMMON MISPERCEPTIONS

People get confused about mindfulness. They think that if they just do one thing at a time, like eating without reading, or if they move *veeerrry* slowly and carefully, they are being mindful. We could stop reading, close the book, and then eat slowly but still not be mindful of what we are eating. It depends upon what our mind is doing as we eat. Are we just eating or are we thinking and eating? Is our mind in our mouth, or somewhere else? This is a crucial difference.

As we begin to practice mindfulness it does help a lot to slow down and to do only one thing at a time. In fact there are two essential aspects of becoming mindful as we eat. They are slowing down and eating without distractions. As we become more skilled in being present, we can be mindful and speedy. In fact we discover that when we are moving quickly we need to be much more mindful. To be mindful means to have the mind full, completely full, of what is happening *now.* When you're chopping vegetables with a large sharp knife, the faster you slice, the more attentive you have to be, if you want to keep your fingers!

It's also important to understand that mindful eating includes mindless eating. Within the wide field of mindfulness we can become aware of the pull toward mindless eating and notice when and how we slip into it. We can also decide, according to this situation and time, how we're going to approach eating. Part of my work as a doctor involves testifying in court cases as an expert witness. Maybe

I'm on the way to court and I haven't had time for lunch. I know it will be hard to stay clear on the witness stand and that court is unpredictable. I may be there for hours. I mindfully decide to undertake mindless eating and order a veggie burger from a fast-food window to eat in the car, trying to at least be mindful about not spilling the special sauce on my one good suit. Mindfulness gives us awareness of what we're doing and, often, why we're doing it.

Establishing a Healthier Relationship with Food

When our relationship to food falls out of harmony, we lose our innate enjoyment of eating. When the relationship has been disordered for many years, it is easy to forget what "normal" eating is like. Actually it's what "normal" eating *was* like, because in infancy almost everyone experienced a natural happiness with eating and an instinctive awareness of how much was satisfying.

Here are some elements of a healthy relationship to food.

- You feel happy and fully engaged in life when you are not eating. (Food is not your only reliable source of pleasure and satisfaction.)

- If you are not feeling hungry, you don't eat.

- You stop eating when you feel full and are able to leave food on the plate.

- You have intervals of at least several hours when you are not hungry or thinking about food, punctuated by (meal) times when you do feel hungry and take enjoyment in eating.

- You enjoy eating many different kinds of foods.

- You maintain a healthy weight that is steady or fluctuates within a range of five to seven pounds. You don't need to weigh yourself more than once every few months or years.

- You don't obsess about food or count calories in order to decide if you can "afford" to eat something or not.

If some or all of the items on this list don't apply to you, you're not alone. Many of us have developed unhealthy habits due to a variety of influences in our lives. Fortunately, mindful eating can help restore your natural sense of balance, satisfaction, and delight with food.

The Basic Mindful Eating Meditation

Anything that we attend to carefully and patiently will open itself up to us. Once we are able to apply the power of a concentrated, focused mind, anything, potentially all things, will reveal their true hearts to us. It is that heart-to-heart connection with ourselves, with our loved ones, and with the world itself that all of us so dearly long for. All it takes is a little bit of courage and the willingness to begin the most delightful of all adventures, the journey of looking, smelling, tasting, and feeling.

In this mindful eating exercise we will experiment with bringing our full awareness to eating a very small amount of food. It is best to have someone read this exercise aloud to you, one step at a time.

Preparation: For this exercise you will need a single raisin. Other foods will also work, such a dried cranberry, a single strawberry, a cherry tomato, or an unusual type of cracker.

1. Begin by sitting quietly and assessing your baseline hunger: How hungry are you, on a scale of zero to ten? Where do you "look" in your body to decide how hungry you are?

2. Imagine that you are a scientist on a mission to explore a new planet. Your spaceship has landed and found the planet to be quite hospitable. You can breathe the air and walk around without any problem. The surface of the planet seems to be bare dirt and rock, and no one has seen any obvious life forms yet. The food supplies on your spaceship are running low, however, and everyone is getting

hungry. You have been asked to scout out this planet to look for anything that might be edible.

As you walk around you find a small object lying on the ground, and you pick it up. Place the raisin (or other food item) on your palm. You are going to investigate it with the only tools you have, your five senses. You have no idea what this object is. You have never seen it before.

3. *Eye hunger.* First you investigate this object with your eyes. Look at its color, shape, and surface texture. What does the mind say that it could be? Now rate your eye hunger for this item. On a scale of zero to ten, how much hunger do you have for this object based upon what your eyes see?

4. *Nose hunger.* Now you investigate it with your nose. Smell it, refresh the nose, and sniff it again. Does this change your idea of whether it might be edible? Now rate nose hunger. On a scale of zero to ten, how much hunger do you have for this object based upon what your nose smells?

5. *Mouth hunger.* Now you investigate this object with your mouth. Place it in your mouth but *do not bite it.* You can roll it around and explore it with the tongue. What do you notice?

Now you can bite this mysterious object, but only once. After biting it once, roll it around again in the mouth and explore it with the tongue. What do you notice?

Now rate mouth hunger. On a scale of zero to ten, how much hunger do you have for this object based upon what the mouth tastes and feels? In other words, how much does the mouth want to experience more of it?

6. *Stomach hunger.* Now you decide to take a risk and eat this unknown object. You chew it slowly, noticing the changes in the mouth in texture and taste. You swallow it. You notice whether there are still any bits in the mouth. What does the tongue do when you have finished eating it? How long can you detect the flavor?

Now rate stomach hunger. Is the stomach full or not, satisfied or not? On a scale of zero to ten, rate stomach hunger. In other words, how much does the stomach want more of this food?

7. *Cellular hunger.* Become aware of this food passing into the body. Absorption begins as soon as we begin chewing. Are there any sensations that tell you that this food is being absorbed? How is it being received by the cells in the body? Now rate cellular hunger. On a scale of zero to ten, how much would the cells like to have more of this food?

8. *Mind hunger.* Can you hear what the mind is saying about this food? (Hint: Often the mind talks in "shoulds" or "should nots.") Now rate mind hunger. On a scale of zero to ten, how much would the mind like you to have more of this food?

9. *Heart hunger.* Is the heart saying anything about this food? On a scale of zero to ten, how soothing or comforting is it? Would the heart like you to have more of this food? You might like to repeat this exercise with liquid. Pick a drink you have never had before, such as an exotic fruit juice. Take your time and assess each kind of thirst separately.

At first we might find this exercise difficult. As with all aspects of practice, the more you do it, the more your awareness opens up. If you try this exercise with many kinds of food and drink, gradually you will be able to sense and rate the different kinds of hunger more easily. As you continue to practice mindful eating you will develop skill and confidence in a new and more balanced relationship with food. You will be able to nourish the body, heart, and mind, and to regain a sense of ease and enjoyment with eating.

Burning Alive

Andrew Olendzki

From belief in the self comes attachment to pleasure, repulsion to pain, and indifference to that which does not affect us. These are called the three poisons—greed, hatred, and delusion—and they are the real cause of our own and the world's problems. The world is aflame with these destructive emotions, ever more so as the historical stakes rise, but as the Buddhist scholar Andrew Olendzki writes, the good news is that the fires can be quelled.

Everything is burning!" said the Buddha almost twenty-five centuries ago. "Burning with what? Burning with the fires of greed, hatred, and delusion" (*Samyutta Nikaya* 35.28). These words seem prophetic today, as our planet is slowly warmed by the fires blazing in our furnaces and engines, by the explosion of our bullets and bombs, and by the raging delusions around which our entire world seems to be organized. There is not a single problem we face as human beings—other than the tectonic (earthquakes), the astronomical (meteor strikes), or the existential (aging and death)—that does not find its origin in greed, hatred, or delusion, whether of people or their institutions.

Like a fire, greed is more a process than a thing. It is the state of combustion, the activity of consumption, the procedure by means of which organic resources are quickly reduced to a heap of ash. It is insatiable by nature, since the moment one desire is gratified another flares up, demanding also to be sated. Greed drives an unquenchable compulsion to consume, and as the guiding hand of our economic system, its reach is rapidly becoming global. As it burns it throws off a compelling light, dazzling us with the pleasure of its shapes and colors. We delight in playing with this fire.

Hatred is a hotter, bluer, more sinister flame. It seethes among the coals, preserving its heat over time, until blasting forth suddenly with a surge of the bellows. It can simmer as discontent, smolder as suppressed rage, or lurk hot underground as a molten river of loathing. When it does flare up, the fire of hatred scorches all in its path indiscriminately, often searing the innocent bystander with the ferocity of its angry flames.

Delusion is subtler. Like the lamp behind the projector or a reflection in a mirror, delusion shines with a soft light and illuminates indirectly. It shows things as other than they are—as stable, satisfying, personal, and alluring. Its optical tricks are endearingly creative, so much so that sometimes we hardly know where the light leaves off and the darkness begins. Delusion leads us to revel in wielding the fires of greed and hatred, oblivious of the harm inflicted both on ourselves and on those around us.

The Buddha identifies these three fires as the origin of both individual and collective suffering. Things do not become the way they are by chance, for no reason, or because a deity makes them so. It is the quality of our intention that shapes the world we inhabit, and our world is burning up because of the fires smoldering in our hearts. Resources are being depleted because people greedily consume them and lust for the money produced thereby. People are being killed, raped, tortured, and exploited because they are hated, because other people do not regard them as worthy of respect or basic rights. And the world blindly, stupidly, deceptively plods along this path to destruction because people do not know—or do not want you to know—any better.

And you know what? This is good news. Why? Because the causes of all the trouble have been exposed, and by knowing them we stand a chance of overcoming them. Just think if our problems were due to continental drift, or to an approaching meteor—then we would really be cooked. Fire is actually a very fragile phenomenon. Diminish its heat, starve it of oxygen, or take away its fuel, and it cannot sustain itself. In fact, it is entirely dependent upon external conditions; change these conditions, and it will go out. The Buddha put out the fires of greed, hatred, and delusion in himself and showed us all how to do the same thing. Perhaps we can use this knowledge to quench the fires that are heating our planet and devouring our world.

Something empowering happens when we begin to see these problems as internal rather than external. We have access to ourselves. We have the ability to make internal changes when the mechanisms for change are within our reach. A slight shift of attitude, a minor adjustment of priorities, an occasional opening to a wider perspective, the glimpse of a good greater than the merely personal—these all contribute in a small way to turning down the heat. And since we are faced not with a single enormous fire but with billions of little fires, each one ablaze in one person, miniscule changes in one mind here and one heart there can add up to a dramatic reduction of greenhouse defilements.

All it would take is a gradual increase in generosity and an incremental reduction of the need for gratification to begin to turn down the heat of greed's fire. Planting a tree rather than cutting one down engages a different quality of mind, an attitude of giving rather than of taking. Appreciating when we get what we need, instead of demanding always to get what we want, removes fuel from the fire instead of stoking it. The flames of hatred are banked when we shoot a picture instead of an animal, when we fight injustice rather than our neighbor, when we include someone different in our circle, or even when we relinquish our hold, ever so slightly, on something that annoys us in a mundane moment of daily life. Just as heat is pumped into the system each and every moment through inattention, so also can heat be consistently and inexorably extracted as we bring more mindfulness to what we think, say, and do. A tranquil mind is a cooler mind, and the Buddha has described the movement toward awakening as "becoming cool" (*siti-bhuta*).

The solution to all our (nonexistential) problems is very close at hand. Look within, reach within, each and every moment—and turn down the thermostat just a degree or two. The fires consuming our world are not sustainable. If we do not feed the fires, they will go out.

The Shitty Monk

Shozan Jack Haubner

What can be said about this story? It's true. It's really funny. It shows that no matter how long you've been practicing, life can still bite you in the end. By the way, "Shozan Jack Haubner" is the pseudonym of an author who for obvious reasons wants to be anonymous. But those who were there will certainly be able to sniff him out.

This past winter, as the temperature shriveled along with my remaining illusions about Zen practice, the great wheel of dharma turned once again here at the monastery and I rotated into the officer position of *jikijitsu.*

The jikijitsu is the bad-ass father figure in charge of making sure meditation in the *zendo* hall is tight, strong, and clear. He shouts corrections—"No moving! Breathe quietly!" and so on. He carries a big stick and hits people with it. He leads all of the sits, as well as walking meditation and formal meals. Don't F with him. His is the most distilled embodiment of the spirit of Rinzai, or samurai, Zen.

Rinzai Zen practice can be brutal, savage even. It is designed to bring you to a crisis within yourself, to trigger a dark night of the soul. Zen attacks that one last thing you hold dear: your precious self-conception. It unravels any notion of a freestanding, unconditional "I" and shows it to be a lie, a fabrication, a construction. True realization, the old masters tell us, takes bone-crushing effort. We pulverize the very skeleton of ego—upon which the meat and skin and organs of our illusions hang—and we do it through intense, hurtle-yourself-off-the-cliffs-and-into-the-chasm practice. To prepare for my training as jikijitsu I decided to get tough with myself. I loaded up daily on protein drinks and vitamins, threw away that Anne Lamott book I was reading, quit e-mail cold turkey, and prohibited myself from partaking in all pleasures of the flesh, self-induced or otherwise. I was going to need a backlog of strong, masculine *chi* energy. I was like a boxer who steers clear of his girl-friend before the big fight.

"You're a train wreck of overzealousness," decided my mentor, a sinewy, green-eyed lesbian from Vancouver. "You've got a little power now. Don't abuse it. The primary ass you should be whipping in the zendo is . . . ?"

"That of those noisy, unfocused students?" I tried, smacking my fist into my palm.

"Your own," she growled. "Don't bring your personal shit into it."

The following weekend I was patrolling the zendo when I passed the meditating form of Tico, our most eccentric student, a formerly homeless physicist. That morning he had tried to shave his head, but he'd left patches of soft, curly, gray-black down, which gave him that *One Flew over the Cuckoo's Nest* fresh-from-electroshock-therapy look. He was quivering and shaking, his eyes rolling back into his head, his mouth open and frozen in an Edvard Munch-ian silent scream. Clearly, he was convinced that he was in the throes of spiri-tual-mojo overload. How much, I wondered, do you let people drift into their own flames, like moths, before you shake them and say, "Enough!"?

In a shamanistic culture Tico might be revered for the trances he slips into. Ours, however, was a shared environment and he was rupturing its equanimity by deviating from the etiquette. It's not about your own little personal trip. The body of practitioners is your body, and you really don't want to be that one area of the body that's an irritation, the inner-ear itch or belly rash. This is the reason for the rules. We move as one, act as one, function as one, and as one we beat our egos down like the redheaded stepchildren they are.

But I began to develop a creeping ambivalence about the inexhaustible ferociousness of this style of Zen. "Eyes down," I grumbled incessantly. "Don't sniff. Wake up!" I began to feel like a priest from some Neil Jordan movie about 1950s Ireland. "Keep yer hands in *gassho*, boyo, or I'll rap 'em! Erin McMurphy, did I see ya dippin' yer fingers in yer green tea at breakfast now? I know yer mum. Ya weren't raised in a barn!"

The truth is, like many underweight, overread *sensitivos*, I've always seen myself as an outsider, a nonconformist. My heroes have always been the rebels, the applecart upsetters—Nietzsche, Ikkyu, Cool Hand Luke. It's ironic that so many of us who are attracted to a tough, no-nonsense discipline like Zen also happen to be repulsed by the practice's endless formal punctilios and ornamented, brocaded behavior.

The battle between these two opposing sides of myself—zendo cop and irreligious rebel—began to take its toll. This is the monk-in-training's challenge. The middle way isn't all nicely laid out for him, like an insurance plan, as though to be enlightened is to sign on the dotted line—"Here ya go, here's my desire, my self-interest: Take 'em all. They're my down payment on satori!" No, he has to establish the middle way within himself by testing the extremes. He has to constantly put himself out there. This is the true meaning of that religious catchall "self-sacrifice." The monk puts himself on the altar, or else he's a liar and a fake.

Which is what I felt like as jikijitsu—a liar and a fake. I felt wimpy half the time, sadistic the rest. I couldn't strike the right balance. I couldn't be *strong*. The truth was becoming clear; I'd been a rebel my whole life not because I was idealistic or original, but because I simply didn't have the guts to stand *for* anything—only *against*. Ikkyu? Nietzsche? Please. Try Eddie Haskell meets Woody Allen. I was a coward. A coward and a bully.

Full of self-hate and self-pity, desperate for warmth, for a warm body, I did what we all do when we don't want to face ourselves in the zendo. I fell in love with a new student. She was a carrot-topped, foggy-skinned Dane who had buoyed her smile with some recent cosmetic dental work. It was a welcome diversion, this *dharmamour*. We made love on every continent, grew old together. She got a dramatic disease; I stood over her fresh grave with flowers. Then I deeply regretted our time together and considered myself fortunate for only having lived it in my head for several sits, the downside being the arousal that made it awkward to take my rest periods standing up.

One evening she visited me in my cabin, where I cracked open a bottle of Jack Daniels. "When I got ordained," I laughed over my shoulder, trying to be worldly-wise and charming, "all the junior monks got me books and all the senior monks got me booze. What does *that* tell you about this path? Ha ha ha!"

Alas, she had no interest in me except as a sounding board for various reconciliation scenarios revolving around her estranged boyfriend. The evening ended with her backing out of the room while thanking me for the drink, after a charged silence I had foolishly hoped would lead to a kiss.

I had barely crawled under my quilt with every intention of breaking my pleasure fast when my new roommate—a Frenchman—arrived. For the month.

"Ha-loo!" he chirped, his air-travel BO filling the room as he took in its dimensions. "Tiny!" he whistled, looking askance.

Jacques-san is no doubt someone's idea of a tall, cool drink of water. Sinewy and athletic, he stripped to his Skivvies, hit the lights, lit a candle, and started in with his ritual nightly asanas, standing on his head and scissoring those graceful, giraffe-neck limbs, which practically touched both walls. I rolled to my side and pretended to sleep. Blown up on the wall in monstrously immense proportions just inches from my face, the bulging shadow of his manly midsection bobbed up and down in the candlelight. It was like a soft porn image dreamed up by some cigar-chewing cinematographer.

Even in my bed, facing the wall, there was no denying that I was trapped on a macho, male-heavy mountain with a squad of spiritual

Green Berets. I fled my cabin for the monastery's small library, a run-down cottage nestled in a womb of conifers. My eyes flitted across the shelves, where the spiritually desperate (but always literarily sensible) had for more than forty years buried their intellectual discards. My fingers paused over a slim, turquoise volume by Pema Chödrön. I'd once perused an essay in which she was gracious and respectful toward Zen, but not without leveling a subtle criticism, which I would paraphrase as: "Geez, lighten up. You guys can be really asshole-ish!"

Pema Chödrön was just what I needed. Even her author photo on the book back was encouraging. First off, she was grinning. "Come on in," she seemed to be saying. "The water's warm. I'll be your dharma momma and I'll scrub you clean." Second of all, she had a sensible haircut. Short, but not shaved raw to the skull, not revealing every crinkle and crease, every bony flaw, like the lack-of-hairdos in our Zen tradition. Pema was even showing a little bit of her bare shoulder in the photo.

Wild! Take me to your buddha-breast, earth mother!

Like a little boy perving on *Hustler*, I crawled under my covers that night, clicked on a book-light and poured through *The Wisdom of No Escape*. "If you are alive, if you have heart, if you can love, if you can be compassionate . . . then you won't have any resentment or resistance," Pema purred. "Loving-kindness is the sense of satisfaction with who we are and what we have . . . fear has to do with wanting to protect your heart: you feel something is going to harm your heart, and therefore you protect it."

Surfeited, I laid the book aside and trembled with satisfaction. Were a cigarette handy I would have blown smoke rings and played with my chest hairs. But the following morning, bitterly ashamed, I vowed never to touch her tome again. It was schmaltz, I told myself. A onetime thing. I was perfectly happy with the husky-voiced, thick-ankled practice I'd taken vows to honor. I returned the book to the library—only to furtively yank it from the shelf again that evening.

And so I began an affair with her lush, seething dharma, cheating on my frigid-but-loyal Zen practice. On the cushion, supposedly steadfast in my *zazen* meditation, I was really thinking of paramour Pema's vivacious birdsong prose and rich, voluptuous metaphors. "Go ahead," I thought to the students, my jikijitsu practice going to seed, "move around all you want. Have a good cry while you're at it!" Pema hit my G-spot: *gentleness.*

And yet it was the great soft one herself who ultimately sold me on the rigors of Zen life. Toward the end of her slim volume of talks she extols the virtues of inconvenience. "Opting for coziness, having that as your prime reason for existing, becomes a continual obstacle to taking a leap and doing something new, something unusual, like going as a stranger into a strange land."

"Stick with one boat," one practice, she suggests, and let it "put you through your changes." If you continue to "shop around" you learn a lot about different religions, but very little about your true self.

Inspired, I redoubled my efforts as jikijitsu, refusing to don my skullcap during walking meditation one evening as moonlit frost crunched under our sandals. By the time the last winter retreat rolled around I'd contracted the dreaded flu-cold and achieved great enervation instead of great enlightenment. This, combined with my militant new desire to do everything by the book, set off a chain reaction. It led to the low point in a quota-busting winter of lows, when forty of my peers witnessed—to hearken back to my mentor's warning—my "personal shit."

During the evening bathroom break of the final retreat, I didn't doff my robes and try to navigate the sea of students and their teeming bladders. Instead, I snuck down into a dank and grungy storage space behind our solar-panel shed. I made for a dusty corner and hiked up my robes to relieve myself.

After a few preliminary squirts I had an ominous, involuntary sphincter contraction, and instantly my priorities changed. I needed to get to a stall. There was no denying this call of nature; no single-pointed Zen concentration would make it go away. This point was driven home with the first round of wet gas.

"Oh, you gotta be kidding me," I cried inside. "You gotta be friggin' kidding me."

I looked at my watch. The ten minute mark! Everyone was in the zendo right now, waiting for me to start the sit. Via a bowlegged crab-walk—an embarrassing proposition to begin with but made all the worse by my heavy, multilayered big-deal/Mr. Important robes—I awkwardly exited the storage shed into a flood of harsh winter light.

I contracted and released the appropriate muscles. But there seemed to be no denying it. I'd shit myself. A man's life is made up of choices like this: Right, the zendo. Left, the bathroom. I never made it to the bathroom.

I can handle this, I told myself, slipping my boots off on the zendo porch. The *shoji*—the zendo's kindly mother figure—opened the door for me and I took my seat with alacrity next to the co-jiki-jitsu, effectively corking my bottom on the cushion beneath me. That's cool, I thought. I can sit this out, then dash to the can during the next break. Before my co-jiki peer rang the bell to start the sit, however, she turned and gave me a small bow.

No. *No!* It was my turn to carry the *keisaku.* During sits before koan meetings with the master, a member of the jiki staff patrols the room with the keisaku, a long, thick ruler-like stick tapering from handle to end. When he comes to a student or monk who looks too loose—or too tense—he taps him or her on the shoulder. They bow together, and then the recipient bends to one side and *whack! whack! whack!* Other side: *whack! whack! whack!*

A zendo is not a place to space out. To take your seat and catch up on personal fantasies or zone out for a week. *Get out of your heads and into your* haras! the "encouragement stick" cries with every crack. *Activate your viscera with your breath. Gut-sit!*

I got up. There was diarrhea running down my leg. It was terrible. I could smell it. I reeked of fresh human shit. I had the dubious good luck to be wearing Hot Chilly thermals and all the excrement running down my legs puddled at the elastic at my ankles.

I stood there at the front of the zendo, holding the stick.

There's no rule saying the jikijitsu has to venture out to walk amongst the meditators. I could just stand there for the whole twenty-five-minute sit if I chose, but Pema's words came back to me: "Opting for coziness, having that as your prime reason for existing, becomes a continual obstacle to taking a leap and doing something new, something unusual, like going as a stranger into a strange land."

Perhaps Suzuki Roshi put it best: "Zen is the path of no turning back."

When I first started practicing there was one struggling student in particular who remained unconvinced by "boot-camp spirituality." He carried on every chance he got about how artificial the extreme discipline was, how "not me" the *kanji* chanting and fierce sitting/koan meetings were. He respected the practice but he couldn't "get into it." It wasn't his thing.

That student was me, a million lifetimes ago, it seems.

What I failed to realize was that my resistance was in itself a pose, a stance—a result of my conditioning as a free-spirited, individualistic American prone to respecting all paths and choosing none. I'd never been stripped of myself, and so I mistook a cleverly embroidered outfit of attitudes for my deepest self, which I had to "be true to." Through the path of negation of self, I began to get an inkling of just how thoroughly cloaked I was in attitudes and platitudes—in my own bullshit—and I also learned that despite this, I had to keep going.

Way down at the other end of the zendo, shivering, shaking, lost in himself, was Tico, the eccentric student. My sphincter spasmed briefly in rage. He'd been a thorn in my authoritarian side all winter. Now, however, instead of a threat to be quelled, he merely looked like his head was about to spin around in circles. I knew the feeling.

Standing there holding that stick, reeking like my nephew after he's filled his diaper, I realized that this is when true practice begins: when you are officially in way over your head. "To be fully alive, fully human, and completely awake," Pema tells us in *When Things Fall Apart*, "is to be continually thrown out of the nest. To live fully is to be always in no-man's-land, to experience each moment as completely new and fresh. To live is to be willing to die over and over again."

Zen is the practice of coming up out of yourself and into the situation, *any* situation, meeting it fully, with a complete heart—no holding back, no half-measures, no room for doubt or selfishness. You run the razor of practice from ear to ear, decapitating the dualistic dictator within so that the blood of ego flows forth as the milk of self-sacrifice, nourishing the world.

OK, maybe that's a little dramatic. I simply went amongst some Zen students with a load in my pants. This was my humble contribution to whatever they learned that day: how to move forward despite your imperfections, despite the fact that you're covered in your shit.

Contributors

DIANE ACKERMAN is a poet, essayist, and naturalist, and the best-selling author of *A Natural History of the Senses, The Zookeeper's Wife,* and *Dawn Light,* excerpted here. Ackerman lives in Ithaca, New York, and Palm Beach, Florida, with her partner of forty years, the novelist Paul West. She has the unusual distinction of having a molecule named after her—dianeackerone.

JAN CHOZEN BAYS is co-abbot of Great Vow Zen Monastery in Clatskanie, Oregon. She received priest's ordination and dharma transmission from the late Taizan Maezumi Roshi. She is also a pediatrician, wife, mother, and the author of *Jizo Bodhisattva* and *Mindful Eating.*

VENERABLE BHIKKHU BODHI, an American Buddhist monk, was ordained in Sri Lanka in 1972. He has translated several important works from the Pali Canon, including the *Sumyatta Nikaya* ("The Connected Discourses of the Buddha"). He is the president of the Buddhist Publication Society and chair of the Buddhist Global Relief organization.

SYLVIA BOORSTEIN, PhD, is a cofounding teacher at Spirit Rock Meditation Center in Woodacre, California. She is the author of many best-selling books, including *Pay Attention, for Goodness' Sake* and *Happiness Is an Inside Job.* She lives in California and France and travels widely teaching meditation and loving-kindness.

ELIZABETH BROWNRIGG is a novelist and essayist. Her first novel, *Falling to Earth*, published by Firebrand Books in 1998, was a Lambda Literary Award finalist. Her second novel, *The Woman Who Loved War*, was published in 2004. She received her MFA in creative writing from the Program for Writers at Warren Wilson College.

PEMA CHÖDRÖN is one of America's leading Buddhist teachers and the author of many best-selling books, including *The Places That Scare You, When Things Fall Apart*, and *Start Where You Are*. Born Deirdre Blomfield-Brown in 1936, she raised a family and taught elementary school before becoming ordained as a nun in 1981. Pema Chödrön's root teacher was Chögyam Trungpa Rinpoche, who appointed her abbess of the monastery he founded in Cape Breton, Nova Scotia. Since his death in 1987, she has studied with Trungpa Rinpoche's son, Sakyong Mipham Rinpoche, and her current principal teacher, Dzigar Kongtrül Rinpoche.

GAYLON FERGUSON is an *acharya* (senior teacher) in the Shambhala Buddhist tradition and a faculty member in Religious Studies and Interdisciplinary Studies at Naropa University. He has a doctorate in cultural anthropology from Stanford and was a contributor to *Dharma, Color, and Culture: New Voices in Western Buddhism*. *Natural Wakefulness*, excerpted here, is his first book.

ZOKETSU NORMAN FISCHER is the founder and teacher of the Everyday Zen Foundation, whose mission is to open and broaden Zen practice through what he calls "engaged renunciation." Fischer practiced and taught at the San Francisco Zen Center for twenty-five years and served as abbot from 1995–2000. His many books include *Sailing Home: Using Homer's* Odyssey *to Navigate Life's Perils and Pitfalls* (prose) and *I Was Blown Back* (poetry).

LAURA FRASER is a freelance writer whose work has appeared in many national publications. Her most recent books are a travel memoir, *An Italian Affair* (2002), and its sequel, *All Over the Map*

(2010). In 2008 she won the International Association of Culinary Professionals' Bert Greene Award for Essay Writing.

CAROLYN ROSE GIMIAN is an author and editor living in Halifax, Nova Scotia, and the editor of many of Chögyam Trungpa Rinpoche's books, including his *Collected Works* and *Smile at Fear: Awakening the True Heart of Bravery.* She is also the founding director of the Shambhala Archives, dedicated to the collection and preservation of the teachings and artifacts of Trungpa Rinpoche and associated teachers.

STAN GOLDBERG is a professor emeritus of communicative disorders at San Francisco State University. The most recent of his six books is *Lessons for the Living,* excerpted here. He consults and leads workshops on change and has been a bedside hospice volunteer for seven years.

SHOZAN JACK HAUBNER is a pseudonym. He is a Zen practitioner living in the United States.

DZONGSAR JAMYANG KHYENTSE RINPOCHE was born in Bhutan and recognized as the main incarnation of the Khyentse lineage of Tibetan Buddhism. He supervises his traditional seat of Dzongsar Monastery in eastern Tibet and Buddhist colleges in India and Bhutan. He has founded three nonprofit organizations and established Buddhist centers in Australia, North America, and the Far East. He is the author of *What Makes You Not a Buddhist* and the director of the acclaimed films *The Cup* and *Travelers and Magicians.*

DZIGAR KONGTRÜL RINPOCHE is the founder of Longchen Jigmé Samten Ling, a mountain retreat center in Crestone, Colorado, where he lives with his wife, Elizabeth Mattis-Namgyel, author of *The Power of an Open Question.* Dzigar Kongtrül Rinpoche is the author of *It's Up to You* and *Light Comes Through.*

JOHN DAIDO LOORI ROSHI (1931–2009) was a dharma heir of the revered Zen Master Taizan Maezumi Roshi and received transmission in both the Rinzai and Soto lines of Zen. He was the founder of the Mountains and Rivers Order and the abbot of Zen Mountain Monastery in Mount Tremper, New York. He was the author of many books and an award-winning photographer and videographer.

DAVID LOY is one of contemporary Buddhism's leading thinkers. His books include *A Buddhist History of the West: Studies in Lack; The Great Awakening: A Buddhist Social Theory*; and *Money, Sex, War, Karma: Notes for a Buddhist Revolution.* He spent the early part of 2009 in Jerusalem, contributing as a Buddhist scholar to a research project on Jewish mysticism in comparative perspective. A Zen practitioner for many years, he is qualified as a teacher in the Sanbo Kyodan tradition of Japanese Zen Buddhism.

JARVIS JAY MASTERS is a prisoner on death row at San Quentin State Prison in California and a student of the late Chagdud Tulku Rinpoche. His first book, *Finding Freedom: Writings from Death Row,* described his conversion to and practice of Buddhism in prison. His second book, *That Bird Has My Wings,* excerpted here, is an autobiography.

YONGEY MINGYUR RINPOCHE is a teacher in the Karma Kagyu school of Tibetan Buddhism. He teaches throughout the world, bringing together traditional Buddhist practice and contemporary culture and science, and has centers on four continents. His best-selling book, *The Joy of Living: Unlocking the Secret and Science of Happiness,* has been translated into over twenty languages. His most recent book is *Joyful Wisdom: Embracing Change and Finding Freedom,* excerpted here.

SAKYONG MIPHAM RINPOCHE is the spiritual leader of Shambhala, an international network of Buddhist meditation and retreat centers. He is the son of the late Chögyam Trungpa Rinpoche and was recognized as the incarnation of the important Tibetan teacher Mipham Jamyang Gyatso Rinpoche. Sakyong Rinpoche teaches throughout North America, Europe, and Asia and is the author of the best-seller *Turning the Mind Into an Ally* and *Ruling Your World.*

THICH NHAT HANH is one of the world's leading Buddhist teachers. He is a Zen Master, poet, and founder of the Engaged Buddhist movement. A social and antiwar campaigner in his native Vietnam, he was nominated for the Nobel Peace Prize in 1967 by Martin Luther King Jr. He is the author of more than forty books, including *You Are Here* and *Answers from the Heart,* both excerpted here. Still teaching actively at the age of 84, Thich Nhat Hanh resides at practice centers in France and the United States.

ANDREW OLENDZKI, PhD, is the executive director and senior scholar at the Barre Center for Buddhist Studies in Barre, Massachusetts. He is the editor of *Insight Journal* and the author of *Unlimiting Mind: The Radically Experiential Psychology of Buddhism.*

MARY PIPHER, PhD, is a psychologist and anthropologist whose special area of interest is how American culture influences the mental health of its people. Pipher travels all over the world sharing her ideas with community groups, schools, and health care professionals. Three of her books, *Reviving Ophelia, The Shelter of Each Other,* and *Another Country,* have been *New York Times* best sellers. Her most recent book, the memoir *Seeking Peace: Chronicles of the Worst Buddhist in the World,* is excerpted in this volume.

DANIEL ASA ROSE has won an O. Henry Award, two PEN Fiction Awards, and an NEA Fellowship. He is the editor of the international literary magazine *The Reading Room* and has written for the *New Yorker, Esquire,* the *New York Times Magazine,* and other national publications. Rose's first novel, *Flipping for It,* was a black comedy about divorce from the man's point of view and a *New York Times* New and Noteworthy Paperback. His most recent novel,

Larry's Kidney, is about how he found himself in China with his cousin and his cousin's mail-order bride, illegally trying to arrange a life-saving transplant.

DANIEL DOEN SILBERBERG teaches and directs his own Zen group, Lost Coin, which has students throughout the U.S. and Europe. He received a BA in English with an emphasis in Eastern literature and an MA and PhD in psychology. He has had a successful career as a musician and has spent twenty-five years as a psychotherapist, coach, and consultant in New York and Salt Lake City.

STEVE SILBERMAN'S articles on science, literature, music, and Buddhism have appeared in *Wired,* the *New Yorker,* the *Shambhala Sun, GQ,* and other national publications. Silberman is writing a book on neurodiversity and lives with his husband, Keith, in San Francisco.

JOAN SUTHERLAND is the founder of The Open Source, a network of practice communities emphasizing the confluence of Zen koans, creativity, and companionship. Before becoming a Zen teacher, she worked as a scholar and teacher in the field of archaeomythology, and for nonprofit organizations in the feminist antiviolence and environmental movements. Sutherland is interested in what becomes possible when ancient methods of meditation and inquiry are brought into contemporary Western lives.

JOHN TARRANT, ROSHI, is the director of the Pacific Zen Institute. He has a PhD in psychology and is the author of *Bring Me the Rhinoceros* and *The Light Inside the Dark: Zen, Soul, and the Spiritual Life.* He also teaches at the Duke Center for Integrative Medicine at Duke University Medical School. Tarrant's work is centered on the transformation of consciousness and he is considered one of the foremost koan teachers in the United States.

HANNAH TENNANT-MOORE lives in Brooklyn, New York, where she is at work on a book of essays about modern women in love. She received her MFA in nonfiction from the Bennington Writing Seminars. Her work has appeared in the *Shambhala Sun, Tricycle, The Best Buddhist Writing* 2008, and elsewhere.

ANAM THUBTEN RINPOCHE was born in Tibet and recognized as an incarnate lama (*tulku*) when he was a young boy. He has been teaching in the West since the 1990s and serves as the main dharma teacher for the Dharmata Foundation, based in Point Richmond, California. He is a Buddhist scholar and writer whose first book in English is *No Self, No Problem*, excerpted here. Anam Thubten's teachings mainly draw from the *Prajnaparamita*, the timeless nonconceptual wisdom of Buddha. He lives in the San Francisco Bay Area.

JAIMAL YOGIS is an award-winning journalist and author who spends a good deal of his spare time surfing and traveling the globe. He has a master's degree in journalism from Columbia University and his work has been published in the *Washington Post, Chicago Tribune, The Surfer's Journal, Beliefnet*, and elsewhere. His first book, the memoir *Saltwater Buddha*, excerpted here, is the subject of a forthcoming documentary. He is now working on his second book.

Credits

John Daido Loori, Roshi, "The Way of Mountains and Rivers." From *The Way of Mountains and Rivers: Teachings on Zen and the Environment* by John Daido Loori. © 2009 by John Daido Loori. Reprinted with permission of Dharma Communications Press.

David Loy, "Why Buddhism Needs the West." From the Spring 2009 issue of *Tricycle: The Buddhist Review.*

Jarvis Jay Masters, "That Bird Has My Wings." From *That Bird Has My Wings* by Jarvis Jay Masters. © 2009 by Jarvis Jay Masters. Reprinted by permission of HarperCollins Publishers.

Yongey Mingyur Rinpoche, "Joyful Wisdom." From *Joyful Wisdom: Embracing Change and Finding Freedom* by Yongey Mingyur Rinpoche. © 2009 by Yongey Mingyur Rinpoche. Published by Harmony Books, a division of Random House, Inc.

Sakyong Mipham Rinpoche, "How Will I Use This Day?" From the February 2009 issue of the *Shambhala Sun.*

Thich Nhat Hanh, "Answers to Children's Questions." From *Answers From the Heart: Compassionate and Practical Responses to Life's Burning Questions* by Thich Nhat Hanh. Copyright © 2009 by Unified Buddhist Church. With permission from Parallax Press. www.parallax.org.

Thich Nhat Hanh, "You Are Here." From *You Are Here: Discovering the Magic of the Present Moment* by Thich Nhat Hanh. © 2001 by Editions Dangles and Unified Buddhist Church, Inc. English translation © 2009 by Shambhala Publications, Inc. Reprinted with permission of Shambhala Publications, Inc., Boston, Mass. www.shambhala.com.

Andrew Olendzki, "Burning Alive." From the Summer 2009 issue of *Tricycle: The Buddhist Review.*